W9-DCZ-875

Yet once more O ye laurells and once more
ye myrtl's browne wth Ivie never sere
I come to pluck yor berries harsh and crude
~~before the mellowing yeare~~ and wth forc't fingers rude
~~and crop yor young~~ shatter yor leaves before ye mellowing yeare
bitter constraint, and sad occasion deare
compells me to disturbe yor season due
for ~~young~~ Lycidas is dead, dead ere his prime
young Lycidas and hath not left his peere
who would ^not sing for Lycidas he well knew
himselfe to sing & build the loftie rime
he must not flote upon the watrie beare
unwept, and welter to the parching wind
without the meed of some melodious teare

Bring the rathe primrose tha~~t~~ unwedded dies
~~collu~~ colouring the pale cheeke of uninjoyd love
and that sad floure that strove
to write his owne woes on the vermeil graine
next adde Narcissus y^ still weeps in vaine
the woodbine and ye pansie freak't wth jet
the glowing violet
the cowslip wan that hangs his pensive head
and every bud that sorrows liverie weares
let Daffadillies fill thire cups ^with teares
bid Amaranthus all his beautie shed
to strew the laureat herse &c.

Bring the rathe primrose that forsaken dies
the tufted crowtoe and pale Gessamin
the white pinke, and ye pansie freakt wth jet
the glowing violet
                    the well-attir'd woodbine
the muske rose and ~~the gorish columbine~~
wth cowslips wan that hang the pensive head
                              • weare   weares
  and every flower that sad escutcheon ~~beare~~ • imbroidrie ~~beares~~
2 &~~let~~ daffadillies fill thire cups wth teares
1 bid Amaranthus all his beauties shed
   to strew &c.

  • what could the muse her selfe that Orpheus bore
    the muse her selfe for her inchanting son.
    ~~for her inchanting son~~
                          did
    whome universal nature ~~might~~ lament
    when by the rout that made the hideous roare
         •   gorie
goarie his ~~divine~~ visage downe the streame was sent
        downe the swift Herbus to ye Lesbian shoare

Milton's "LYCIDAS"

Milton's

"LYCIDAS"

EDITED TO SERVE AS

AN INTRODUCTION TO CRITICISM

PR3558.A1E45   ST. JOSEPH'S UNIVERSITY   STX

Lycidas,

3 9353 00024 5025

SCOTT ELLEDGE

Professor of English
Cornell University

79170

PR3558
.A45
.E45

HARPER & ROW, PUBLISHERS, NEW YORK & LONDON

Milton's "LYCIDAS": EDITED TO SERVE AS AN INTRODUCTION TO CRITICISM
Copyright © 1966 by Scott Elledge
Printed in the United States of America. All rights reserved. No part of this book may be used or reproduced in any manner whatsoever without written permission except in the case of brief quotations embodied in critical articles and reviews. For information address Harper & Row, Publishers, Incorporated, 49 East 33rd Street, New York, N.Y. 10016.

Library of Congress Catalog Card Number: 66-11463

This book is for my mother
Eva Bowen Elledge

CONTENTS

PREFACE   xi
EPIGRAPH I   xix
EPIGRAPH II   xxi

The Poem

"Lycidas" (1638 text)   3
Textual Variations   10

The Tradition

FIVE CLASSICAL PASTORAL ELEGIES   15
     Theocritus *The First Idyl*   15
     Bion *The Lament for Adonis*   21
     Moschus *The Lament for Bion*   25
     Virgil *Pastoral V*   30
         Pastoral X   36

TWO CLASSICAL CONSOLATIONS   41
     Seneca *from To Marcia, on Consolation*   41
     Statius *from The Poet's Lament for His Father*   42

NINE RENAISSANCE PASTORALS   45
     Petrarch *Eclogue VI*   45
         Eclogue VII   52
     Boccaccio *Eclogue XIV*   54
     Castiglione *Alcon*   67
     Marot *from De Madame Loyse de Savoye, Mère du Roy, en forme d'eclogue*   72

from Concerning Madame Louise of Savoy, Mother of the King, in the form of an Eclogue   74

Ronsard   *from Eclogue I*   76
Angelot's Lament   79

Spenser   *Ægloga Vndecima: Nouember*   82
Ægloga Quinta: Maye   92

Lodowick Bryskett   *A Pastorall Æglogue vpon the Death of Sir Phillip Sidney Knight, &c.*   95

Glossary   102

The Theory of the Monody

Julius Caesar Scaliger   *from The Poetics*   107

George Puttenham   *from The Arte of English Poesie* (1598)   112

Contemporary Elegies

THREE ELEGIES ON THE DEATH OF PRINCE HENRY, 1612

Giles Fletcher   *Upon the Most Lamented Departure of the Right Hopefull, and Blessed Prince Henrie, Prince of Wales*   117

Cyril Tourneur   *A Griefe on the Death of Prince Henrie, Expressed in a Broken Elegie, According to the Nature of Such a Sorrow*   121

John Donne   *Elegie upon the Untimely Death of the Incomparable Prince Henry*   126

TWO ELEGIES ON THE DEATHS OF CLOSE FRIENDS

John Milton   *Epitaphium Damonis*   130

Abraham Cowley   *On the Death of Mr. William Hervey*   139

Justa Edovardo King

Edward King   147
Selections from Justa Edovardo King   150
    Obsequies to the Memorie of Mr. Edward King   151

John Milton

Milton's Life from 1608 to 1637   163
Milton's Own Account of His Early Training and Aspirations
    167
    from An Apology for Smectymnuus   167
    from A Revised Draft of a Letter to a Friend   170
    from A Letter to Charles Diodati   173
    *from The Reason of Church Government Urged Against
      Prelaty*   174

England in 1637

Trevelyan *from England Under the Stuarts*   179
William Prynne *from A Breviate of the Prelates intolerable
  usurpations, both upon the Kings Prerogative Royall, and the
  Subjects Liberties*   197
*from A Briefe Relation Of certain speciall and most materiall
  passages, and speeches in the Starre-Chamber . . .*   207
John Milton *from Of Reformation Touching Church-
  Discipline in England and the Causes that hitherto have
  hindered it*   220

Commentaries and Notes

SELECTIONS FROM COMMENTARY ON
 "*LYCIDAS*"   227
   Joseph Warton   227
   Thomas Newton   227
   Richard Hurd   228
   Samuel Johnson   230
   Thomas Warton   231
   William Hazlitt   235
   Henry Hallam   236
   Thomas Keightly   237
   John Ruskin   244
   Mark Pattison   244
   Arthur Machen   244
   Robert Graves   248
   W. H. Auden   249
A List of Abbreviations Used in the Notes   249
Line Notes   251
Principal Editions from Which Notes Have Been Taken   317

Bibliographies

Books and Articles on Pastoral Poetry   321
Books and Articles About "Lycidas"   322
   Index   329

PREFACE

When I first collected some of the materials that make up this book, I thought the time was ripe for a small counter-reformation in the teaching of literature. Some six or seven years earlier *Understanding Poetry* had revealed to English instructors a ready and easy way to purge the study of literature and return the academic priesthood to the original purity of worship, freed from the confusing, question-begging and corrupting influences of pedantic paraphernalia. We converts had embraced a faith that the lives of the poets, the history of literature, and the study of sources were all "wind and rank mist," and that if *our* sheep were not unfed, it was because we had learned to tend the homely slighted shepherd's trade. Brooks and Warren had shown us how to strictly meditate the *poem*, in its bare beauty, without the aid or intervention of other authority than, perhaps, the *Oxford English Dictionary* and *Understanding Poetry*. We believed in simply reading the poem hard and well with the same confidence in our ability to find the truth that characterized the Puritans' exegesis of the Holy Scripture.

Fifteen years ago I felt certain, as I do today, that the reformation was good for literature, good for criticism, good for pedagogy, good for education. But I was beginning to mistrust some of the effects of Brooks and Warren's success. For like other puritans, we had carried the new dogma to extremes. In our zealous care to avoid talking around the poem and about the genre and the poet and his times, we neglected the truth that great works of art are also humanistic monuments more beautiful and more meaningful when they are seen in relation to the aesthetic and intellectual tradition they are a part of. No doubt it *was* wrong to smother a poem with historical, biographical, and critical comment; no doubt reading the poem carefully and making it mean as much as possible by itself *was* the first and hardest task of teachers and students. But no doubt, also, it was wrong to leave the impression that the limits of criticism were a solid Brooks and Warren reading, or that history, biography, literary theory, and literary history were as supererogatory as scholastic commentary, or were like the Arminian heresy in their vain emphasis on good works. After all, I thought, T. S. Eliot had made the point clear in "Tradition and the Individual Talent," and all one needed to do to correct our excesses was to illustrate that essay by a study of "Lycidas."

So I made this collection and tried to find a publisher who would share my belief that other English teachers felt the same need to temper their puritanism with some demonstrations of the value of traditional literary scholarship and humanistic criticism. Others, I thought, would welcome a convenient means to illustrate the ways literary conventions influence works of art, the ways the life in and around a poet colors, if not shapes, his poem, the way a knowledge of a body of literature and a period of history can sharpen a reader's faculties for enjoying and understanding a poem—to show why, perhaps, Doctor Johnson thought a study of a poet's work might properly lead finally to a study of the poet.

"Lycidas" is better suited for this purpose than any other work I know. Because it is so short, an intense and comprehensive study is more practicable than it would be with a play or novel. Because it was written in 1637, when the literary tradition was three hundred years shorter than it is today, one can more nearly master all the essential elements in its literary tradition than one could for a work written later. Because it is a pastoral elegy, it is in a small class nearly all of whose chief members can be examined. "Lycidas" has the important distinction of being an exaggerated (and therefore clinically useful) example of the effect of tradition on the poet and poem, for Milton knew well nearly all the poems of the genre, both classical and renaissance, and he had a strong sense of what he called "decorum," the principle that implies, among other things, that certain styles and conventions are appropriate to certain kinds of poems, and that a poet about to write a pastoral elegy, for instance, should look for the rules for that genre in the best elegies already written. Milton was unusually careful; other poets have not defined decorum quite so strictly as Milton did, but it is a rare poet, probably, who can think of the poem he is writing without some sense of the kind of poem it will be; and "kind" implies a class, no matter how large.

Perhaps what most recommended "Lycidas" for this introduction to criticism was its greatness. Teachers deceive themselves, I know, but I think no poem I teach so generally moves students to immediate and lasting admiration as "Lycidas." Like other highly allusive poems, like much modern poetry, it moves admiration before it produces understanding. And its perfection is so sturdy that no amount of study of it can taint its beauty. At least so my students report.

I thought, therefore, that my collection of materials would present a context sufficiently varied and extensive and not too artificially constructed by means of which any student could discover for himself some of those things about the study of literature that he was not likely to learn from Brooks and Warren. First, he might better understand Eliot's essay and he might see, at least dimly, not only the way Milton composed, the way "Lycidas" was written, but also the way many poets have composed, the way many poems have been written. In short, he might pick up some clues to the mystery of literary creation. And second, he might discover what remains to be done with any work of the past after innocence, intelligence, and hard work have found all the meaning and pleasure they can: that is, to learn what comparative literary study will produce, what a knowledge of several kinds of history can contribute to the value of the work.

During the fifteen years since I first tried to persuade a publisher that such a book would find an audience, several things have happened to encourage me to try again. First, there was my continuing satisfaction with the use of these materials and with the method of study they implemented. Year after year I have put my two typescript copies on the reserve shelf in the college library, and year after year my classes in Milton have been excited by what they themselves *discover* as they work on a wide variety of problems I assign them. Year after year when we finish our study of "Lycidas" I feel that I have been about the proper work of a teacher of literature and that my students have learned something I find it hard to teach in other ways, in other courses, with other works.

Second, during this period three essays on "Lycidas" have shown, in three quite different ways, what insights the study of these materials can produce not only into Milton and seventeenth-century aesthetics, but into the nature of poetry as well. Ruth Wallerstein's "The Laureat Hearse: The Funeral Elegy and Seventeenth-Century Aesthetic," the first part of her book entitled *Studies in Seventeenth-Century Poetic* (Madison, 1950), illustrates not only the value of comparative study but the neatness of "Lycidas" and its immediate context (the volume to King) as a model for study and demonstration. But Miss Rosemund Tuve's essay on "Lycidas" in *Images and Themes in Five poems by Milton* (Cambridge, Mass., 1957) was an even greater stimulus to reconsider publishing this collection. No college student should hope to equal the wisdom, learning, and literary tact of this distinguished piece of scholarship, nor could Miss Tuve have written her essay simply from the materials in this book. And no one but a mature scholar could equal the work of D. C. Allen in *The Harmonius Vision* (Baltimore, 1954). But college students, with my collection, could at least make their own modest beginnings in this kind of criticism. It would be good exercise. And students who wished to play the game (that academic exercises often are) would not read Wallerstein or Tuve or Allen until they had finished their own work.

Third, the antithetical movement to the thesis of "New Criticism" seems almost complete, and few English teachers now will deny the values of the kinds of criticism this book will enable students to practice. The success of the counter-reformation has, however, made the task of the teacher harder because he now needs more context than most editions can give and he is frustrated by the limitations of reserve-shelf assignments. My hope is that this book, supplemented, perhaps, by the modern critical essays in C. A. Patrides's *Milton's Lycidas: The Tradition and the Poem* (New York, 1961), will furnish all materials necessary for an elementary anatomy of criticism.

Fourth, the rapid growth of honors courses in undergraduate programs of study has created a possible audience for this book much larger than it would have had fifteen years ago. And finally, collections of source materials prepared for use in college courses are now so common that all teachers of English are familiar with the method of study implied by this book.

It would be inconsistent with the purpose of the book to explain in any detail how it should be used or why any of the selections were included; consequently, instead of an Introduction, I add only a note on how, in general, I think the book can be most useful.

First, I should say I naturally hope the book will be interesting to any serious common reader of poetry—in or out of a course or college. The relationships between a work of art and its milieu, culture, or background are more easily and more usefully illustrated than described; and no one who knows "Lycidas" fairly well can miss the scores of connections between it and the material in the collection, or, I think, fail to be excited by this opportunity to come so close to seeing the process of creation. More particularly, of course, I think the book will be useful to students of Milton. I begin my own course in Milton with the study of "Lycidas" because the poem serves as an introduction to Milton's art limited enough in scope to be encompassed in a short time. Several of Milton's most characteristic ideas and modes, found in all his works, are in this poem, and it is, therefore, a good point of departure, and of reference, throughout the course. The critiques which students can write simply from knowledge of the poem and the materials in this collection will serve as small-scale models for the essays they may later attempt on the major poems, as well as for more ambitious or more general papers on Milton's thought and art.

But chiefly, I should think, the book will be useful in those introductions to the serious study of literature that are somewhat more sophisticated than the great sophomore survey courses, and that are introductions for honors candidates into the methods and aims of the study of literature. Many kinds of critical questions can be considered. First, there is what was once called grammatical criticism, which includes the intensive study of the language— diction, syntax, rhetorical figures—all that can be discovered simply by a careful study of the poem in itself, with the help of a good knowledge of English and the use of the Oxford English Dictionary. Many of the notes in my "variorum" will be interesting in this kind of criticism. Another kind of study examines the poem as an example of a genre—what were other poems of this kind like and what does a comparison between them and this poem reveal? Third, what will a knowledge of the poet's life and of his other works add to the meaning of the poem? And fourth, how is the poem related to the culture in which it was produced—i.e., how can a knowledge of the times enhance our experience of the poem? Such questions do not so much comprehend or define the limits of criticism as suggest the concentric circles, or the spirals, that make criticism seem more like an expanding universe than a closed system. The facsimile of the manuscript of the poem furnishes material for answers to other critical questions. Nothing in the collection, I think, is insignificant; everything in it will reward careful study. And after solving a series of problems suggested by the existence of these materials, a student should have a good notion of the nature, the variety, the rewards of criticism. The little anthology of critical comments from Joseph Warton to W. H. Auden, the notes variorum selected from the many editors of the poem, and the bibliographies, have been put at the end to suggest that they are all *post facto*; many of the tangential questions they raise, though they take us away from "Lycidas," keep us nevertheless in the orbit of criticism in general.

The two epigraphs and the table of contents will, to a thoughtful teacher or student, speak sufficiently for the *idea* of the book, but of course only a careful study will reveal why these particular materials were included.

Among the many who in one way or another helped me in making this little book I gratefully mention a few: Professor Andrew Bongiorno, who first led me to Milton; the late Lane Cooper, who taught me useful ways to learn and teach; Professor Douglas Bush, who first encouraged me to publish such an edition as this and with characteristic generosity suggested several ways to improve my first version; and those students at Carleton College and Cornell University who helped me discover new ways to make discoveries. To all the editors of Milton I am, of course, greatly indebted, as I am to several contemporary Milton scholars whose studies pointed out some of the materials I have included. Finally, I wish to thank Mrs. Henry Guerlac for her translation of passages from Scaliger, and Professors Paul MacKendrick and Robert Durling for their translations from Petrarch and Castiglione.

S. E.

Ithaca, New York
December, 1965

EPIGRAPH I

We might remind ourselves that criticism is as inevitable as breathing, and that we should be none the worse for articulating what passes in our minds when we read a book and feel an emotion about it, for criticizing our own minds in their work of criticism. One of the facts that might come to light in this process is our tendency to insist, when we praise a poet, upon those aspects of his work in which he least resembles any one else. In these aspects or parts of his work we pretend to find what is individual, what is the peculiar essence of the man. We dwell with satisfaction upon the poet's difference from his predecessors, especially his immediate predecessors; we endeavour to find something that can be isolated in order to be enjoyed. Whereas if we approach a poet without this prejudice we shall often find that not only the best, but the most individual parts of his work may be those in which the dead poets, his ancestors, assert their immortality most vigorously. . . .

* * *

There is a great deal, in the writing of poetry, which must be conscious and deliberate. In fact, the bad poet is usually unconscious where he ought to be conscious, and conscious where he ought to be unconscious. Both errors tend to make him "personal." Poetry is not a turning loose of emotion, but an escape from emotion; it is not the expression of personality, but an escape from personality. But, of course, only those who have personality and emotions know what it means to want to escape from these things. . . .

* * *

To divert interest from the poet to the poetry is a laudable aim;

From *Selected Essays of T. S. Eliot,* new ed., copyright, 1932, 1936, 1950, by Harcourt, Brace & World, Inc.; copyright, 1960, 1964 by T. S. Eliot. Reprinted by permission of the publishers and Faber and Faber, Ltd., London.

for it would conduce to a juster estimation of actual poetry, good and bad. There are many people who appreciate the expression of sincere emotion in verse, and there is a smaller number of people who can appreciate technical excellence. But very few know when there is an expression of *significant* emotion, emotion which has its life in the poem and not in the history of the poet. The emotion of art is impersonal. And the poet cannot reach this impersonality without surrendering himself wholly to the work to be done. And he is not likely to know what is to be done unless he lives in what is not merely the present, but the present moment of the past, unless he is conscious, not of what is dead, but of what is already living.

T. S. Eliot, "Tradition and the Individual Talent"

EPIGRAPH II

We have got something out of the lines [*Lycidas*, 108–129], I think, and much more is yet to be found in them; but we have done enough by way of example of the kind of word-by-word examination of your author which is rightly called "reading"; watching every accent and expression, and putting ourselves always in the author's place, annihilating our own personality, and seeking to enter into his, so as to be able assuredly to say, "Thus Milton thought," not "Thus I thought, in mis-reading Milton." And by this process you will gradually come to attach less weight to your own "thus I thought" at other times. You will begin to perceive that what *you* thought was a matter of no serious importance;— that your thoughts on any subject are not perhaps the clearest and wisest that could be arrived at thereupon:—in fact, that unless you are a very singular person, you cannot be said to have any "thoughts" at all; that you have no materials for them, in any serious matters;—no right to "think," but only to try to learn more of the facts. Nay, most probably all your life (unless, as I said, you are a singular person) you will have no legitimate right to an "opinion" on any business, except that instantly under your hand. What must of necessity be done, you can always find out, beyond question, how to do. Have you a house to keep in order, a commodity to sell, a field to plough, a ditch to cleanse? There need be no two opinions about these proceedings; it is at your peril if you have not much more than an "opinion" on the way to manage such matters. . . . [But] respecting religions, governments, sciences, arts, you will find that, on the whole, you can know NOTHING,— judge nothing; that the best you can do, even though you may be a well-educated person, is to be silent, and strive to be wiser every day, and to understand a little more of the thoughts of others, which so soon as you try to do honestly, you will discover that the thoughts even of the wisest are very little more than pertinent questions. To put the difficulty into a clear shape, and exhibit to you the grounds for *in*decision, that is all they can generally do for you!—and well for them and for us, if indeed they are able "to mix the music with our thoughts, and sadden us with heavenly doubts."

John Ruskin, *Sesame and Lilies*

The Poem

"LYCIDAS"

In this Monody the Author bewails a learned Friend, unfortunately drown'd in his passage from Chester on the Irish Seas, 1637. And by occasion foretells the ruine of our corrupted Clergie then in their height.

YET once more, O ye Laurels, and once more
Ye Myrtles brown, with Ivy never sear,
I com to pluck your Berries harsh and crude,
And with forc'd fingers rude,
Shatter your leaves before the mellowing year.   5
Bitter constraint, and sad occasion dear,
Compells me to disturb your season due:
For *Lycidas* is dead, dead ere his prime,
Young *Lycidas*, and hath not left his peer:
Who would not sing for *Lycidas*? he knew   10
Himself to sing, and build the lofty rhyme.
He must not flote upon his watry bear
Unwept, and welter to the parching wind,
Without the meed of som melodious tear.
　　Begin then, Sisters of the sacred well,   15
That from beneath the seat of *Jove* doth spring,
Begin, and somewhat loudly sweep the string.

Hence with denial vain, and coy excuse,
So may some gentle Muse
20   With lucky words favour my destin'd Urn,
And as he passes turn,
And bid fair peace be to my sable shrowd.
For we were nurst upon the self-same hill,
Fed the same flock; by fountain, shade, and rill.
25   Together both, ere the high Lawns appear'd
Under the opening eye-lids of the morn,
We drove a field, and both together heard
What time the Gray-fly winds her sultry horn,
Batt'ning our flocks with the fresh dews of night,
30   Oft till the Star that rose, at Ev'ning, bright,
Toward Heav'ns descent had slop'd his westering
      wheel.
Mean while the Rural ditties were not mute,
Temper'd to th' Oaten Flute,
Rough *Satyrs* danc'd, and *Fauns* with clov'n heel,
35   From the glad sound would not be absent long,
And old *Damœtas* lov'd to hear our song.
      But O the heavy change, now thou art gon,
Now thou art gon, and never must return!
Thee Shepherd, thee the Woods, and desert Caves,
With wilde Thyme and the gadding Vine
40   o'regrown,
And all their echoes mourn.
The Willows, and the Hazle Copses green,
Shall now no more be seen,
Fanning their joyous Leaves to thy soft layes.
45   As killing as the Canker to the Rose,
Or Taint-worm to the weanling Herds that graze,
Or Frost to Flowers, that their gay wardrop wear,

When first the White Thorn blows;
Such, *Lycidas*, thy loss to Shepherds ear.
   Where were ye Nymphs when the remorseless
      deep   50
Clos'd o're the head of your lov'd *Lycidas*?
For neither were ye playing on the steep,
Where your old *Bards*, the famous *Druids*, ly,
Nor on the shaggy top of *Mona* high,
Nor yet where *Deva* spreads her wisard stream: 55
Ay me, I fondly dream!
Had ye bin there—for what could that have don?
What could the Muse her self that *Orpheus* bore,
The Muse her self for her inchanting son
Whom Universal nature did lament,   60
When by the rout that made the hideous roar,
His goary visage down the stream was sent,
Down the swift *Hebrus* to the *Lesbian* shore.
   Alas! What boots it with uncessant care
To tend the homely slighted Shepherds trade,   65
And strictly meditate the thankless Muse,
Were it not better don as others use,
To sport with *Amaryllis* in the shade,
Or with the tangles of *Neæra's* hair?
Fame is the spur that the clear spirit doth raise   70
(That last infirmity of Noble mind)
To scorn delights, and live laborious dayes;
But the fair Guerdon when we hope to find,
And think to burst out into sudden blaze,
Comes the blind *Fury* with th' abhorred shears,   75
And slits the thin spun life. But not the praise,
Phœbus repli'd, and touch'd my trembling ears;
Fame is no plant that grows on mortal soil,

Nor in the glistering foil
80   Set off to th' world, nor in broad rumour lies,
But lives and spreds aloft by those pure eyes,
And perfet witnes of all-judging *Jove*;
As he pronounces lastly on each deed,
Of so much fame in Heav'n expect thy meed.

85   O Fountain *Arethuse*, and thou honour'd floud,
Smooth-sliding *Mincius*, crown'd with vocal reeds,
That strain I heard was of a higher mood:
But now my Oat proceeds,
And listens to the Herald of the Sea
90   That came in *Neptune's* plea,
He ask'd the Waves, and ask'd the Fellon Winds,
What hard mishap hath doom'd this gentle swain?
And question'd every gust of rugged wings
That blows from off each beaked Promontory;
95   They knew not of his story,
And sage *Hippotades* their answer brings,
That not a blast was from his dungeon stray'd,
The Air was calm, and on the level brine,
Sleek *Panope* with all her sisters play'd.
100   It was that fatal and perfidious Bark
Built in th' eclipse, and rigg'd with curses dark,
That sunk so low that sacred head of thine.

Next *Camus*, reverend Sire, went footing slow,
His Mantle hairy, and his Bonnet sedge,
105   Inwrought with figures dim, and on the edge
Like to that sanguine flower inscrib'd with woe.
Ah; Who hath reft (quoth he) my dearest pledge?
Last came, and last did go,
The Pilot of the *Galilean* lake,
110   Two massy Keyes he bore of metals twain,

(The Golden opes, the Iron shuts amain)
He shook his Miter'd locks, and stern bespake,
How well could I have spar'd for thee, young swain,
Anow of such as for their bellies sake,
Creep and intrude, and climb into the fold?   115
Of other care they little reck'ning make,
Then how to scramble at the shearers feast,
And shove away the worthy bidden guest;
Blind mouthes! that scarce themselves know how
      to hold
A Sheep-hook, or have learn'd ought els the least   120
That to the faithful Herdmans art belongs!
What recks it them? What need they? They are sped;
And when they list, their lean and flashy songs
Grate on their scrannel Pipes of wretched straw,
The hungry sheep look up, and are not fed,   125
But swoln with wind, and the rank mist they draw,
Rot inwardly, and foul contagion spread:
Besides what the grim Woolf with privy paw
Daily devours apace, and nothing sed,
But that two-handed engine at the door,   130
Stands ready to smite once, and smite no more.
      Return *Alpheus*, the dread voice is past,
That shrunk thy streams; Return *Sicilian* Muse,
And call the Vales, and bid them hither cast
Their Bells, and Flourets of a thousand hues.   135
Ye valleys low where the milde whispers use,
Of shades and wanton winds, and gushing brooks,
On whose fresh lap the swart Star sparely looks,
Throw hither all your quaint enameld eyes,
That on the green terf suck the honied showres,   140
And purple all the ground with vernal flowres.

Bring the rathe Primrose that forsaken dies.
The tufted Crow-toe, and pale Gessamine,
The white Pink, and the Pansie freakt with jeat,
145   The glowing Violet.
The Musk-rose, and the well attir'd Woodbine,
With Cowslips wan that hang the pensive head,
And every flower that sad embroidery wears:
Bid *Amarantus* all his beauty shed,
150   And Daffadillies fill their cups with tears,
To strew the Laureat Herse where *Lycid* lies.
For so to interpose a little ease,
Let our frail thoughts dally with false surmise.
Ay me! Whilst thee the shores, and sounding Seas
155   Wash far away, where ere thy bones are hurl'd,
Whether beyond the stormy *Hebrides*
Where thou perhaps under the whelming tide
Visit'st the bottom of the monstrous world;
Or whether thou to our moist vows deny'd,
160   Sleep'st by the fable of *Bellerus* old,
Where the great vision of the guarded Mount
Looks toward *Namancos* and *Bayona's* hold;
Look homeward Angel now, and melt with ruth.
And, O ye *Dolphins*, waft the haples youth.
165   Weep no more, woful Shepherds weep no more,
For *Lycidas* your sorrow is not dead,
Sunk though he be beneath the watry floar,
So sinks the day-star in the Ocean bed,
And yet anon repairs his drooping head,
170   And tricks his beams, and with new spangled Ore,
Flames in the forehead of the morning sky:
So *Lycidas* sunk low, but mounted high,
Through the dear might of him that walk'd the waves

Where other groves, and other streams along,
With *Nectar* pure his oozy Lock's he laves,   175
And hears the unexpressive nuptial Song,
In the blest Kingdoms meek of joy and love.
There entertain him all the Saints above,
In solemn troops, and sweet Societies
That sing, and singing in their glory move,   180
And wipe the tears for ever from his eyes.
Now *Lycidas* the Shepherds weep no more;
Henceforth thou art the Genius of the shore,
In thy large recompense, and shalt be good
To all that wander in that perilous flood.   185

    Thus sang the uncouth Swain to th' Okes and rills,
While the still morn went out with Sandals gray,
He touch'd the tender stops of various Quills,
With eager thought warbling his *Dorick* lay:
And now the Sun had stretch'd out all the hills,   190
And now was dropt into the Western Bay;
At last he rose, and twitch'd his Mantle blew:
To morrow to fresh Woods, and Pastures new.

"Lycidas" was published three times during Milton's life: in the volume of verses in memory of King, *Justa Edvardo King* (Cambridge, 1638), in the first collection of Milton's poems, POEMS/ OF/ Mr. *John Milton*,/ BOTH/ ENGLISH and LATIN,/ Compos'd at several times (London, 1645), and in the second edition of that collection (London, 1673). Our text is that of 1673, transcribed from *John Milton's Complete Poetical Works, Reproduced in Photographic Facsimile*, ed. Harris Fletcher, 4 vols. (Urbana, 1943), Vol. I. The variations among the three texts are chiefly in spelling and punctuation; several are clearly printer's errors. Below are listed the more interesting variant readings, taken from Fletcher's collation:

> *In this Monody . . . height.*]   1638 omits

2 never sear,]   1638 never sere

9 Young *Lycidas*,]   1638 (Young Lycidas!)

14 som]   1638 some

19 some]   1645 som

26 opening]   1638 glimmering

30 1638 Oft till the ev'n starre bright

31 westering   1638 burnisht

36 *Damætas*]   1645 *Damœtas*   1638 *Dametas*

39 Shepherd,]   1638 shepherds,

51 lov'd]   1638 lord

53 your]   1638 the

56 Ay]   1638 Ah

65 tend]   1673 end   1638 and 1645 tend

67 use]   1638 do

69 Or with]   1638 Hid in

   Neæra's]   1638 *Neera's*

82 perfet]   1628 perfect

10

103 *Camus*, reverend Sire,]   1638 *Chamus* (reverend sire)

107 Ah;]   1638 Ah!

114 Anow]   1638 Enough

129 nothing]   1638 little

149 *Amarantus*]   1638 and 1645 *Amaranthus*

157 whelming]   1638 humming

    1638 is signed J.M.

The Tradition

FIVE CLASSICAL PASTORAL ELEGIES

THEOCRITUS[1]

THE FIRST IDYL

The shepherd Thyrsis meets a goatherd, in a shady place beside a spring, and at his invitation sings the Song of Daphnis. This ideal hero of Greek pastoral song had won for his bride the fairest of the Nymphs. Confident in the strength of his passion, he boasted that Love could never subdue him to a new affection. Love avenged himself by making Daphnis desire a strange maiden, but to this temptation he never yielded, and so died a constant lover. The song tells how the cattle and the wild things of the wood bewailed him, how Hermes and Priapus gave him counsel in vain, and how with his last breath he retorted the taunts of the implacable Aphrodite.
The scene is in Sicily.

Thyrsis. Sweet, meseems, is the whispering sound of yonder pine tree, goatherd, that murmureth by the wells of water; and sweet are thy pipings. After Pan the second prize shalt thou bear away,

---

[1]Theocritus was born about 315 B.C. in Syracuse, where flowed the fountain Arethusa. Among the thirty idyls that have been attributed to him, the first is probably the best known. The argument and the translation from the Greek (made about 1880) are by Andrew Lang: *Theocritus, Bion and Moschus* (London, 1924).

15

and if he take the hornéd goat, the she-goat shalt thou win; but if he choose the she-goat for his meed, the kid falls to thee, and dainty is the flesh of kids e'er the age when thou milkest them.

The Goatherd. Sweeter, O shepherd, is thy song than the music of yonder water that is poured from the high face of the rock! Yea, if the Muses take the young ewe for their gift, a stall-fed lamb shalt thou receive for thy meed; but if it please them to take the lamb, thou shalt lead away the ewe for the second prize.

Thyrsis. Wilt thou, goatherd, in the nymph's name, wilt thou sit thee down here, among the tamarisks, on this sloping knoll, and pipe while in this place I watch thy flocks?

Goatherd. Nay, shepherd, it may not be; we may not pipe in the noontide. 'Tis Pan we dread, who truly at this hour rests weary from the chase; and bitter of mood is he, the keen wrath sitting ever at his nostrils. But, Thyrsis, for that thou surely wert wont to sing *The Affliction of Daphnis*, and hast most deeply meditated the pastoral muse, come hither, and beneath yonder elm let us sit down, in face of Priapus and the fountain fairies, where is that resting-place of the shepherds, and where the oak trees are. Ah! if thou wilt but sing as on that day thou sangest in thy match with Chromis out of Libya, I will let thee milk, ay, three times, a goat that is the mother of twins, and even when she has suckled her kids her milk doth fill two pails. A deep bowl of ivy-wood, too, I will give thee, rubbed with sweet bees'-wax, a twy-eared bowl newly wrought, smacking still of the knife of the graver. Round its upper edges goes the ivy winding, ivy besprent with golden flowers; and about it is a tendril twisted that joys in its saffron fruit. Within is designed a maiden, as fair a thing as the gods could fashion, arrayed in a sweeping robe, and a snood on her head. Beside her two youths with fair love-locks are contending from either side, with alternate speech, but her heart thereby is all untouched. And now on one she glances, smiling, and anon she lightly flings the other a thought, while by reason of the long vigils of love their eyes are heavy, but their labour is all in vain.

Beyond these an ancient fisherman and a rock are fashioned, a rugged rock, whereon with might and main the old man drags a great net for his cast, as one that labours stoutly. Thou wouldst say that he is fishing with all the might of his limbs, so big the sinews swell all about his neck, grey-haired though he be, but his strength is as the strength of youth. Now divided but a little space from the sea-worn old man is a vineyard laden well with fire-red clusters, and on the rough wall a little lad watches the vineyard, sitting there. Round him two she-foxes are skulking, and one goes along the vine-rows to devour the ripe grapes, and the other brings all her cunning to bear against the scrip, and vows she will never leave the lad, till she strand him bare and breakfastless. But the boy is plaiting a pretty locust-cage with stalks of asphodel, and fitting it with reeds, and less care of his scrip has he, and of the vines, than delight in his plaiting.

All about the cup is spread the soft acanthus, a miracle of varied work, a thing for thee to marvel on. For this bowl I paid to a Calydonian ferryman a goat and a great white cream cheese. Never has its lip touched mine, but it still lies maiden for me. Gladly with this cup would I gain thee to my desire, if thou my friend, wilt sing me that delightful song. Nay, I grudge it thee not at all. Begin, my friend, for be sure thou canst in no wise carry thy song with thee to Hades, that puts all things out of mind!

The Song of Thyrsis

Begin, ye Muses dear, begin the pastoral song!

Thyrsis of Etna am I, and this is the voice of Thyrsis. Where, ah! where were ye when Daphnis was languishing; ye Nymphs, where were ye? By Peneus's beautiful dells, or by dells of Pindus? for surely ye dwelt not by the great stream of the river Anapus, nor on the watch-tower of Etna, nor by the sacred water of Acis.

Begin, ye Muses dear, begin the pastoral song!

For him the jackals, for him the wolves did cry; for him did even the lion out of the forest lament. Kine and bulls by his feet right many, and heifers plenty, with the young calves bewailed him.

Begin, ye Muses dear, begin the pastoral song!

Came Hermes[2] first from the hill, and said, "Daphnis, who is it that torments thee; child, whom dost thou love with so great desire?" The neatherds came, and the shepherds; the goatherds came: all they asked what ailed him. Came also Priapus[3],—

Begin, ye Muses dear, begin the pastoral song!

And said: "Unhappy Daphnis, wherefore dost thou languish, while for thee the maiden by all the fountains, through all the glades is fleeting, in search of thee? Ah! thou art too laggard a lover, and thou nothing availest! A neatherd wert thou named, and now thou art like the goatherd:

Begin, ye Muses dear, begin the pastoral song!

"For the goatherd, when he marks the young goats at their pastime, looks on with yearning eyes, and fain would be even as they; and thou, when thou beholdest the laughter of maidens, dost gaze with yearning eyes, for that thou dost not join their dances."

Begin, ye Muses dear, begin the pastoral song!

Yet these the herdsman answered not again, but he bare his bitter love to the end, yea, to the fated end he bare it.

---

[2]Hermes, the messenger of the Gods, was believed also to be the protector of animals used in sacrifice; hence he was a favorite deity among shepherds.

[3]Priapus, son of Dionysus (Bacchus) and Aphrodite (Venus), was also a protector of flocks of sheep and goats.

Begin, ye Muses dear, begin the pastoral song!

Ay, but she too came, the sweetly smiling Cypris[4], craftily smiling she came, yet keeping her heavy anger; and she spake, saying: "Daphnis, methinks thou didst boast that thou wouldst throw Love a fall; nay, is it not thyself that hast been thrown by grievous Love?"

Begin, ye Muses dear, begin the pastoral song!

But to her Daphnis answered again: "Implacable Cypris, Cypris terrible, Cypris of mortals detested, already dost thou deem that my latest sun has set; nay, Daphnis even in Hades shall prove great sorrow to Love.

Begin, ye Muses dear, begin the pastoral song!

"Where it is told how the herdsman with Cypris—Get thee to Ida, get thee to Anchises[5]! There are oak trees—here only galingale blows, here sweetly hum the bees about the hives!

Begin, ye Muses dear, begin the pastoral song!

"Thine Adonis, too, is in his bloom, for he herds the sheep and slays the hares, and he chases all the wild beasts. Nay, go and confront Diomedes[6] again, and say, 'The herdsman Daphnis I conquered, do thou join battle with me.'

Begin, ye Muses dear, begin the pastoral song!

"Ye wolves, ye jackals, and ye bears in the mountain caves, farewell! The herdsman Daphnis ye never shall see again, no more in the dells, no more in the groves, no more in the woodlands. Farewell Arethusa, ye rivers, good-night, that pour down Thymbris your beautiful waters.

[4]Cypris is another name for Aphrodite.
[5]Anchises, who dwelt on Mt. Ida, was beloved by Aphrodite, by whom she bore Aeneas.
[6]Diomedes was a Greek warrior who incurred the anger and suffered the revenge of Aphrodite.

Begin, ye Muses dear, begin the pastoral song!

"That Daphnis am I who here do herd the kine, Daphnis who water here the bulls and calves.

"O Pan, Pan! whether thou art on the high hills of Lycæus, or rangest mighty Mænalus, haste hither to the Sicilian isle! Leave the tomb of Helice, leave that high cairn of the son of Lycaon, which seems wondrous fair, even in the eyes of the blessed.[7]

Give o'er, ye Muses, come, give o'er the pastoral song!

"Come hither, my prince, and take this fair pipe, honey-breathed with wax-stopped joints; and well it fits thy lip: for verily I, even I, by Love am now haled to Hades.

Give o'er, ye Muses, come, give o'er the pastoral song!

"Now violets bear, ye brambles, ye thorns bear violets; and let fair narcissus bloom on the boughs of juniper! Let all things with all be confounded,—from pines let men gather pears, for Daphnis is dying! Let the stag drag down the hounds, let owls from the hills contend in song with the nightingales."

Give o'er, ye Muses, come, give o'er the pastoral song!

So Daphnis spake, and ended; but fain would Aphrodite have given him back to life. Nay, spun was all the thread that the Fates assigned, and Daphnis went down the stream. The whirling wave closed over the man the Muses loved, the man not hated of the nymphs.

Give o'er, ye Muses, come, give o'er the pastoral song!

And thou, give me the bowl, and the she-goat, that I may milk her and pour forth a libation to the Muses. Farewell, oh, farewells manifold, ye Muses, and I, some future day, will sing you yet a sweeter song.

[7]Lang says "These are places famous in the oldest legends of Arcadia."

The Goatherd. Filled may thy fair mouth be with honey, Thyrsis, and filled with the honeycomb; and the sweet dried fig mayst thou eat of Ægilus, for thou vanquishest the cicala in song! Lo here is thy cup; see, my friend, of how pleasant a savour! Thou wilt think it has been dipped in the well-spring of the Hours. Hither, hither, Cissætha: do thou milk her, Thyrsis. And you young she-goats, wanton not so wildly lest you bring up the he-goat against you.

BION[1]

THE LAMENT FOR ADONIS

This poem was probably intended to be sung at one of the spring celebrations of the festival of Adonis. The story is traditional; Adonis, a favorite of Aphrodite, was killed by a boar while hunting.

WOE, woe for Adonis, he hath perished, the beauteous Adonis, dead is the beauteous Adonis, the Loves join in the lament. No more in thy purple raiment, Cypris[2], do thou sleep; arise, thou wretched one, sable-stoled, and beat thy breasts, and say to all, "He hath perished, the lovely Adonis!"

---

[1]The authorship of this elegy is uncertain, though it was for long attributed to Bion, who is supposed to have died about 300 B.C. This poem may have been written as late as 100 B.C. The argument and translation from the Greek are by Andrew Lang, *op. cit.*
[2]I.e., Venus, or Aphrodite.

Woe, woe for Adonis, the Loves[3] *join in the lament!*

Low on the hills is lying the lovely Adonis, and his thigh with the boar's tusk, his white thigh with the boar's tusk is wounded, and sorrow on Cypris he brings, as softly he breaths his life away.

His dark blood drips down his skin of snow, beneath his brows his eyes wax heavy and dim, and the rose flees from his lip, and thereon the very kiss is dying, the kiss that Cypris will never forego.

To Cypris his kiss is dear, though he lives no longer, but Adonis knew not that she kissed him as he died.

Woe, woe for Adonis, the Loves join in the lament!

A cruel, cruel wound on his thigh hath Adonis, but a deeper wound in her heart doth Cytherea[4] bear. About him his dear hounds are loudly baying, and the nymphs of the wild wood wail him; but Aphrodite with unbound locks through the glades goes wandering,—wretched, with hair unbraided, with feet unsandaled, and the thorns as she passes wound her and pluck the blossom of her sacred blood. Shrill she wails as down the long woodlands she is borne, lamenting her Assyrian lord, and again calling him, and again. But round his navel the dark blood leapt forth, with blood from his thighs his chest was scarlet, and beneath Adonis's breast, the spaces that afore were snow-white, were purple with blood.

Woe, woe for Cytherea, the Loves join in the lament!

She hath lost her lovely lord, with him she hath lost her sacred beauty. Fair was the form of Cypris, while Adonis was living, but her beauty has died with Adonis! *Woe, woe for Cypris*, the mountains all are saying, and the oak-trees answer, *Woe for Adonis*. And the rivers bewail the sorrows of Aphrodite, and the wells are weeping Adonis on the mountains. The flowers flush red for

[3]I.e., cupids.
[4]Another name for Aphrodite.

anguish, and Cytherea through all the mountain-knees, through every dell doth shrill the piteous dirge.

Woe, woe for Cytherea, he hath perished, the lovely Adonis!

And Echo cried in answer, *He hath perished, the lovely Adonis.* Nay, who but would have lamented the grievous love of Cypris? When she saw, when she marked the unstaunched wound of Adonis, when she saw the bright red blood about his languid thigh, she cast her arms abroad and moaned, "Abide with me, Adonis, hapless Adonis abide, that this last time of all I may possess thee, that I may cast myself about thee, and lips with lips may mingle. Awake Adonis, for a little while, and kiss me yet again, the latest kiss! Nay kiss me but a moment, but the lifetime of a kiss, till from thine inmost soul into my lips, into my heart, thy life-breath ebb, and till I drain thy sweet love-philtre, and drink down all thy love. This kiss will I treasure, even as thyself, Adonis, since, ah ill-fated, thou art fleeing me, thou art fleeing far, Adonis, and art faring to Acheron, to that hateful king and cruel, while wretched I yet live, being a goddess, and may not follow thee! Persephone[5], take thou my lover, my lord, for thy self art stronger than I, and all lovely things drift down to thee. But I am all ill-fated, inconsolable is my anguish, and I lament mine Adonis, dead to me, and I have no rest for sorrow.

"Thou diest, O thrice-desired, and my desire hath flown away as a dream. Nay, widowed is Cytherea, and idle are the Loves along the halls! With thee has the girdle of my beauty perished. For why, ah overbold, didst thou follow the chase, and being so fair, why wert thou thus overhardy to fight with beasts?"

So Cypris bewailed her, the Loves join in the lament:

Woe, woe for Cytherea, he hath perished, the lovely Adonis!

A tear the Paphian[6] sheds for each blood-drop of Adonis, and

---

[5]The wife of Hades, king of the lower regions.
[6]Another name for Aphrodite.

tears and blood on the earth are turned to flowers. The blood
brings forth the rose, the tears, the wind-flower.

Woe, woe for Adonis, he hath perished, the lovely Adonis!

No more in the oak-woods, Cypris, lament thy lord. It is no fair
couch for Adonis, the lonely bed of leaves! Thine own bed,
Cytherea, let him now possess,—the dead Adonis. Ah, even in
death he is beautiful, beautiful in death, as one that hath fallen
on sleep. Now lay him down to sleep in his own soft coverlets,
wherein with thee through the night he shared the holy slumber
in a couch all of gold, that yearns for Adonis, though sad is he to
look upon. Cast on him garlands and blossoms: all things have
perished in his death, yea all the flowers are faded. Sprinkle him
with ointments of Syria, sprinkle him with unguents of myrrh.
Nay, perish all perfumes, for Adonis, who was thy perfume, hath
perished.

He reclines, the delicate Adonis, in his raiment of purple, and
around him the Loves are weeping, and groaning aloud, clipping
their locks for Adonis. And one upon his shafts, another on his
bow is treading, and one hath loosed the sandal of Adonis, and
another hath broken his own feathered quiver, and one in a golden
vessel bears water, and another laves the wound, and another
from behind him with his wings is fanning Adonis.

Woe, woe for Cytherea, the Loves join in the lament!

Every torch on the lintels of the door has Hymenaeus [7] quenched,
and hath torn to shreds the bridal crown, and *Hymen* no more,
Hymen no more is the song, but a new song is sung of wailing.

"*Woe, woe for Adonis,*" rather than the nuptial song the Graces
are shrilling, lamenting the son of Cinyras, and one to the other
declaring, *He hath perished, the lovely Adonis*.

And *woe, woe for Adonis*, shrilly cry the Muses, neglecting
Pæan [8], and they lament Adonis aloud, and songs they chant to

[7] The god of marriage.
[8] A surname of Apollo.

him, but he does not heed them, not that he is loth to hear, but that the Maiden of Hades doth not let him go.

Cease, Cytherea, from thy lamentations, to-day refrain from thy dirges. Thou must again bewail him, again must weep for him another year.

MOSCHUS[1]

THE LAMENT FOR BION

WAIL, let me hear you wail, ye woodland glades, and thou Dorian[2] water; and weep ye rivers, for Bion, the well beloved! Now all ye green things mourn, and now ye groves lament him, ye flowers now in sad clusters breathe yourselves away. Now redden ye roses in your sorrow, and now wax red ye wind-flowers, now thou hyacinth, whisper the letters on thee graven, and add a deeper *ai ai*[3] to thy petals; he is dead, the beautiful singer.

Begin, ye Sicilian Muses, begin the dirge.

Ye nightingales that lament among the thick leaves of the trees, tell ye to the Sicilian waters of Arethusa the tidings that Bion the herdsman is dead, and that with Bion song too has died, and perished hath the Dorian minstrelsy.

---

[1]This poem, attributed to Moschus, was probably written by a follower of Bion about 100 B.C. The translation is by Andrew Lang, *op. cit.*

[2]Doris was a region in Greece, whence came the dialect in which these idyls were written.

[3]See note to "Lycidas," line 106.

Begin, ye Sicilian Muses, begin the dirge.

Ye Strymonian[4] swans, sadly wail ye by the waters, and chant with melancholy notes the dolorous song, even such a song as in his time with voice like yours he was wont to sing. And tell again to the Œagrian[5] maidens, tell to all the Nymphs Bistonian,[6] how that he hath perished, the Dorian Orpheus.

Begin, ye Sicilian Muses, begin the dirge.

No more to his herds he sings, that beloved herdsman, no more 'neath the lonely oaks he sits and sings, nay, but by Pluteus's[7] side he chants a refrain of oblivion. The mountains too are voiceless: and the heifers that wander by the bulls lament and refuse their pasture.

Begin, ye Sicilian Muses, begin the dirge.

Thy sudden doom, O Bion, Apollo himself lamented, and the Satyrs mourned thee, and the Priapi in sable raiment, and the Panes[8] sorrow for thy song, and the fountain fairies in the wood made moan, and their tears turned to rivers of waters. And Echo in the rocks laments that thou art silent, and no more she mimics thy voice. And in sorrow for thy fall the trees cast down their fruit, and all the flowers have faded. From the ewes hath flowed no fair milk, nor honey from the hives, nay, it hath perished for mere sorrow in the wax, for now hath thy honey perished, and no more it behoves men to gather the honey of the bees.

Begin, ye Sicilian Muses, begin the dirge.

Not so much did the dolphin mourn beside the sea-banks, nor ever sang so sweet the nightingale on the cliffs, nor so much lamented the swallow on the long ranges of the hills, nor shrilled so loud the halcyon o'er his sorrows;

[4]The Strymon, a river in Thrace.
[5]I.e., Thracian.
[6]Also Thracian.
[7]I.e., Hades'.
[8]Effigies of Priapus and Pan stood in the pastures.

(Begin, ye Sicilian Muses, begin the dirge.)

Nor so much, by the grey sea-waves, did ever the sea-bird sing, nor so much in the dells of dawn did the bird of Memnon bewail the son of the Morning, fluttering around his tomb, as they lamented for Bion dead.

Nightingales, and all the swallows that once he was wont to delight, that he would teach to speak, they sat over against each other on the boughs and kept moaning, and the birds sang in answer, "Wail, ye wretched ones, even ye!"

Begin, ye Sicilian Muses, begin the dirge.

Who, ah who will ever make music on thy pipe, O thrice desired Bion, and who will put his mouth to the reeds of thine instrument? who is so bold?

For still thy lips and still thy breath survive, and Echo, among the reeds, doth still feed upon thy songs. To Pan shall I bear the pipe? Nay, perchance even he would fear to set his mouth to it, lest, after thee, he should win but the second prize.

Begin, ye Sicilian Muses, begin the dirge.

Yea, and Galatea laments thy song, she whom once thou wouldst delight, as with thee she sat by the sea-banks. For not like the Cyclops[9] didst thou sing—him fair Galatea ever fled, but on thee she still looked more kindly than on the salt water. And now hath she forgotten the wave, and sits on the lonely sands, but still she keeps thy kine.

Begin, ye Sicilian Muses, begin the dirge.

All the gifts of the Muses, herdsman, have died with thee, the delightful kisses of maidens, the lips of boys; and woful round thy tomb the loves are weeping. But Cypris loves thee far more than the kiss where with she kissed the dying Adonis.

[9]A one-eyed giant who vainly loved the nymph Galatea.

Begin, ye Sicilian Muses, begin the dirge.

This, O most musical of rivers, is thy second sorrow, this, Meles,[10] thy new woe. Of old didst thou lose Homer, that sweet mouth of Calliope,[11] and men say thou didst bewail thy goodly son with streams of many tears, and didst fill all the salt sea with the voice of thy lamentation—now again another son thou weepest, and in a new sorrow art thou wasting away.

Begin, ye Sicilian Muses, begin the dirge.

Both were beloved of the fountains, and one ever drank of the Pegasean[12] fount, but the other would drain a draught of Arethusa. And the one sang the fair daughter of Tyndarus, and the mighty son of Thetis, and Menelaus Atreus's son,[13] but that other,—not of wars, not of tears, but of Pan, would he sing, and of herdsmen would he chant, and so singing, he tended the herds. And pipes he would fashion, and would milk the sweet heifer, and taught lads how to kiss, and Love he cherished in his bosom and woke the passion of Aphrodite.

Begin, ye Sicilian Muses, begin the dirge.

Every famous city laments thee, Bion, and all the towns. Ascra laments thee far more than her Hesiod, and Pindar is less regretted by the forests of Bœotia. Nor so much did pleasant Lesbos mourn for Alcæus, nor did the Teian town so greatly bewail her poet, while for thee more than for Archilochus doth Paros yearn, and not for Sappho, but still for thee doth Mytilene wail her musical lament;[14]

[10]A river in Thrace.

[11]The muse of epic poetry. Smyrna, Bion's birthplace, is according to Lang "one of the towns which claimed the honor of being Homer's birthplace."

[12]A fountain sacred to the muses, created when Pegasus struck the spot with his hoof. Hippocrene and Arethusa produced different kinds of inspiration and consequently different kinds of poetry: epic or tragic, and pastoral.

[13]Helen, Achilles, and Menelaus were chief characters in Homer's *Iliad*.

[14]Hesiod, Pindar, Alcæus, Anacreon (of Teos), Archilochus, and Sappho were famous Greek poets.

[Here seven verses are lost.]

And in Syracuse Theocritus; but I sing thee the dirge of an Ausonian sorrow, I that am no stranger to the pastoral song, but heir of the Doric Muse which thou didst teach thy pupils. This was thy gift to me; to others didst thou leave thy wealth, to me thy minstrelsy.

Begin, ye Sicilian Muses, begin the dirge.

Ah me, when the mallows wither in the garden, and the green parsley, and the curled tendrils of the anise, on a later day they live again, and spring in another year; but we men, we, the great and mighty, or wise, when once we have died, in hollow earth we sleep, gone down into silence; a right long, and endless, and unawakening sleep. And thou too, in the earth wilt be lapped in silence, but the nymphs have thought good that the frog should eternally sing. Nay, him I would not envy, for tis no sweet song he singeth.

Begin, ye Sicilian Muses, begin the dirge.

Poison came, Bion to thy mouth, thou didst know poison. To such lips as thine did it come, and was not sweetened? What mortal was so cruel that could mix poison for thee, or who could give thee the venom that heard thy voice? surely he had no music in his soul.

Begin, ye Sicilian Muses, begin the dirge.

But justice hath overtaken them all. Still for this sorrow I weep and bewail thy ruin. But ah, if I might have gone down like Orpheus to Tartarus,[15] or as once Odysseus, or Alcides of yore, I too would speedily have come to the house of Pluteus, that thee perchance I might behold, and if thou singest to Pluteus, that I might hear what is thy song. Nay, sing to the Maiden[16] some strain of Sicily, sing some sweet pastoral lay.

[15]Hell. See note to *Lycidas*, 1. 58.
[16]Persophone, wife of Pluto.

And she too is Sicilian, and on the shores by Aetna she was
wont to play, and she knew the Dorian strain. Not unrewarded will
thy singing be; and as once to Orpheus's sweet minstrelsy she gave
Eurydice to return with him, even so will she send thee too, Bion,
to the hills. But if I, even I, and my piping had aught availed,
before Pluteus I too would have sung.

VIRGIL[1]

PASTORAL V

*Mopsus and Menalcas, two very expert shepherds at a song,
begin one by consent to the memory of Daphnis, who is supposed
by the best critics to represent Julius Cæsar. Mopsus laments
his death; Menalcas proclaims his divinity; the whole eclogue
consisting of an elegy and an apotheosis.*

Menalcas.

Since on the downs our flocks together feed,
And since my voice can match your tuneful reed,
Why sit we not beneath the grateful shade,
Which hazels, intermixed with elms, have made?

Mopsus.

Whether you please that sylvan scene to take,
Where whistling winds uncertain shadows make;

[1]Virgil (born 70 B.C., died 19 B.C.) wrote, in addition to the epic poem the
Aeneid and other, shorter poems, ten eclogues, or pastoral poems. The trans-
lations from the Latin and the arguments of the fifth and tenth eclogues are by
John Dryden.

Or will you to the cooler cave succeed,
Whose mouth the curling vines have overspread?

Menalcas.

Your merit and your years command the choice;
Amyntas only rivals you in voice.

Mopsus.

What will not that presuming shepherd dare,
Who thinks his voice with Phœbus may compare?

Menalcas.

Begin you first; if either Alcon's praise,
Or dying Phyllis, have inspired your lays;
If her you mourn, or Codrus you commend,
Begin, and Tityrus your flock shall tend.

Mopsus.

Or shall I rather the sad verse repeat,
Which on the beech's bark I lately writ?
I writ, and sung betwixt. Now bring the swain,
Whose voice you boast, and let him try the strain.

Menalcas.

Such as the shrub to the tall olive shows,
Or the pale sallow to the blushing rose;
Such is his voice, if I can judge aright,
Compared to thine, in sweetness and in height.

Mopsus.

No more, but sit and hear the promised lay;
The gloomy grotto makes a doubtful day.
The nymphs about the breathless body wait

Of Daphnis, and lament his cruel fate.
The trees and floods were witness to their tears;
At length the rumour reached his mother's ears.
The wretched parent, with a pious haste,
Came running, and his lifeless limbs embraced.
She sighed, she sobbed; and, furious with despair,
She rent her garments, and she tore her hair,
Accusing all the gods, and every star.
The swains forgot their sheep, nor near the brink
Of running waters brought their herds to drink.
The thirsty cattle, of themselves, abstained
From water, and their grassy fare disdained.
The death of Daphnis woods and hills deplore;
They cast the sound to Libya's desert shore;
The Libyan lions hear, and hearing roar.
Fierce tigers Daphnis taught the yoke to bear,
And first with curling ivy dressed the spear.
Daphnis did rites to Bacchus first ordain,
And holy revels for his reeling train.
As vines the trees, as grapes the vines adorn,
As bulls the herds, and fields the yellow corn;
So bright a splendour, so divine a grace,
The glorious Daphnis cast on his illustrious race.
When envious Fate the godlike Daphnis took,
Our guardian gods the fields and plains forsook;
Pales no longer swelled the teeming grain,
Nor Phœbus fed his oxen on the plain;
No fruitful crop the sickly fields return,
But oats and darnel choke the rising corn;
And where the vales with violets once were
　　crowned,
Now knotty burs and thorns disgrace the ground.

Come, shepherds, come, and strew with leaves
    the plain;
Such funeral rites your Daphnis did ordain.
With cypress-boughs the crystal fountains hide,
And softly let the running waters glide.
A lasting monument to Daphnis raise,
With this inscription to record his praise:—
"Daphnis, the fields' delight, the shepherds' love,
Renowned on earth, and deified above;
Whose flock excelled the fairest on the plains,
But less than he himself surpassed the swains."

Menalcas.

O heavenly poet! such thy verse appears,
So sweet, so charming to my ravished ears,
As to the weary swain, with cares opprest,
Beneath the sylvan shade, refreshing rest;
As to the feverish traveller, when first
He finds a crystal stream to quench his thirst.
In singing, as in piping, you excel;
And scarce your master could perform so well.
O fortunate young man! at least your lays
Are next to his, and claim the second praise.
Such as they are, my rural songs I join,
To raise our Daphnis to the powers divine;
For Daphnis was so good, to love whate'er was
    mine.

Mopsus.

How is my soul with such a promise raised!
For both the boy was worthy to be praised,
And Stimicon has often made me long
To hear, like him, so soft, so sweet a song.

Menalcas.

Daphnis, the guest of heaven, with wondering
    eyes,
Views, in the milky way, the starry skies,
And far beneath him, from the shining sphere,
Beholds the moving clouds, and rolling year.
For this with cheerful cries the woods resound,
The purple spring arrays the various ground,
The nymphs and shepherds dance, and Pan
    himself is crowned.
The wolf no longer prowls for nightly spoils,
Nor birds the springes fear, nor stags the toils;
For Daphnis reigns above, and deals from thence
His mother's milder beams, and peaceful
    influence.
The mountain-tops unshorn, the rocks, rejoice;
The lowly shrubs partake of human voice.
Assenting Nature, with a gracious nod,
Proclaims him, and salutes the new-admitted
    god.
Be still propitious, ever good to thine!
Behold! four hallowed altars we design;
And two to thee, and two to Phœbus rise;
On both is offered annual sacrifice.
The holy priests, at each returning year,
Two bowls of milk, and two of oil, shall bear;
And I myself the guests with friendly bowls will
    cheer.
Two goblets will I crown with sparkling wine,
The generous vintage of the Chian vine;
These will I pour to thee, and make the nectar
    thine.

In winter shall the genial feast be made
Before the fire; by summer, in the shade.
Damœtas shall perform the rites divine,
And Lyctian Ægon in the song shall join.
Alphesibœus, tripping, shall advance,
And mimic Satyrs in his antic dance.
When to the nymphs our annual rites we pay,
And when our fields with victims we survey;
While savage boars delight in shady woods,
And finny fish inhabit in the floods;
While bees on thyme, and locusts feed on dew—
Thy grateful swains these honours shall renew.
Such honours as we pay to powers divine,
To Bacchus and to Ceres, shall be thine.
Such annual honours shall be given; and thou
Shalt hear, and shalt condemn thy suppliants to
     their vow.

Mopsus.

What present, worth thy verse, can Mopsus find?
Not the soft whispers of the southern wind,
That play through trembling trees, delight me
     more;
Nor murmuring billows on the sounding shore;
Nor winding streams, that through the valley
     glide,
And the scarce-covered pebbles gently chide.

Menalcas.

Receive you first this tuneful pipe, the same
That played my Corydon's unhappy flame;
The same that sung Neæra's conquering eyes,
And, had the judge been just, had won the prize.

Mopsus.

Accept from me this sheep-hook in exchange;
The handle brass, the knobs in equal range.
Antigenes, with kisses, often tried
To beg this present, in his beauty's pride,
When youth and love are hard to be denied.
But what I could refuse to his request,
Is yours unasked, for you deserve it best.

PASTORAL X

Gallus, a great patron of Virgil, and an excellent poet, was very deeply in love with one Cytheris, whom he calls Lycoris, and who had forsaken him for the company of a soldier. The poet therefore supposes his friend Gallus retired, in his height of melancholy, into the solitudes of Arcadia (the celebrated scene of pastorals), where he represents him in a very languishing condition, with all the rural deities about him, pitying his hard usage, and condoling his misfortune.

THY sacred succour, Arethusa, bring,
To crown my labour ('tis the last I sing),
Which proud Lycoris may with pity view:—
The Muse is mournful, though the numbers few.
Refuse me not a verse, to grief and Gallus due.
So may thy silver streams beneath the tide,

Unmixed with briny seas, securely glide.
Sing then my Gallus, and his hopeless vows;
Sing, while my cattle crop the tender browse.
The vocal grove shall answer to the sound,
And echo, from the vales, the tuneful voice
    rebound.

What lawns or woods withheld you from his aid,
Ye nymphs, when Gallus was to love betrayed,
To love, unpitied by the cruel maid?
Not steepy Pindus could retard your course,
Nor cleft Parnassus, nor the Aonian source:
Nothing, that owns the Muses, could suspend
Your aid to Gallus:—Gallus is their friend.
For him the lofty laurel stands in tears,
And hung with humid pearls the lowly shrub
    appears.

Mænalian pines the godlike swain bemoan,
When, spread beneath a rock, he sighed alone;
And cold Lycæus wept from every dropping
    stone.

The sheep surround their shepherd, as he lies:
Blush not, sweet poet, nor the name despise.
Along the streams, his flock Adonis fed;
And yet the queen of beauty blest his bed.
The swains and tardy neat-herds came, and last
Menalcas, wet with beating winter mast.
Wondering, they asked from whence arose thy
    flame.

Yet more amazed, thy own Apollo came.
Flushed were his cheeks, and glowing were his
    eyes:

"Is she thy care? is she thy care?" he cries.
"Thy false Lycoris flies thy love and thee,
And, for thy rival, tempts the raging sea,
The forms of horrid war, and heaven's
        inclemency."
Silvanus came: his brows a country crown
Of fennel, and of nodding lilies, drown.
Great Pan arrived; and we beheld him too,
His cheeks and temples of vermilion hue.
"Why, Gallus, this immoderate grief?" he cried.
"Think'st thou that love with tears is satisfied?
The meads are sooner drunk with morning dews,
The bees with flowery shrubs, the goats with
        browse."
Unmoved, and with dejected eyes, he mourned:
He paused, and then these broken words
        returned:—
"'Tis past; and pity gives me no relief:
But you, Arcadian swains, shall sing my grief,
And on your hills my last complaints renew:
So sad a song is only worthy you.
How light would lie the turf upon my breast,
If you my sufferings in your songs exprest!
Ah! that your birth and business had been mine—
To pen the sheep, and press the swelling vine!
Had Phyllis or Amyntas caused my pain,
Or any nymph or shepherd on the plain,
(Though Phyllis brown, though black Amyntas
        were,
Are violets not sweet, because not fair?)
Beneath the sallows and the shady vine,
My loves had mixed their pliant limbs with mine:

Phyllis with myrtle wreaths had crowned my hair,
And soft Amyntas sung away my care.
Come, see what pleasures in our plains abound;
The woods, the fountains, and the flowery
    ground.
As you are beauteous, were you half so true,
Here could I live, and love, and die with only
    you.
Now I to fighting fields am sent afar,
And strive in winter camps with toils of war;
While you, (alas, that I should find it so!)
To shun my sight, your native soil forego,
And climb the frozen Alps, and tread the eternal
    snow.
Ye frosts and snows, her tender body spare!
Those are not limbs for icicles to tear.
For me, the wilds and deserts are my choice;
The Muses, once my care; my once harmonious
    voice.
There will I sing, forsaken, and alone:
The rocks and hollow caves shall echo to my
    moan.
The rind of every plant her name shall know;
And, as the rind extends, the love shall grow.
Then on Arcadian mountains will I chase
(Mixed with the woodland nymphs) the savage
    race;
Nor cold shall hinder me, with horns and hounds
To thrid the thickets, or to leap the mounds.
And now methinks o'er steepy rocks I go,
And rush through sounding woods, and bend the
    Parthian bow;

As if with sports my sufferings I could ease,
Or by my pains the god of love appease.
My frenzy changes: I delight no more
On mountain tops to chase the tusky boar:
No game but hopeless love my thoughts pursue:
Once more, ye nymphs, and songs, and sounding
    woods, adieu!
Love alters not for us his hard decrees,
Not though beneath the Thracian clime we freeze,
Or Italy's indulgent heaven forego,
And in mid-winter tread Sithonian snow;
Or, when the barks of elms are scorched, we keep
On Meroë's burning plains the Libyan sheep.
In hell, and earth, and seas, and heaven above,
Love conquers all; and we must yield to Love."

   My Muses, here your sacred raptures end:
The verse was what I owed my suffering friend.
This while I sung, my sorrows I deceived,
And bending osiers into baskets weaved.
The song, because inspired by you, shall shine;
And Gallus will approve, because 'tis mine—
Gallus, for whom my holy flames renew,
Each hour, and every moment rise in view;
As alders, in the spring, their boles extend,
And heave so fiercely, that the bark they rend.

   Now let us rise; for hoarseness oft invades
The singer's voice, who sings beneath the shades.
From juniper unwholesome dews distil,
That blast the sooty corn, the withering herbage
    kill.
Away, my goats, away! for you have browsed
    your fill.

TWO CLASSICAL CONSOLATIONS

SENECA[1]

🌿 🌿 🌿

from "TO MARCIA, ON CONSOLATION"

There is no need, therefore, for you to hurry to the tomb of your son; what lies there is his basest part and a part that in life was the source of much trouble—bones and ashes are no more parts of him than were his clothes and the other protections of the body. He is complete—leaving nothing of himself behind, he has fled away and wholly departed from earth; for a little while he tarried above us while he was being purified and was ridding himself of all the blemishes and stain that still clung to him from his mortal existence, then soared aloft and sped away to join the souls of the blessed. A saintly band gave him welcome—the Scipios and the Catos and, joined with those who scorned life and through a draught of poison found freedom, your father, Marcia. Although there all are akin with all, he keeps his grandson near him, and, while your son rejoices in the new found light, he instructs him in the movement of the neighbouring stars, and gladly initiates him into Nature's secrets, not by guesswork, but by experience having true knowledge of them all; and just as a stranger is grateful for a guide through an unknown city, so your son, as he searches

[1]Written about 40 A.D. This prose passage comes from Book VI. par. xxv, of The Dialogues of Lucius Annæus Seneca, trans. John W. Basore, in Seneca, *Moral Essays*, The Loeb Classical Library (New York, 1932), Vol. II, pp. 89–91.

into the causes of celestial things, is grateful for a kinsman as his instructor. He bids him also turn his gaze upon the things of earth far below; for it is a pleasure to look back upon all that has been left behind. Do you therefore, Marcia, always act as if you knew that the eyes of your father and your son were set upon you— not such as you once knew them, but far loftier beings, dwelling in the highest heaven. Blush to have a low or common thought, and to weep for those dear ones who have changed for the better! Throughout the free and boundless spaces of eternity they wander; no intervening seas block their course, no lofty mountains or pathless valleys or shallows of the shifting Syrtes; there every way is level, and, being swift and unencumbered, they easily are pervious to the matter of the stars and, in turn, are mingled with it.

STATIUS[1]

🌾 🌾 🌾

from "*THE POET'S LAMENT FOR HIS FATHER*"

Do thou thyself, most learned sire, vouchsafe me from Elysian springs a bitter potency in the music of grief, and the touch of an ill-omened lyre. For without thee I may not move the Delian grottoes, or awake Cirrha to wonted strains. All that Phœbus of late revealed in his Corycian bower,[2] and Euhan upon the hills of

---

[1]Written between 79 and 95 A.D., this passage is the first 65 lines of poem iii in Book V of *Silvæ*, trans. J. H. Mozley, in *Statius*, The Loeb Classical Library (New York, 1928), Vol. I, pp. 303–309.

Reprinted by permission.
[2]On Parnassus.

Ismara,[3] I have unlearnt. The fillets of Parnassus have dropped from my brow, and I have beheld in fear the deadly yew creep in among the ivy-leaves, and the trembling bay—ah! horror!—wither and die. Yet surely I am he who, loftily inspired, essayed to extol the deeds of great-hearted kings, and to raise my song to the height of Mars himself. Who has doomed my spirit to decay? Who has drawn a cold shroud of mist about my blighted heart, and drowned my inspiration? The goddesses stand dismayed around the bard, and with neither voice nor finger make sweet melody. Their queen herself sinks her head upon her silent lyre, as when after Orpheus' loss she halted by thy stream, O Hebrus, and gazed at the troops of beasts that listened no more, and the woods that moved not since the strains were gone.

But thou, whether freed from the body thou soarest to the heights and reviewest the glittering realms and the elements of things, learning what is God, whence cometh fire, what orbit guides the sun, what cause makes Phœbe wane and has power to restore her hidden light, and dost continue the music of renowned Aratus; or whether in the secluded grassy meads of Lethe, among gatherings of heroes and spirits of the blest, thou dost attend the Mæonian and Ascræan sages, thyself no feebler shade, and makest music in thy turn and minglest thy song with theirs: O grant a voice and inspiration, father, to my great grief. For thrice has the moon journeyed o'er the heaven, and thrice displayed her countenance, and still beholds me sluggish, and my sadness unconsoled by any draught of Helicon; ever since thy pyre shed its red light upon my face, and with streaming eyes I gazed upon thy ashes, I have held cheap my poet's art. Scarce do I for the first time free my mind for tasks like this, and (e'en now with failing hand and no tearless eye) essay to shake my silent sorrow from its torpor, leaning against the tomb in which thou dost rest at peace in our own fields,—those fields where after Aeneas' death star-bright Ascanius set Alba upon Latian hills, in hatred of the plains that

[3]In Thrace, with which Bacchus was connected in legend.

Phrygian blood had drenched, the royal dower of his ill-omened stepdame. Here in thy honour—nor softer is the fragrant breath of Sicanian crocus, nor the rare cinnamon that rich Sabæans pluck thee, nor perfumed blossoms of Arabia—O thou who deservest full meed of holy offerings, do I make musical lament; ah! receive the groans and the anguish of thy son, and tears such as have been shed for but few fathers. Would it were my fortune, to build an altar to thy shade, a work that would match temples, to raise high the soaring fabric, higher than Cyclopean rock or the Pyramids' bold masonry, and plant a mighty grove about thy tomb. There had I surpassed the tribute of the Sicilian sepulchre, and Nemea's precinct and the rites of maimed Pelops. There no naked bank of Grecian athletes would cleave the air with the Œbalian disk, no sweat of steeds would water the ground or hoof-beat ring upon the crumbling track; there would be but the choir of Phœbus, and I would duly sing thy praise, O father, and bind on thee the minstrel's prize of leaves. I myself, as priest of the dead and of thy soul, would with moist eyes lead a mournful dirge, from which neither Cerberus with all his mouths nor Orpheus' cruel bond could keep thee. There as I sang of thy goodness and thy deeds perchance thy love had deemed me not second to Homer's mighty utterance, ay, would even fain hold me equal to Maro's solemn chant.

NINE RENAISSANCE PASTORALS

PETRARCH[1]

ECLOGUE VI[2]

PAMPHILIUS.   MITIO.

Pamphilius. [Aside] Who has allowed the unrestrained flocks[3] to tear up all the grove?[4] Is this the proper treatment for the

[1]Of Petrarch's twelve Latin eclogues, numbers VI and VII are of most interest to students of "Lycidas." They were written sometime between 1346 and 1352, at about the mid-point of the seventy-year, self-imposed exile of the papacy in Avignon, and during the time of Pope Clement VI. They are thinly veiled satires on the corruption of the papal court. Petrarch called Avignon "the sink of every vice, the haunt of all iniquities, a third Babylon, the Babylon of the West." Such a metaphor suggests not only the captivity suffered by the Hebrews, but also that part of St. John's revelation in which he sees the whore of Babylon (Revelation xvii, and Ezekiel xxiii). In Eclogue VI the two shepherds Pamphilius and Mitio represent St. Peter and Pope Clement VI. Some of the allegory is now difficult to discover, but the main outline is clear. Clement prefers luxury to the hard, unrewarding work of a conscientious pastor; under the patronage of the King of France he has found it easy to become wealthy and popular by means of simony, bribery, and nepotism; having relaxed the discipline of the cardinals and prelates, he knows that his flocks (the people) are not being guided in the Christian way. But preferring goods here to the good hereafter, he affirms his devotion to Epy (Epicura), "the famous whore," whom Petrarch, remembering the scriptural allegory, uses to represent the corrupt state of the church.

Apparently no English translation of Eclogues VI and VII has ever been published; the one presented here is a somewhat free rendering of a literal translation by Professor Paul MacKendrick.

[2]Petrarch's title is *Pastorum Pathos*.
[3]The cardinals and prelates.
[4]The church.

pasture which Jove[5] watered with celestial dew, and his uncouth wife[6] constantly sprinkled with foaming streams, and Pyrius[7] and Phanius[8] once did water?[9] While the bitter grasses[10] are quietly growing, what madness defeats our hope for a good crop in the field which fair Hyber,[11] our delight and glory, was not afraid at plowing time[12] to burn off by applying live coals to the crackling laurel?[13] . . .

Mitio. [Aside] The lot of shepherds is too hard! Hobble the goats, restrain the wild flocks, and at the same time make the udders flow with quantities of milk![14] We know no magic arts. And now this mad man plots quarrels and hurls insults; as he brandishes that stone[15] and that knotty bolt.[16] May he merit whatever curses he is preparing; may he die by his own sword; may he drink the poison he carries. Still, I shall address him with flattery. [To Pamphilius] Where have you come from Pamphilius, and where are you going? Where have you been staying? You are closing your folds late! Why are you trembling, and why is your mouth spattered with foam?

Pamphilius. You evil rogue! Hasn't the earth yet swallowed you up? As if it were not enough that the groves, the harvest, and every perverted thing mock my hopes! To whom (alas!) was the guardianship of the fields entrusted? To whom, the flock that was to be pastured in the meadow? The lambs have met untimely deaths, and the oxen have died of exhaustion. The goats have survived;

[5]God.
[6]The early church.
[7]St. Paul.
[8]St. Stephan.
[9]With the blood of martyrdom.
[10]Unholy riches.
[11]St. Laurence.
[12]During the earliest days of the church.
[13]A reference to the martyrdom of St. Laurence, who was burned to death. The poet seems to have punned on *lauris* for *Laurence* and *laurel.*
[14]Keep the church wealthy.
[15]"Thou art Peter, and upon this rock (*petrus*) I will build my church." Matthew xvi. 18.
[16]The key or bar to the gates of heaven.

and the filthy swine—a destructive flock—nourished by riotousness and ease, run unrestrained through the fields. They stunt the sapplings with their nibbling, and already their smell[17] infects the mountains[18] and our peace.

Mitio. [Aside] I expected these insults; for some time I have had a foreboding that he would return angry and determined to be relentless to both the back of a slave and the reputation of a friend, and to show no affection. [To Pamphilius] How easy it is to carp at another's life! How hard to take care of your own! If you happened to be the shepherd, would the flocks live any longer, or would the wolf rush at the flocks any less violently? By no means, in spite of your threatening staff and your menacing look. At your command grim winter would not become more kind (though its rigor is less than yours), nor doubtful spring, nor deathlike autumn, nor violent summer; nor would the birds spare the grain; nor would there be more shade for the tender, young grape-vines; nor would the goat spare the trees, nor the heifer the grasses.

Pamphilius. Was I not a shepherd, you vilest of men, when surly Nereus,[19] pasturing his bulls[20] on the opposite hill,[21] threw me to the earth and was preparing to steal my whole flock? I fought until he, the more violent, ripped off my hairy tunic and left me naked.[22]

Mitio. Why do you not rather consider, I pray you, how many of our flock fell in that short time? The valley is still rich with the blood, the bones lie hastily stuffed into blind caverns.[23] Did not you and others send the animals to the butcher? The wolves and the lions scattered them!

[17]Infamy.

[18]Altars.

[19]Nero.

[20]Powerful Romans.

[21]The Capitoline, not the Vatican.

[22]After the burning of Rome, Nero accused the Christians of setting fire to the city and ordered them sought out and slain. Though not supported by any scriptural record, the tradition is that Peter himself suffered martyrdom at the same time or shortly afterward.

[23]The catacombs.

Pamphilius. May the gods be your enemies! The shepherds and their dogs did not sit idly by. We all did what we could: we stripped the fallen and sent the snowy pelts to the city and the lord. What did you save, except the horns taken from the bullocks?[24]

Mitio. I kept the gold we were paid for the tender lambs, and I kept the artful cups, for unlike my rude ancestors I scorn the simple things. In fact, under me art has much enhanced the lot of all shepherds. Look, my feet are girt with many-colored sandals in the Tyrrhenian style; I wear a garland made of gleaming jasper;[25] I have dyed my white woolen robe thrice in Sidonian purple; and I have won great friends with gifts of milk.[26] My bride glitters with jewels and necklaces, and she lies with me safe in the dusky shade, neither shivering with cold and snows, nor sunburned like your squalid old woman, when you lived in the country. When you look, she seems my queen, not merely my wife. Now the kids[27] play everywhere in the grassy valleys, and with innate pleasure the slothful swine wallow in their sties. No strange shepherd enters our cool cave; and with no cares about tomorrow I lie there singing love songs. Or sometimes I go out to judge the games or battles of the flocks. Stay, sad complainer, you who are always ready to nip with the tooth of a mad dog.

Pamphilius. Then, vile one, will you interweave our thorns with gold? That your wife may strut in her dishonest finery? That you may lay your limbs on a better couch, and take upon your eyes that sleep which, if your mind were watchful, would be fleeting; and that wild visions may make you weary? That you may drink from beautiful cups, and that both the beauty of the house and the expensive furniture may themselves be causes of fear? What foolish labor, to pile up danger with your gold! And your crowning madness—to obey a mad bride! Can you hide your adulteries and

[24]Cardinals' hats, the shape of which suggested horns.
[25]The second crown in the papal tiara was indicative of the Pope's temporal power.
[26]Simony.
[27]Cardinals.

the many sins of a shameful marriage chamber? Indeed, those whom you imagine to be friends have already raped the easy virtue of your unchaste wife; and now they are setting a trap for you, too. Lift up your eyes, downcast by too much drinking. The wolf[28] threatens the fold, and thieves surround your rich cave.

Mitio. With those thieves I have made a treaty, signed in pig's blood and written upon the altar of the king of the world below; and though it may be hated by the gods above, it is honored by those below, before whom suits are settled with money. Let hungry tigers run through the rich folds, and raging hail descend, and a bitter season kill the cattle, I shall never be poor: I have buried so much in the black pits!

Pamphilius. Away, criminal, with your wild oath, which would make Jove,[29] the sun,[30] and even light itself[31] blush for shame! But I shall not dwell on such a grievous subject. You, who used to be a shepherd, now ship your treasures along the shores; you will succeed in neither enterprise. Dare now to forsake the woods and see distant cities; to spread your sail to the winds and face the violent storms; for your wife has long been wandering on unknown hills, and leaving her ancestral threshold and chaste chamber, that famous whore will follow joyfully and bring with her the ardent suitors and the reeking goats, to whom the grass of alien fens is already pleasant.[32]

Mitio. Why, father, do you fill my mind with dark ambiguities? Why do you now interrupt my long leisure with these tardy complainings? Stop attacking the happy with sad words. Come, say whatever is on your mind.

[28]The king of France.
[29]God.
[30]Christ.
[31]The Holy Ghost.
[32]Apparently, Pamphilius in this speech says, "Go ahead—follow your foolish course; you are no good as a shepherd, and you will be equally a failure in your commercial enterprises (as head of the highly mercenary papal court at Avignon). But then, it's an old story; the corruption of the church (the Whore of Babylon) is not new."

Pamphilius. You deserve to be whipped, then thrown into irons, or to be imprisoned then crucified; but such punishment would be too brief! Nay, rather the endless pains of the eternal prison, or whatever is more grim, you faithless steward, you deserter, you wretch ungrateful to a kind lord!

Mitio. Cruel old man, only fortune kept you yourself from being crucified: all the meadows know how in fear of proud Nereus you would have deserted the flock if Apollo in his anger had not ordered you to stop in your tracks and not leave the battle. How faithful to the lord you had been in earlier times I shall not mention, lest the shepherds should discover that also.[33]

Pamphilius. Though I fled, I returned. I was afraid of the whips of that wicked shepherd,[34] a fear that no one can condemn me for. In the river I soon washed off the stains, and my pallor disappeared. But what caused your flight? Why did you leave the quiet folds? Why did you scorn your ancestral oaks and wander far afield? Whither have you taken the keys? Give them up if they are such a great burden, lest the wandering sheep be forced to return home by a leap over the wall.

Mitio. At the moment, great matters occupy me; I shall not always be the slave of a penniless sheepfold. I have, by singing, got me a sweet mistress; and I long to become beautiful. Whereas I used to be burned by the sun, I now keep to my shady cave, and wash my hands with fresh spring water, and delight myself by looking into that mirror which Corydon[35] the Byzantine gave me.[36] My wife knows and submits to everything, since I in my turn endure at her hands much that is hard. Brag of your unknown mistresses;[37] let my epicurean one [Epy] only comfort me with everlasting embraces.

[33]A reference to Peter's denial of Christ; see Matthew xxvii. 69 ff.
[34]Nero.
[35]Constantine.
[36]The Donation of Constantine, a forged document in which Constantine the Great appears to give extensive temporal rights to the papacy, among them the government of Rome and certain other lands in Italy.
[37]Glory and beatitude, unknown to us in this world.

Pamphilius. An infamous woman, unlucky to many lovers, fondles you, madman. That former Epicurus,[38] fallen into those profane embraces, sang through country and city how noble a wife he had. He took her away with him to watered gardens. But living and dead, he was held in scorn; and as he lay dead, the dogs ate him and befouled his tomb. It was hardly happier for others after him. But your adulteress perhaps is faithful to you; enjoy her; and keep your Corydon's mirror—may that wretch groan forever who first gave shepherds the evil gift of a palace! While you seek to be considered handsome and upon your snowy head put tiaras (something unknown to your predecessors), while you deck the cave with flowers, and your crook with woodland roses, everything is going madly to rack and ruin. When impious stars conquer in the sky, and impious fate on earth, no one cares for the flocks or herds, and no one works in the field.

[Ten lines omitted.]

Mitio. Though I die sorrowing, I shall live happily. You are sad both ways; I know not what purpose your confused dreams serve.

Pamphilius. It is enough to remember through what dangers the good master provided all this! We saw him scourged with sharp thorns! Ah, how dearly the merchant coming from high Olympus, in his mercy, bought the lost herds! How modest his fare; how humble the life of the true Lord of the countryside! You riot in his fields while he is thirsting and sober in his own hall.

Mitio. He was unmindful of his interests: when the miser is afraid of losing a little, he may lose much. Ceaselessly he fills his shepherds with awful voices. You can judge from this: always immerse sick sheep in a fountain, keep them shorn lest vermin worm their way into the fleece, keep the goats away from the hedges, beware of blackberry bushes and the fruitless tamarisk. He wears out his servants with starvation and cold, and teaches them to bear hunger, vigil, and thirst. He adds threats, and his voice thunders; forbidding all delights, he requires difficult tasks: haunt the untrodden,

[38]Boniface VII.

climb difficult mountains, and tread barefoot upon sharp stones. Can any mortal follow this rule? Or is it any wonder that his friends are few? I, on the other hand, remember that I serve a powerful master,[39] that I lost a magnificent one, that it is fitting to have pleased many.

Where no force oppresses, who will eat up so many sheaves? What flock could possibly get through so much grain? Let the flocks wander lustful, and the eager goats rejoice in copulation. I shall sport as well, as long as my mistress, my Epy, succors me; keep your ways, leave me to mine.

Pamphilius. Unhappy one, are you so ignorant of our master? While you think that you stand safe in the shade, he will come, turning joy into sorrow.

Mitio. What, are you trying to frighten me with words? The brave despise what is before their faces; the timid fear even distant dangers.

ECLOGUE VII

MITIO.   EPY.

Mitio. My noble Epy, sweeter than these woods or the grass of the fields, pleasanter than these caves or the sounding stream, only stay with me here while I am alone.

Epy. Let no day, Mitio, interrupt our loving; let no day take your head from my bosom. I am, and always shall be, happy by your side; nor shall I of my own will ever be borne away.

---

[39]The devil or the King of France.

Mitio. O my own (for it is sweet to unburden the mind by speaking), how angry I am! How full of gall is my heart! Pamphilius has bitterly attacked me unaware and carried the quarrel deep. At the end he tried to make me afraid of the absent master, though I was fearless; this brow of mine fronted him courageously. Now, dear one, who has shared so many delights with me, so many happy days, share what threatens. Let us not be lazy, let us count our sheep, let us number our goats.[1] If that solemn one returns, or perhaps that fearsome one,[2] we may hide our crimes with fiction: only let our attitude and our story be the same.

Epy. Whatever wool-bearing flock you used to keep is now either sick or dead; on the river-bank feed whatever fate has left of the other flock. Wasting fever, deep-seated itch, and racking cough already ravage the empty fields: thick sweat weighs down the fleece, and stiff thorns transfix the coats. We are safer if they are far off, lest grim destruction run secret through the few remaining sheep. . . . You may know the rest; turn your eyes to it in its enormity. . . . That goat you see far off sporting, with tawny back, noticeable because of his height, whose cheeks and chin are covered with a pepper and salt beard, is known far and wide through the pastures as merciless and wanton. Even the eager nanny-goats fear to choose him, he so rushes with his whole weight lying upon the wretched creatures, nor scorns any love-making whatever. . . .[3]

Mitio. What is there that long passage of time does not snatch away as the ages flit past? Behold how the flock has wasted away. Whose fault? Nothing of man's is deathless: we ourselves shall die. My counsel is to enjoy ourselves, and not lose the hour of passing time in sloth: to reject empty worries—unless you, my dear, think otherwise.

Epy. Nay, I agree. For what is there left? What end of evils? Let

[1]The cardinals.
[2]Christ.
[3]In the next forty-five lines Petrarch continues this kind of allegorical satire on the luxury of over a dozen cardinals.

that solemn one continue to press upon us his ambiguous promises and his threats of judgment; the case is pending; it's best to take our pleasure meanwhile, and take from death its first share. I say nothing about how wise I have been, always your faithful urger-on, and at one with you: to take advantage of present goods, and enjoy them: to consign the future to fate, to recall fleeting youth with constant caresses, to stand against old age. . . .[4] But we have given enough time to our cares, and already the hour of quiet summons us. Hurry: let the chilling air of night settle down on the hills, so long as locked in one another's arms we may lie upon the soft grass.

BOCCACCIO[1]

ECLOGUE XIV

This fourteenth Eclogue is called Olympia, from the Greek Olympus, signifying in Latin splendidus *or* lucidus, & *so Heaven. Hence the name Olympia is given to this Eclogue, since much is told herein concerning the heavenly realm. The speakers are four in number: Silvius, Camalus, Therapon, and Olympia. By Silvius I mean myself, and so I name myself here, because the first thought of this Eclogue came to me in a wood. Camalos*

[4]In the next forty-six lines Epy advises Mitio which cardinals to favor and which to sacrifice.

[1]Boccaccio, a friend of Petrarch's, wrote *Olympia* about 1361, a few years after the death of his five-year-old daughter. The argument here reproduced is an extract from one of the poet's letters. The translation (from Latin) of both the argument and the ecologue is by Sir Israel Gollancz: *Boccaccio's Olympia* (Methuen, London, 1904; Barnes & Noble, New York). Reprinted by permission.

is from a Greek word signifying hebes *or* torpens, *that is, dull or sluggish—a type of the lazy servant. Of Therapon I am not giving you the meaning: indeed I cannot recall it unless I refer to the book whence I took the rest. So this you will not learn from me. You know how slippery is memory, and especially the memory of old men. By Olympia I mean my little daughter, who died at that age at which, as we believe, those who die become the citizens of heaven. And so for Violante, as she was named when living, I call her now Olympia—the angelic.*

SILVIUS. CAMALUS. THERAPON. OLYMPIA.

Silvius. If I err not, the sylvan sprites rejoice.
List, boys, with song of birds the grove is filled.
With gentle whine Luke scampers to and fro;
Something he sees; as for a friend he wags.
Bright day, long heralded, bestreaks the shades:
Go, seek ye what it is, and what good Luke
Yonder has seen; and quickly bring me word.
Camalus. Our master, when—alack!—he cannot
    lull
His aching heart to sleep, from downy bed
Gives orders, and poor we, toil-weary boys,
—What recketh he?—must forth & view dread
    night.
Silvius. In Western Ocean when the Dawn's first
    streak
Illumines Earth, when Delia[2] westward leads
Her brother's[3] team, when hinds o'er lions vaunt,
A servant then perchance will do as bid.

[2]I.e., Diana, the goddess of hunting.
[3]Apollo, or Phœbus, often confused with Helios, the god who drove the chariot of the sun in its daily course.

But, Therapon,[4] do thou unbar the door!
Fear not; see thou, I pray, what Luke has seen.—
Therapon. Haste, sir, arise, come forth! Our
  ancient oaks
Are all by fire possessed; light conquers night.
The grove is all a-glow; fierce flames now lap
The very gods within. Awed by the sight,
I hied me thence. The flames the gods now lap!
Silvius. Pan, holy God of shepherds, be my help!
Go ye, my boys, with water face the flames.
Stay, Therapon! stay here awhile.—What is't?
What see I? Am I sane? Perchance I sleep.
Nay, yonder light, it is nor flame nor fire.
Seest not the branches fair, the hazels green
Amid the glow, the beech-trees all about
Inviolate? Here burns no evil heat.
Therapon. Look skyward! Spangled stars betoken
  night.
Daylight the wood illumes. What wonder next?
Silvius. So Nature marks her changes; day and
  night
Commingled she displays. But here I see
Nor Phœbe's[5] beams nor Sol's. Rare fragrances
Feel'st not, as if Dame Nature here had made
A grove of Araby? What flowers fresh
Has Night brought forth? What strains hear I
above?
God-haunted spots & pastures these things show.—
Olympia. Hail, chiefest glory, dearest father, hail!

---

[4]The Greek word for *attendant*.
[5]I.e., Diana, also goddess of the moon.

Fear not, I am thy daughter. Why this look?
Silvius. I' faith, I know not, do I wake or dream!
My child's voice hear I, and her image sweet
Stands here before me. Fool! Too oft the gods
With shadows trick dull mortals. Let us home!
Olympia. Silvius, doubt not! Think'st thou
    Olympia
Would mock her father, or herself reveal
Against God's will? To dry thy tears I come.
Silvius. Now know I, 'tis no trick of love or
    dream.
O too beloved! thy father's dearest hope!
What god restrained thee, child? Me Fusca[6] told
That, whilst I journey'd to Campania's hills,
Vesuvian pastures, thou from us wast reft,
And, hid in sacred soil, wast lost to sight.
Thinking 'twas so, in misery I mourned;
I wailed thee, daughter mine, on mountain
    heights,
In woods and far-off glades, and called thee oft.
But me, if I be worthy, tell what haunts
Have held thee this long day. Who gave to thee
Thy robe so white, entwined with yellow gold?
What light shines in thine eyes, ne'er seen before?
Thy comrades—who? Wondrous, how grown art
    thou
In so brief time! Thou seem'st for spousal fit.
Olympia. The vestments, sire, which thou to me
    didst give,
Great Mother Earth holds in her mighty lap.

[6]Gollancz notes, "Probably the child's mother."

These robes, this form, this beauty, heavenly bright,
The Virgin gave; with Her I was. But, lo,
My comrades hast ne'er seen before? Rejoice!
Silvius. I call them not to mind. More beauteous
    sure
Was not Narcissus, nor was Daphnis such,
The wood-nymphs' darling, nor Alexis fair![7]
Olympia. Know'st thou thy Marius not, thy Julus,
    too,
And these sweet sisters mine? Thy dear ones all!
Silvius. The down-soft cheeks I knew, their
    image lacks;
Beshaded cheeks I see. Now join we hands;
Embrace we now; and come, let kisses sweet
Be pressed, to sate my soul. Thy praises, Pan,
How shall I sing, and thine, Sylvanus? Boys,
Strip you for wrestling; lead our ancient games!
From sacred beeches hang the victors' meeds!
Let beakers foam; and jocund Bacchus laud!
With garlands deck the gods; with grassy turf
Heap high their altars! To Diana slay
A heifer white; to Night a tawny beast!
Reeds for the lads good youth; for lasses wreaths!
Olympia. Reeds, Silvius, have we here, & goodly
    wreaths;
And, if so please thee festal cheer to stir,
Strains will we chant these woods have never
    known.
Silvius. Hushed is the wood; Arno flows silently;
Hushed are the fields; & hushed be ye, my boys.

[7]A beautiful youth beloved by a shepherd, in Virgil's *Eclogue II*.

Olympia. "Endless our life by Codrus'[8] grace
    divine!
He, sent of late from high Olympus down
Into the Maid, the Golden Age recalled;
Shepherds' vile scorn He dreed,[9] on cedar hung;
A triumph gave He Death, of His free will.
Endless our life by Codrus' grace divine!

"So from the blemished sheep He washed old taints,
    Old maladies and sores, with His bright blood;
    Then sought He Pluto's dales, broke up his
        folds,
    And brought to light the Father's flocks and
        herds.
    Endless our life by Codrus' grace divine!

"Death slain, Elysium's[10] fragrant fields He oped;
To gardens honey-sweet His host He led,
Victor all-bright with laurel and with oak,
And gave us evermore the wished-for homes.
Endless our life by Codrus' grace divine!

"At doomsday, when their slough all kinds
    resume,
He comes again, to part the lambs from goats,—
These to wild beasts, to Thrones eternal those:
Anon a heaven new will compass them.
Endless our life by Codrus' grace divine!"

---

[8] An Athenian king who sacrificed himself for his country's sake—here, of course, another name for Christ.

[9] I.e., *suffered.*

[10] I.e., Heaven's.

Silvius. What fools be we, to think that Latin
          swains
Can pipe and sing! Their notes are out of time.
Arcadian youths upon their mountain-slopes,
The Thracian sire[11] who with his song drew
          rocks,
All have I known; yet none so high I hold
As like unto these youths. What throats! what
          tones!
What harmony! What music from their reeds!
The Guardian of the Grove,[12] the Queen of Song,
Calliope, nor e'en the God who rules
O'er Helicon,[13] could vie! The oaks bent low,
And tender wood-nymphs sought the silent glades
Unto the light; yea, wolves and hounds stood
          mute.
Tell me, ye youths, caught ye the heavenly sense
Of yon sweet strain? Ne'er Tityrus[14] sang so,
Nor aged Mopsus[15] in his sunny wood.
Sacred it is, to be remembered aye!
Unto the maids, from me, give snow-white doves;
Unto the lads strong bows from Ischiros![16]
Olympia. Hold thou them! To the glorious
          climes we haunt
Nought mortal comes. Immortals shun things
          frail.

[11]Orpheus.
[12]Sylvanus.
[13]Apollo.
[14]Virgil.
[15]Homer.
[16]The Greek word for *strong*.

Silvius. What climes, oh, daughter mine, what
    climes, I pray?
Yon roof us all will cover; quiet sleep
Green sward will give; a turf 'neath oak our
    board;
The crystal brook our fount of richest draughts;
And our wild woodlands chestnuts ripe will bring,
And apples fresh; our fruitful herd young kids
And cheese. What other climes, then, would ye
    seek?
Olympia. Have I not told thee, father dear, that
    Earth
The trappings keeps that thou to me didst give?
I am not what I was, the child thou knewest;
Now am I numbered with the god-like throng.
Me fair Olympus calls, my comrades eke;
Homeward we turn. Sweet father mine, farewell!
Silvius. Leav'st thou me wretched thus, I weep
    to death.
Olympia. Away with grief! Think'st thou to burst
    thy fate
With tears? As many as created be,
We all are born for death. I have but done
What thou shalt do. Rate not with spleen, I pray,
The god's eternal years. Trow peace is thine
Hereafter; render praise to Heav'n for me,
That, dying, I 'scaped death and toils below.
Awhile apart, sure thou wilt see me soon,
And lead with me in bliss unending years.
Silvius. Mine eyes will waste with tears, mine
    age will pine.

After life's woes in what wood shall I seek
Thee, fleeing hence, twice reft from these mine
    arms?
Olympia. Elysium I seek, where thou wilt come.
Silvius. Elysium! The Mantuan bard,[17] methinks,
Sang once & piped thereof; was none more skilled.
Is thine the spot he sang? Fain would I learn.
Olympia. His mighty mind, indeed, some glories
    grasped,
Some beauties of the place; he sang but few
Of all the many joys Elysium holds,—
Home of the blest, our Gods' most fair abode!
Silvius. What mountains hath it? In what
    regions set?
What he saw not, or what he left unsung,
Tell me! To hear was oft sweet balm for toil.
Perchance the soul will yearn those sights to see.
Olympia. Remote, beyond the reach of sickly sheep
Bright with perpetual light, a mountain rears;
There Phœbus first, from Earth below, ascends;
On topmost peak a wood, with towering palms,
With festal laurels, cedars ever-green,
Peace-loving olive-trees, to Pallas[18] dear.
Who could describe the many flowers? the scents
The zephyrs waft? and who the silvery streams,
Their wondrous waters sprinkling all about,
Meandering here and there with murmur sweet,
And drawing in their course full many a bough?

[17]Virgil, in the *Æneid*, describes Æneas' visit to Elysium.

[18]I.e., the goddess Minerva, victor in a heavenly contest to discover who could invent the most useful present to mankind. Minerva won because the olive is not only a very useful tree but the symbol of peace.

Such golden fruit th'Hesperides[19] ne'er saw;
Gold-hued are birds there, and the gold-hornèd
    goats
And gentle deer; moreover, lambs are there
Whose snowy fleeces gleam with brightest gold;
And oxen, too, and bulls, and fatted cows,
Resplendent all with gold; yea, lions tame,
And griffins tame, their manes with gold all bright.
Golden our sun, and silvern is our moon;
Grander than yours the stars that shine on us.
'Tis ever Spring; no southern gale strikes there;
A joyous calm the place pervades. Earth's mist,
And Night, all things that jar, are banished
    thence.
Death comes not to the flocks, nor ailing Age;
And far are grievous cares, and want, and grief.
Things wished for freely come to all. What more?
The air, so soft, with sweet-toned song resounds.
Silvius. Marvels thou tell'st! Sure, sacred is that
    wood,
The Gods' abode! But who o'errules it, say;
Who dwell therein, and what the usages?
Olympia. High, on a grassy mound, in glory sits
Arcesilas,[20] shepherding flocks and worlds.
But verily, would'st thou His aspect know,
It were in vain; the mind this cannot grasp.
All life is He, too fair, wholly serene;
And in His bosom rests a Lamb, milk-white,
Sweet Sustenance for folk, whereby we live;

[19]Guardians of the golden apple, which Juno gave to Jupiter on their wedding-day.
    [20]*Chieftan,* i.e., *God.*

Thence comes our weal, and life to those re-born.
And from Them both alike there flames a fire,
Wondrous to trow! To all things spreads that
>   light:
The sad it comforts, purges the mind's eye,
Counsels the wretched, strengthens those that fall,
With sweetest love informs the souls of men.
An aged band of Satyrs, suppliant,
Their hoary locks with rosy chaplets crowned,
Stand there; with lute & song the Lamb they praise.
And then the Purple Order, well revered,
Their temples all engirt with laurel green;
At cross-roads these with pipes the true God sang,
And, strong of soul, they conquered cruel toils.
Then come the Snow-white Host; lilies their brows
Enwreathe. To these is joined our little band,
Thy children fair. The Saffron Order next,
Illustrious, resplendent, with loud voice
Sing praises of the Gods, and serve the King.
'Mong these Asylas[21] sang; how calm his look,
When first the mount received me from the
>   woods!
Silvius. Did my Asylas then ascend the mount?
Worthy was he, gentle, of ancient faith
A noble type. God grant we meet again!
But knew he thee, when to the heights thou
>   camest?
Olympia. Gleeful, he threw his arms about my
>   neck;
Kissed me a hundred times, embraced me oft;

---

[21]Gollancz notes that this is " Evidently a reference to Boccaccio's father."

And then, a mighty concourse with him, said:
"Hast come, my Silvius' beloved child?
'Come hither, love,'[22] and Hymen's holy lays
Sing we; and Manhood's Mother honour thou!"
Then me he led, and down I knelt where sat
The Virgin beauteous. Joyful She clasped
Her maid, & kindly spake: "Now, daughter
    mine,
Enter Our blissful choirs; thou shalt enjoy
Eternal Spousal, as Olympia
In Heaven known, who Violante wast."
The raiment that thou seest she gave me then.
Were I to tell the strains the woods then gave,
The tuneful Shepherds' notes, thou'dst scarce
    believe.
The mountain's song resounded through the cave;
And fire so flashed, that all things seemed a-glow;
And scattered from above fell roseate flowers.
Silvius. Who is the Virgin? Tell me now, I pray.
Olympia. Jove's Gracious Mother She, His
    Daughter eke,
The Gods' Queen-Mother, Heaven's Gem,
    Night's Bane,
Celestial Star, the Shepherds' certain hope,
Their flocks' sure guard, their wished-for rest
    from toil!
Fauns Her adore, and nymphs; Apollo great
With lute exalts Her praise, and owns Her Queen.
She, worshipful, upon the Father's throne,

---

[22]From *Song of Songs*, 4.8—Gollancz. The reference, of course, is to Olympia's metaphysical marriage to Christ.

On right-hand of the Son, full brightly shines.
Her look the woods and mountains, hills and poles,
Makes glad. Too fair is She. About Her fly
White swan-like bands; as Mother hail they Her,
As Spouse and Daughter of Eternal Light!
Silvius. And what do ye, while thus the swans
        acclaim?
Olympia. We youths cull flowers; and, with
        the wreaths we make,
Our unshorn locks we crown. With dances glad
We circle woods and founts and sounding brooks;
And, sporting 'mid the grasses, with loud voice
We chant due praises of the gentle Maid;
And eke the Son we laud. The wood's delights
Who can recount? Who tell in words? Not one!
First must he put on wings, as bird, by flight
To seek and see the heights; else all is vain.
Silvius. 'T were to be wished! But who, as
        Dædalus,[23]
Will give me agile wings, and bind them on,
Show me the easy way, and teach me flight?
Olympia. Thy brother feed, give to the weary
        milk,
To prisoners alms; the naked clothe, the fallen
Raise, while thou canst; and list to those who
        plead.
Such offices will give thee eagle's wings;
And, God thy guide, thou wilt to Heaven fly.—
Silvius. Whither, my daughter, whither fleest thou,
Leaving thy father tearful?—Ah, she passed

---

[23]According to mythology the first man to fly.

To upper air, and drew the scents she brought.
With tears my life I'll dree, and fare to death.
Boys, drive the calves afield! Lo, Phosphor[24]
    gleams,
And Sol emerges now from misty shades.

CASTIGLIONE

ALCON[1]

The shepherds were bewailing Alcon, pride
Of the forest and comfort of sad lovers,
Torn away by the Fates in his youth's bloom;
Whose songs the Fauns and Dryads often heard,
Whom Apollo, whom Pan so marveled at.
More than the rest, him mourned his loved Iolas,
With trickling tears called cruel the gods and stars,
As Philomela bewails in the shadows
Her lost child, or the widowed turtledove
His mate whom, seen afar in the high oak,
The cruel shepherd with his dart has slain:
He rests no longer on the grass or green
Branches, nor drinks from the sweet crystal stream,
But publishes with sighs his loved one vanished,

[24]The morning star.

[1]Translated from the Latin by Robert M. Durling and published here by
his kind permission. Castiglione (1478–1529), the author of *The Courtier*, wrote
excellent poetry in Latin and Italian. In this eclogue Iolas (the speaker) laments
the death of his friend Alcon.

And fills the high groves with his stricken moan.
No day saw sad Iolas cease from tears,
At morn nor at its sinking in the west:
No longer his the care to pasture sheep
Or lowing bulls, and lead them, fed, to drink,
Nor to protect with folds the calves and kids:
Among the woods or on the lonely shore,
Sunk in himself, not ceasing with deepest
Night, thus to the deaf sands and cliffs he cried:
    Alcon, joy of the Muses and of Phœbus,
The better share of my heart and soul, Alcon,
My grief, for whom these tears shall ever flow,
What god, or what unhappy chance has seized you?
Does cruel fate, then, plunder all our jewels?
Is some malicious god the foe of good?
The reaper spares the unripe grain, the rude
Farmer leaves on its native tree the green
Fruit; but you early death has drowned in dark
Avernus, gripping with fierce hands your growing
Youth. Alas, luckless boy! with you the mildness
Of fields, with you Love, the Graces, and all
Our joys are gone. The glory of the trees
Lies scattered, and the wood denies its shade.
The empty pastures wither to the wind,
For the fountains have run dry, the streams fail.
The promised harvest, eaten by foul rust,
Yields but the mangled stalk of sterile grain.
The flocks shudder, their feeble masters pine;
And the unfed wolf rages in the folds,
Rends with their dams the sucklings, fearless braves
Both dogs and men, and carries off his prey.
No gladness sounds from forest, field, or river;

The sweet-flowing streams mourn your bitter fate,
The sweet springs, the forest, field, and river.
Alas, unhappy youth! the very gods
Do mourn; the farmer hears in the grove weeping
The woodnymphs, Pan, Sylvanus, and the Fauns.
But not by tears or wailing are the Fates
Moved, merciless, and Death is deaf to pleas.
Cut by the plow, the grass dies on its field,
Yet rises once again from the live sod;
But once our thread of life is broken, fate
Joins it no more. See, on the heavenly slope
The sun sinks down, and dying lights the stars;
And yet, once sunk beneath the western wave,
He visits earth anew with brighter beams.
But we, once the black flood of death has closed
Over us, once the unrelenting gate
Swings to, we see no more the lands of light;
Eternal sleep wraps us in bitter shade.
Then vainly tears and useless vows pour forth;
The rough wind scatters tears and useless vows.
Alas, wretched youth, stolen by harsh fate!
No more, the shepherd-throng about us crowding,
Shall I see your swift arrow strike the mark
Nor watch you win the rustic wrestling match.
No more, lying at ease in the mild shade,
Shall we together flee July's long suns;
Your oaten flute no more shall soothe the hills,
Nor to your lofty verse the shaded vales
Shall echo; nor shall ever your Lycoris,
Deep though her name be carved in many a tree,
Hear with my Galatea our vying songs.
For we together grew from earliest youth,

Endured together cold, heat, nights, and days,
And by our common toil our flocks were fed;
We bore these fields the same love, we were one;
Why, then, you dying, am I living still?
Alas, it was the angry gods that led me
Far from home, that I might not close the eyes
Of my dying friend, catch his final breath
With my mouth, nor his last kiss with my lips.
I envy you, Leucippus; for his last
Charges the dying Alcon gave to you,
On your face gazed with fading eyes; and you
Placed on the careful hearse his rigid limbs,
Your tears you shed on the sorrowful grave,
And then, the rite of grief being paid, and all
Due ceremony done, a happy comrade
You followed Alcon, not enduring life
Without him, and now pace the Elysian groves
By him companioned, and forever shall.
And perchance, on some flowering bank, some
Shepherd has in the selfsame tomb arranged,
Devout, the bones of both, for both has wept
The same tears, and their sacree shades has honored.
But I that fatal day no sad tears shed,
Nor to my wretched friend did pay his rite,
But, of harsh fate ignorant, vain dreams
In my madness I feigned within myself:
    "Here in these honored fields shall I dwell; soon
Alcon, quitting his hills and barren crags,
Shall come, the infected streams leaving and poisoned
Herbs, and shall visit these fresh brooks and fields.
Him shall I run to greet, far off shall know,
Shall be the first to touch his countenance,

And the strange joy shall bring forth laughing tears.
Sweet discourse shall we thus at last exchange;
Our heavy sorrows and our long-past griefs
Shall we delight to tell and tell again.
Then, speaking, shall our former love renew,
And here, amid the tranquil fields and rural
Ease, shall we live our lives secure from care.
Ceres protects these fields, Bacchus these slopes,
Here Pales brings grass and milk for the lambs;
Upon these nearby hills the nymphs are wont
To drive the hart, or wind their slender dance;
Guarding the glory of an older race, Tiber
Here washes the grey beauty of the ruins;
Here are the shaded groves, the springs, cool Tempe;
Here did Corydon sing the fair Alexis.
Come then, dear youth, the pastures and the streams
Await you, for you the nymphs already weave
Garlands of flowers to display their joy,
Of fresh flowers brought forth by the daedal earth."
    Thus did I, wretched, frame my hopes in vain,
Ignorant of the crimes of fate and death;
But now, since my deluded prayers were scattered
By the rough wind, nor was it granted me
To see him living, to hear and answer him,
May his shade at least come to me with soft
Flight through the ghastly void, and, pitying
My pain, accept my tears and the deep sighs
Torn from my heart, to which these caves reply.
Here on Anio's banks, with my own hands
A tomb shall I build, which, though it be empty,
Some solace shall afford. Here shall I burn
Incense, invoke his shade. Do you now, youths,

With me strew fragrant roses, hyacinth,
Narcissus; and make deep the laurel shade;
Nor cassia be wanting, cinnamon,
Amomum, that the wind may breathe their scent.
For Alcon loved us, worthy of love himself,
And worthy of such honor. Upon the tomb,
Meanwhile, the nymphs shall scatter amaranth
Intwined with violets, and in their sorrow
Engrave upon the tomb this mournful song:
  "Now that unpitying fate has stolen Alcon,
The harsh mountains weep; day is overlaid
With darkness; fair is foul and sweetness bitter."

MAROT[1]

from DE MADAME LOYSE DE SAVOYE, MERE DU ROY, EN FORME D'EGLOGUE

Chantez, mes vers, fresche douleur conceue.
Non, taisez vous, c'est assez deploré:
Elle est aux champs Elisiens receue,
Hors des travaulx de ce monde esploré.
  Là où elle est n'y a rien defloré;

[1]Clément Marot (1496–1544) wrote this poem in 1531; the text comes from *Œuvres Complètes*, ed. M. Pierre Jannet, 4 vols. (Paris, 1878), Vol. II, pp. 266–267. This passage represents about one-fifth of the entire poem.

Jamais le jour et les plaisirs n'y meurent;
Jamais n'y meurt le vert bien coloré,
Ne ceulx avec qui là dedans demeurent.

Car toute odeur ambrosienne y fleurent,
Et n'ont jamais ne deux ne trois saisons,
Mais un printemps, et jamais ilz ne pleurent
Perte d'amys, ainsi que nous faisons.

En ces beaulx champs et nayfves maisons
Loyse vit, sans peur, peine ou mesaise;
Et nous ça bas, pleins d'humaines raisons,
Sommes marrys (ce semble) de son aise.

Là ne veoit rien qui en rien luy desplaise;
Là mange fruict d'inestimable prix;
Là boyt liqueur qui toute soif appaise;
Là congnoistra mille nobles esprits.

Tous animaulx playsans y sont compris,
Et mille oyseaulx y font joye immortelle,
Entre lesquelz vole par le pourpris
Son papegay, qui partit avant elle.

Là elle veoit une lumiere telle
Que pour la veoir mourir devrions vouloir.
Puis qu'elle a donc tant de joye eternelle,
Cessez, mes vers, cessez de vous douloir.

Mettez voz montz et pins en nonchaloir,
Venez en France, ô Nymphes de Savoye,
Pour faire honneur à celle qui valoir
Feit par son loz son pays et sa voye.

Savoysienne estoit, bien le sçavoye,
Si faictes vous; venez donques, affin
Qu'avant mourir vostre oeil par deçà voye
Là où fut mise après heureuse fin.

Portez au bras chascune plein coffin
D'herbes et fleurs du lieu de sa naissance,
Pour les semer dessus son marbre fin,
Le mieulx pourveu dont ayons congnoissance :
   Portez rameaulx parvenuz à croissance:
Laurier, lyerre et lys blancs honorez,
Romarin vert, roses en abondance,
Jaune soucie et bassinetz dorez,
   Passeveloux de pourpre colorez,
Lavende franche, oeilletz de couleur vive,
Aubepins blancs, aubepins azurez,
Et toutes fleurs de grand' beauté nayfve.
   Chascune soit d'en porter attentive,
Puis sur la tumbe en jectez bien espais,
Et n'oubliez force branches d'olive,
Car elle estoit la bergere de paix . . .

from CONCERNING MADAME LOUISE OF SAVOY, MOTHER OF THE KING, IN THE FORM OF AN ECLOGUE [2]

Sing, my verses, fresh sorrow conceived.

No, rather, be silent; there has been enough lamenting. She has been received in the Elysian fields, beyond the labors of this distressful world. There where she is nothing has lost its bloom;

[2]This translation, by Harry Joshua Leon, is reprinted by permission from *The Pastoral Elegy: An Anthology*, ed. Thomas Perrin Harrison, Jr. (Austin: University of Texas Press, 1939), pp. 142–144.

never do the day and its pleasures die there; never dies the richly colored green, nor those with whom they live within that place. For every ambrosial fragrance flourishes there, and they have neither two nor three seasons, but only spring, and never do they mourn for loss of friends, as we do. In those fair fields and natural mansions Louise lives, without fear, suffering or discomfort, and we below, full of human reasons, are grieved (it seems) at her joy. There she sees naught that can in any way displease her; there she eats fruit of inestimable price; there she drinks that which appeases every thirst; there she will know a thousand noble souls. Every pleasant animal is found there, and a thousand birds give immortal joy, and among them about the place flies her parrot, which departed before her. There she beholds a radiance such that to behold it we should wish to die. So then, since she has such eternal joy,

Cease, my verses, cease to be distressed.

Have no care for your mountains and pines; come to France, you Nymphs of Savoy, to do honor to her who through her glory made great her country and her path. She was of Savoy; well I knew it and so do you. Come then, that before dying your eye may here behold where she was placed after a happy end. Let each one bring in her arms a basket filled with herbs and flowers from the place of her birth, to scatter them upon her smooth marble tomb, the finest that we have knowledge of. Bear bouquets that are full blown: laurel, ivy, and glorious white lilies, green rosemary, abundant roses, yellow marigold, and golden crowfoot, coxcombs colored purple, lovely lavender, carnations of bright hue, white hawthorns, blue hawthorns, and every flower of great natural beauty. Let each one be mindful to bring them; then throw them upon the tomb very thickly, and do not forget many olive branches, for she was the shepherdess of peace . . .

RONSARD[1]

from ECLOGUE I

Quand le bon Henriot par fiere destinée
Avant la nuict venuë accomplist sa journée,
Noz troupeaux, prevoyans quelque futur danger,
Languissoient par les champs sans boire ny manger,
Et beslans et crians et tapis contre terre,
Gisoient comme frappez de l'esclat du tonnerre.
Toutes choses ça bas pleuroient en desconfort;
Le Soleil s'en-nua pour ne voir telle mort,
Et d'un crespe rouillé cacha sa teste blonde,
Abominant la terre en vices si feconde.
Les Nymphes l'ont gemy d'une piteuse vois,
Les Antres l'ont pleuré, les rochers et les bois:
Vous le sçavez, forests, qui vistes és bocages
Les loups mesme le plaindre, et les lions sauvages.
Ce fut ce Henriot qui remply de bon-heur
Remist des Dieux banis le service en honneur,
Et se monstrant des arts le parfait exemplaire,
Esleva jusqu'au ciel la gloire militaire.
Tout ainsi que la vigne est l'honneur d'un ormeau,
Et l'honneur de la vigne est le raisin nouveau,
Et l'honneur des troupeaux est le bouc qui les meine,

[1]This passage is the second song of Angelot. The poem was first published in *Les Elegies, Eclogues et mascarades de P. de Ronsard* (Paris, 1578); our text comes from *Ronsard: Œuvres Complètes*, ed. Gustave Cohen, 2 vols. (Paris, 1958), Vol. I, pp. 928–930.

Et comme les espics sont l'honneur de la plaine,
Et comme les fruicts meurs sont l'honneur des vergers,
Ainsi ce Henriot fust l'honneur des Bergers.
Quantesfois nostre soc depuis sa mort cruelle
A fendu les guerets d'une peine annuelle,
Qui n'ont rendu sinon en lieu de bons espics
Qu'yvraie, qu'aubifoin, que ponceaux inutils!
Les herbes par sa mort perdirent leur verdure,
Les roses et les lis prindrent noire teinture,
La belle marguerite en prist triste couleur,
Et l'oeillet sur sa fueille escrivit son malheur.
Pasteurs, en sa faveur semez de fleurs la terre,
Ombragez les ruisseaux de pampre et de lierre,
Et de gazons herbus en toute saison verts
Dressez luy son sepulchre et y gravez ces vers:
L'ame qui n'eut jamais en vertu son egale,
Icy laissa son voile, allant à son repos:
Chesnes, faites ombrage à la tombe Royale,
Et vous, Manne du Ciel, tombez dessus ses os.
O Berger Henriot, en lieu de vivre en terre
Toute pleine de peur, de fraudes et de guerre,
Tu vis là haut au Ciel, où mieux que paravant
Tu vois dessous tes pieds les astres et le vent,
Tu vois dessous tes pieds les astres et les nues,
Tu vois l'air et la mer et les terres cognues,
Comme un Ange parfait deslié du soucy
Et du fardeau mortel qui nous tourmente icy.
O belle ame royale au Ciel la plus haussée,
Qui te mocques de nous et de nostre pensée,
Et des appas mondains qui tousjours font sentir
Apres un court plaisir un tres-long repentir.
Ainsi qu'un beau Soleil entre les belles ames

Environné d'esclairs, de rayons et de flames
Tu reluis dans le Ciel, et loin de toute peur
Fait Ange, tu te ris de ce monde trompeur.
Où tu es, le Printemps ne perd point sa verdure,
L'orage n'y est point, le chaut ny la froidure,
Mais un air pur et net, et le Soleil au soir
Comme icy ne se laisse en la marine choir.
Tu vois autres forests, tu vois autres rivages,
Autres plus hauts rochers, autres plus verds bocages,
Autres prez plus herbus, et ton troupeau tu pais
D'autres plus belles fleurs qui ne meurent jamais.
Et pource nos forests, nos herbes et nos plaines,
Nos ruisseaux et nos prez, nos fleurs et nos fontaines,
Se souvenant de toy, murmurent en tout lieu
Que le bon Henriot est maintenant un Dieu.
Sois propice à nos voeux: je te feray d'yvoire
Et de marbre un beau temple au rivage de Loire
Où sur le mois d'avril, aux jours longs et nouveaux
Je feray des combats entre les pastoureaux
A sauter, à luter sur l'herbe nouvelette,
Pendant au prochain pin le prix d'une musette.
Là sera ton Janot qui chantera tes faits,
Tes guerres, tes combats, tes ennemis desfaits,
Et tout ce que ta main d'invincible puissance
Oza pour redresser la houlette de France.
Or adieu grand Berger! tant qu'on verra les eaux
Soustenir les poissons, et le vent les oiseaux,
Nous aimerons ton nom, et par ceste ramée
D'âge en âge suivant vivra ta renommée.
Nous ferons en ton nom des autels tous les ans
Verds de gazons de terre, et comme aux Egipans
Aux Faunes, aux Satyrs, te ferons sacrifice:

Ton Perrot le premier chantera le service
En long sourpelis blanc, couronné de cyprés
Et au son du cornet nous ferons aux forests
Apprendre tes honneurs, afin que ta loüange
Redite tous les ans, par les ans ne se change,
Plus forte que la mort, fleurissante en tous temps
Par ces grandes forests comme fleurs au Printemps.

ANGELOT'S LAMENT [2]

When good Henriot through cruel destiny ended his journey
before the coming of night, our flocks, foreseeing some future
danger, pined in the fields without drinking or eating; and bleating
and crying and cowering to the earth, they lay as though struck
by the clap of thunder. All things here below wept in distress.
The sun beclouded himself in order not to behold this death, and
with rusty crape hid his fair head, detesting the earth so fruitful
of evil.

The Nymphs lamented him with piteous voice, the caves wept
for him, the rocks and the woods. You know it, forests, who in
the groves saw even the wolves and the savage lions mourning for
him. This was the Henriot who, filled with prosperity, restored
to honor the worship of the banished gods, and while showing
himself the perfect exemplar of the arts, raised military glory to
the sky.

[2]This translation, by Harry Joshua Leon, is reprinted by permission from
The Pastoral Elegy: An Anthology, ed. Thomas Perrin Harrison, Jr. (Austin:
University of Texas Press, 1939), pp. 153–157. *Henriot* is a pastoral form for
Henri, i.e., the name of Henry II, King of France from 1547 till his death in 1559.

Even as the vine is the glory of an elm, and the glory of the vine is the new grape, and the glory of the flocks is the he-goat which leads them, and as the ears of grain are the glory of the field, and as the ripe fruits are the glory of the orchards, so was Henriot the glory of the shepherds.

How many times since his cruel death has our plowshare split the fields with yearly toil, but instead of good grain ears, they have produced only darnel, corn cockles, and useless poppies!

The grasses at his death lost their greenness, the roses and the lilies took on a black hue, the fair marguerite assumed a sad color, and the carnation inscribed its woe upon its leaf.

Shepherds, in his honor strew the ground with flowers, shade the streams with vine branches and ivy, and of grassy turf, green in every season, build his tomb and engrave thereon these verses: "The soul that in virtue never had its equal left its cloak here in going to its repose: oaks, spread shade over the royal tomb, and, Manna, fall from heaven upon his bones."

Shepherd Henriot, instead of living on an earth full of fear, of deceit and of war, thou livest up yonder in Heaven, where better than before thou beholdest beneath thy feet the stars and the wind, thou beholdest beneath thy feet the stars and the clouds, thou beholdest the air and the sea and the known lands, like a perfect Angel released from care and from the mortal burden which torments us here.

Fair royal spirit, most exalted in Heaven, that dost scorn us and our thoughts and those worldly attractions which ever after a brief pleasure make us feel a very long repentance. Even as a fair Sun amid the fair souls, surrounded by lightnings, rays, and flames, thou art radiant in Heaven and far from every fear, now an Angel, thou dost laugh at this deceitful world.

Where thou art, the springtime never loses its verdure, storms do not exist there, nor heat nor cold, but a pure and clear air, and the sun at evening does not, as here, allow himself to sink into the sea.

Thou beholdest other forests, thou beholdest other shores, other higher rocks, other greener groves, other grassier meadows, and thou pasturest thy flock with other fairer flowers that never die.

Therefore our forest, our grasses and our plains, our brooks and our meadows, our flowers and our fountains, recalling thee, murmur in every place that good Henriot is now a God.

Be propitious to our vows. I will build thee a fair temple of ivory and of marble on the bank of the Loire, where in the month of April, when the days are long and new, I will have contests between the shepherd boys, in leaping, in wrestling on the fresh grass, while there hangs on the nearest pine the prize of a pipe.

There shall be thy Janot, who shall sing thy deeds, thy wars, thy battles, thy enemies defeated, and all that thy hand of invincible power dared, in order to raise up again the sheephook of France.

Now farewell, great Shepherd. As long as men shall see the waters maintain the fish and the wind the birds, we shall love thy name, and through this green bower, from age to following age thy renown shall live.

Every year in thy name we shall build altars, green with turf, and as to the Aegipans, the Fauns, and the Satyrs, we shall bear sacrifice to thee. Thy Perrot shall first sing the service in a long white robe and crowned with cypress, and with the sound of the horn we will make known thy honors to the forests, that thy praise, repeated every year, may not change through the years, proving stronger than death, flourishing at all times in these great forests as flowers in the springtime.

SPENSER[1]

ÆGLOGA VNDECIMA
Nouember

*In this xi. Æglogue he bewayleth the death of some mayden of
greate bloud, whom he calleth Dido. The personage is secrete,
and to me altogether vnknowne, albe of him selfe I often
required the same. This Æglogue is made in imitation of Marot
his song, which he made vpon the death of Loys the frenche
Queene. But farre passing his reache, and in myne opinion
all other the Eglogues of this booke.*

THENOT.   COLIN.

COLIN my deare, when shall it please thee sing,
As thou were wont songs of some iouisaunce?
Thy Muse to long slombreth in sorrowing,
Lulled a sleepe through loues misgouernaunce.
Now somewhat sing, whose endles souenaunce,
Emong the shepeheards swaines may aye remaine,
Whether thee list thy loued lasse aduaunce,

---

[1]The twelve eclogues which compose Edmund Spenser's *The Shepheardes
Calender* were published anonymously in 1579, eleven years before the first
installment of *The Faerie Queene.* The difficulty a modern reader may have in
understanding Spenser's language is partly due to the poet's notion that words
already obsolete in his time were appropriate to rustic verse. The footnotes to
the present text are taken from the " glosse" which accompanied the first edition
of the poem and which was written by the "editor," who signed himself "E.K."
A glossary of rare or obsolete words is on p. 102. The passage from *May* is only
the first sixth of that poem.

Or honor *Pan* with hymnes of higher vaine.
Colin. *Thenot,* now nis the time of merimake.
Nor *Pan* to herye, nor with loue to playe:
Sike myrth in May is meetest for to make,
Or summer shade vnder the cocked haye.
But nowe sadde Winter welked hath the day,
And *Phœbus* weary of his yerely taske,
Ystabled hath his steedes in lowlye laye[2]
And taken vp his ynne in *Fishes* haske.[3]
Thilke sollein season sadder plight doth aske:
And loatheth sike delightes, as thou doest prayse:
The mornefull Muse in myrth now list ne maske,
As shee was wont in younth and sommer dayes.
But if thou algate lust light virelayes,
And looser songs of loue to vnderfong
Who but thy selfe deserues sike Poetes prayse?
Relieue thy Oaten pypes, that sleepen long.
Thenot. The Nightingale is souereigne of song,
Before him sits the Titmose silent bee:
And I vnfitte to thrust in skilfull thronge,
Should *Colin* make iudge of my fooleree.
Nay, better learne of hem, that learned bee,
And han be watered[4] at the Muses well:
The kindlye dewe drops from the higher tree,
And wets the little plants that lowly dwell.

---

[2]According to the season of the moneth Nouember, when the sonne draweth low in the South toward his Tropick or returne.

[3]The sonne, reigneth that is, in the signe Pisces all Nouember. A haske is a wicker pad, wherein they vse to cary fish.

[4]For it is a saying of Poetes, that they haue dronk of the Muses well Castalias, whereof was before sufficiently sayd.

But if sadde winters wrathe and season chill,
Accorde not with thy Muses meriment:
To sadder times thou mayst attune thy quill,
And sing of sorrowe and deathes dreeriment.
For deade is Dido, dead alas and drent,
Dido the greate shehepearde[5] his daughter sheene:
The fayrest May she was that euer went,
Her like shee has not left behinde I weene.
And if thou wilt bewayle my wofull tene:
I shall thee giue yond Cosset for thy payne:
And if thy rymes as rownd and rufull bene,
As those that did thy *Rosalind* complayne,
Much greater gyfts for guerdon thou shalt gayne,
Then Kidde or Cosset, which I thee bynempt:
Then vp I say, thou iolly shepeheard swayne,
Let not my small demaund be so contempt.
Colin. Thenot to that I choose, thou doest me tempt,
But ah to well I wote my humble vaine,
And howe my rymes bene rugged and vnkempt:
Yet as I conne, my conning I will strayne.

VP then Melpomene[6] thou mournefulst Muse of nyne,
Such cause of mourning neuer hadst afore:

---

[5]The great shepheard is some man of high degree, and not as
some vainely suppose God Pan. The person both of the shephearde
and of Dido is vnknowen and closely buried in the Authors con-
ceipt. But out of doubt I am, that it is not Rosalind, as some
imagin: for he speaketh soone after of her also.

[6]The sadde and waylefull Muse vsed of Poets in honor of
Tragedies: as saith Virgile Melpomene Tragico proclamat mæsta
boatu.

Vp grieslie ghostes[7] and vp my rufull ryme,
Matter of myrth now shalt thou haue no more.
For dead shee is, that myrth thee made of yore.
    Dido my deare alas is dead,
        Dead and lyeth wrapt in lead:
            O heauie herse,[8]
Let streaming teares be poured out in store:
            O carefull verse.

Shepherds, that by your flocks on Kentish downes abyde,
Waile ye this wofull waste of natures warke:
Waile we the wight, whose presence was our pryde:
Waile we the wight, whose absence is our carke.
The sonne of all the world is dimme and darke:
        The earth now lacks her wonted light,
        And all we dwell in deadly night,
            O heauie herse.
Breake we our pypes, that shrild as lowde as Larke,
            O carefull verse.

Why doe we longer liue, (ah why liue we so long)
Whose better dayes death hath shut vp in woe?
The fayrest floure our gyrlond all emong,
Is faded quite and into dust ygoe.
Sing now ye shepheards, daughters, sing no moe
        The songs that *Colin* made in her prayse,
        But into weeping turne your wanton layes,

---

[7]The maner of Tragicall Poetes, to call for helpe of Furies and damned ghostes: so is Hecuba of Euripides, and Tantalus brought in of Seneca. And the rest of the rest.

[8]The solemne obsequie in funeralles.

O heauie herse,
Now is time to dye. Nay time was long ygoe,
O carefull verse.

Whence is it, that the flouret of the field doth fade,
And lyeth buryed long in Winters bale:
Yet soone as spring his mantle doth displaye,
It floureth fresh, as it should neuer fayle?
But thing on earth that is of most availe,
As vertues braunch and beauties budde,
Reliuen not for any good.
O heauie herse,
The braunch[9] once dead, the budde eke needes must
quaile,
O carefull verse.

She while she was, (that was, a woful word to sayne)
For beauties prayse and plesaunce had no pere:
So well she couth the shepherds entertayne,
With cakes and cracknells and such country chere.
Ne would she scorne the simple shepheards swaine,
For she would cal hem often heme
And giue hem curdes and clouted Creame.
O heauie herse,
Als *Colin cloute* she would not once disdayne.
O carefull verse.

But nowe sike happy cheere is turnd to heauie chaunce,
Such pleasaunce now displast by dolors dint:
All Musick sleepes, where death doth leade the daunce,

---

[9]He meaneth Dido, who being, as it were the mayne braunch now withered the buddes that is beautie (as he sayd afore) can no more flourish.

And shepherds wonted solace is extinct.
The blew in black, the greene in gray is tinct,
    The gaudie[10] girlonds deck her graue,
    The faded flowres her corse embraue.
        O heauie herse,
Morne nowe my Muse, now morne with teares besprint.
        O carefull verse.
O thou greate shepheard *Lobbin*,[11] how great is thy griefe,
Where bene the nosegayes that she dight for thee:
The coulourd chaplets wrought with a chiefe,
The knotted rushrings, and gilte Rosemaree?
For shee deemed nothing too deere for thee.
        Ah they bene all yclad in clay,
        One bitter blast blewe all away.
        O heauie herse,
Thereof nought remaynes but the memoree.
        O carefull verse.

Ay me that dreerie death should strike so mortall stroke,
That can vndoe Dame natures kindly course:
The faded lockes fall from the loftie oke,
The flouds do gaspe, for dryed is theyr sourse,
And flouds of teares flowe in theyr stead perforse.
        The mantled medowes mourne,
        Theyr sondry colours tourne.
        O heauie herse,
The heauens doe melt in teares without remorse.
        O carefull verse.

---

[10]The meaning is, that the things, which were the ornaments of her lyfe, are made the honor of her funerall, as is vsed in burialls.

[11]The name of a shepherd, which seemeth to haue bene the louer and deere frende of Dido.

The feeble flocks in field refuse their former foode,
And hang theyr heads, as they would learne to weepe:
The beastes in forest wayle as they were woode,
Except the Wolues, that chase the wandring sheepe:
Now she is gon that safely did hem keepe,
   The Turtle on the bared braunch,
   Laments the wound, that death did launch.
     O heauie herse,
And *Philomele*[12] her song with teares doth steepe.
     O carefull verse.

The water Nymphs, that wont with her to sing and daunce,
And for her girlond Oliue braunches beare,
Now balefull boughes of Cypres[13] doen aduaunce:
The Muses, that were wont greene bayes to weare,
Now bringen bitter Eldre braunches seare,
   The fatall sisters[14] eke repent,
   Her vitall threde so soone was spent.
     O heauie herse,
Morne now my Muse, now morne with heauie cheare.
     O carefull verse.

---

[12]The Nightingale. Whome the Poetes faine once to haue bene a Ladye of great beauty, till being rauished by hir sisters husbande, she desired to be turned into a byrd of her name.

[13]Vsed of the old Paynims in the furnishing of their funerall Pompe. And properly the signe of all sorow and heauinesse.

[14]Clotho Lachesis and Atropos, daughters of Herebus and the Nighte, whom the Poetes fayne to spinne the life of man, as it were a long threde, which they drawe out in length, till his fatal howre and timely death be come; but if by other casualtie his dayes be abridged, then one of them, that is Atropos, is sayde to haue cut the threde in twain.

O trustlesse state of earthly things, and slipper hope
Of mortal men, that swincke and sweate for nought,
And shooting wide, doe misse the marked scope:
Now haue I learnd (a lesson derely bought)
That nys on earth assurance to be sought:
    For what might be in earthlie mould,
    That did her buried body hould,
      O heauie herse,
Yet saw I on the beare when it was brought
      O carefull verse.

But maugre death, and dreaded sisters deadly spight,
And gates of hel, and fyrie furies[15] forse:
She hath the bonds broke of eternall night,
Her soule vnbodied of the burdenous corpse.
Why then weepes Lobbin so without remorse?
    O Lobb, thy losse no longer lament,
    Dido nis dead, but into heauen hent.
      O happye herse,
Cease now my Muse, now cease thy sorrowes sourse,
      O ioyfull verse.

Why wayle we then? why weary we the Gods with playnts,
As if some euill were to her betight?
She raignes a goddesse now among the saintes,
That whilome was the saynt of shepheards light:
And is enstalled nowe in heauens hight.
    I see thee blessed soule, I see,

---

[15]Of Poetes feyned to be three, Persephone Alecto and
Megera, which are sayd to be the Authours of all euill and mischiefe.

Walke in *Elisian* fieldes[16] so free.
        O happy herse,
Might I once come to thee (O that I might)
        O ioyfull verse.

Vnwise and wretched men to weete whats good or ill,
We deeme of Death as doome of ill desert:
But knewe we fooles, what it vs bringes vntil,
Dye would we dayly, once it to expert.
No daunger there the shepheard can astert:
        Fayre fieldes and pleasaunt layes there bene,
        The fieldes ay fresh, the grasse ay greene:
        O happy herse,
Make hast ye shepheards, thether to reuert,
        O ioyfull verse.
Dido is gone afore (whose turne shall be the next?)
There liues shee with the blessed Gods in blisse,
There drincks she *Nectar* with *Ambrosia*[17] mixt,
And ioyes enioyes, that mortall men doe misse.
The honor now of highest gods she is,
        That whilome was poore shepheards pryde,
        While here on earth she did abyde.
        O happy herse,
Ceasse now my song, my woe now wasted is.
        O ioyfull verse.

---

[16]Be deuised of Poetes to be a place of pleasure like Paradise, where the happye soules doe rest in peace and eternal happynesse.

[17]Be feigned to be the drink and foode of the gods: Ambrosia they liken to Manna in scripture and Nectar to be white like Creme, whereof is a proper tale of Hebe, that spilt a cup of it, and stayned the heauens, as yet appeareth.

Thenot. Ay francke shepheard, how bene thy verses meint
With doolful pleasaunce, so as I ne wotte,
Whether reioyce or weepe for great constrainte?
Thyne be the cossette, well hast thow it gotte.
Vp *Colin* vp, ynough thou morned hast,
Now gynnes to mizzle hye we homeward fast.
Colins Embleme.[18]

La mort ny mord.

ÆGLOGA QUINTA
Maye

*In this fift Æglogue, vnder the persons of two shepheards
Piers and Palinodie, be represented two formes of pastoures or
Ministers, or the protestant and the Catholique: whose chiefe*

---

[18]Which is as much to say, as death biteth not. For although by
course of nature we be borne to dye, and being ripened with age,
as with a timely haruest, we must be gathered in time, or els of
our selues we fall like rotted ripe fruite fro the tree yet death is
not to be counted for euil, nor (as the Poete sayd a little before)
as doome of ill desert. For though the trespasse of the first man
brought death into the world, as the guerdon of sinne, yet being
ouercome by the death of one, that dyed for al, it is now made (as
Chaucer sayth) the grene path way to lyfe. So that it agreeth well
with that was sayd, that Death byteth not (that is) hurteth not at all.

*talke standeth in reasoning, whether the life of the one must
be like the other. With whom hauing shewed, that it is daunger-
ous to mainteine any felowship, or giue too much credit to their
colourable and feyned goodwill, he telleth him a tale of the foxe,
that by such a counterpoynt of craftines deceiued and deuoured
the credulous kidde.*

PALINODE.   PIERS.

IS not thilke the mery moneth of May,
When loue lads masken in fresh aray?
How falles it then, we no merrier bene,
Ylike as others, girt in gawdy greene?
Our bloncket liueryes bene all to sadde,
For thilke same season, when all is ycladd
With pleasaunce: the grownd with grasse, the Woods
With greene leaues, the bushes with bloosming Buds.
Yougthes folke now flocken in euery where,[1]
To gather may buskets and smelling brere:
And home they hasten the postes to dight,
And all the Kirke pillours eare day light,
With Hawthorne buds, and swete Eglantine,
And girlonds of roses and Sopps in wine.
Such merimake holy Saints doth queme,
But we here sytten as drownd in a dreme.
Piers. For Younkers *Palinode* such follies fitte,
But we tway bene men of elder witt.
Palinode. Sicker this morrowe, ne lenger agoe,
I sawe a shole[2] of shepeheardes outgoe,

---

[1] A straunge, yet proper kind of speaking.

[2] A multitude; taken of fishe, whereof some going in great
companies, are sayde to swimme in a shole.

With singing, and shouting, and iolly chere:
Before them yode a lusty Tabrere,
That to the many a Horne pype playd,
Whereto they dauncen eche one with his mayd.
To see those folkes make such iouysaunce,
Made my heart after the pype to daunce.
Tho to the greene Wood they speeden hem all,
To fetchen home May with their musicall:
And home they bringen in a royall throne,
Crowned as king: and his Queene attone
Was Lady Flora, on whom did attend
A fayre flocke of Færies, and a fresh bend
Of louely Nymphs. (O that I were there,
To helpen the Ladyes their Maybush beare)
Ah *Piers*, bene not thy teeth on edge, to thinke,
How great sport they gaynen with little swinck?
Piers. Perdie so farre am I from enuie,
That their fondnesse inly I pitie.
Those faytours little regarden their charge,
While they letting their sheepe runne at large,
Passen their time, that should be sparely spent,
In lustihede and wanton meryment.
Thilke same bene shepeheards for the Deuils stedde,
That playen, while their flockes be vnfedde.
Well is it seene, theyr sheepe bene not their owne,
That letten them runne at randon alone.
But they bene hyred for little pay
Of other, that caren as little as they,
What fallen the flocke, so they han the fleece,
And get all the gayne, paying but a peece.
I muse, what account both these will make,

> The one for the hire, which he doth take,
> And thother for leauing his Lords taske,
> When great Pan[3] account of shepeherdes shall aske.

---

[3]Christ, the very God of all shepheards, which calleth himselfe the greate and good shepherd. The name is most rightly (me thinkes) applyed to him, for Pan signifieth all or omnipotent, which is onely the Lord Iesus. And by that name (as I remember he is called of Eusebius in his fifte booke de Preparat. Euang: who thereof telleth a proper storye to that purpose. Which story is first recorded of Plutarch, in his booke of the ceasing of oracles, and of Lauetere translated, in his booke of walking sprightes. Who sayth, that about the same time, that our Lord suffered his most bitter passion for the redemtion of man, certein passengers sayling from Italy to Cyprus and passing by certain Iles called Paxæ, heard a voyce calling alowde Thamus, Thamus, (now Thamus was the name of an Ægyptian, which was Pilote of the ship,) who giuing eare to the cry, was bidden, when he came to Palodes, to tel, that the great Pan was dead: which he doubting to doe, yet for that when he came to Palodes, there sodeinly was such a calme of winde, that the shippe stoode still in the sea vnmoued, he was forced to cry alowd, that Pan was dead: where-withall there was heard suche piteous outcryes and dreadfull shriking, as hath not bene the like. By whych Pan, though of some be vnderstoode the great Satanas, whose kingdome at that time was by Christ conquered, the gates of hell broken vp, and death by death deliuered to eternall death, (for at that time, as he sayth, all Oracles surceased, and enchaunted spirits, that were wont to delude the people, thenceforth held theyr peace) and also at the demaund of the Emperoure Tiberius, who that Pan should be, answere was made him by the wisest and best learned, that it was the sonne of Mercurie and Penelope, yet I think it more properly meant of the death of Christ, the onely and very Pan, then suffering for his flock.

LODOWICK BRYSKETT[1]

A PASTORALL ÆGLOGUE VPON THE DEATH OF SIR PHILLIP SIDNEY KNIGHT, &C.

LYCON.   COLIN.

Colin, well fits thy sad cheare this sad stownd,
This wofull stownd, wherein all things complaine
This great mishap, this greeuous losse of owres.
Hear'st thou the *Orown*?[2] how with hollow sownd
He slides away, and murmuring doth plaine,
And seemes to say vnto the fading flowres,
Along his bankes, vnto the bared trees;
Phillisides[3] is dead. Vp iolly swaine,
Thou that with skill canst tune a dolefull lay,
Help him to mourn. My hart with grief doth freese,

---

[1]Lodowick Bryskett was a friend of Edmund Spenser during Spenser's stay in Ireland, where both men were English officials. Though he was a man with genuine literary intents, only two of his poems have survived: "The Mourning Muse of Thestylis" and "A Pastorall Aeglogue," both written on the occasion of the death of Sir Philip Sidney, a famous poet and friend to both Spenser and Bryskett. The poems were first published in 1595 (nine years after Sidney's death) in a series of elegies to Sidney collected by Spenser and published with Spenser's poem "*Colin Clout Come Home Again*." Presumably Lycon is Bryskett and Colin is Spenser.

[2]A river in Ireland (?).

[3]Phili(p) Sid(ney) becomes "a lover of a star." Sidney's sonnets are addressed to Stella.

Hoarse is my voice with crying, else a part
Sure would I beare, though rude: But as I may,
With sobs and sighes I second will thy song,
And so expresse the sorrowes of my hart.
Colin. Ah *Lycon, Lycon,* what need skill, to teach
A grieued mynd powre[4] forth his plaints? how long
Hath the pore Turtle gon to school (weenest thou)
To learne to mourne her lost make? No, no, each
Creature by nature can tell how to waile.
Seest not these flocks, how sad they wander now?
Seemeth their leaders bell their bleating tunes
In dolefull sound. Like him, not one doth faile
With hanging head to shew a heauie cheare.
What bird (I pray thee) hast thou seen, that prunes
Himselfe of late? did any cheerfull note
Come to thine eares, or gladsome sight appeare
Vnto thine eies, since that same fatall howre?
Hath not the aire put on his mourning coat,
And testified his grief with flowing teares?
Sith then, it seemeth each thing to his powre
Doth vs inuite to make a sad consort;
Come let vs ioyne our mournfull song with theirs.
Griefe will endite, and sorrow will enforce
Thy voice, and *Eccho* will our words report.
Lycon. Though my rude rymes, ill with thy verses
     frame,
That others farre excell, yet will I force
My selfe to answere thee the best I can,
And honor my base words with his high name.

---

[4]Here and later the sign of the infinitive is omitted.

But if my plaints annoy thee where thou sit
In secret shade or cave; vouchsafe (O *Pan*)
To pardon me, and here this hard constraint
With patience while I sing, and pittie it.
And eke ye rurall *Muses*, that do dwell
In these wilde woods; If euer piteous plaint
We did endite, or taught a wofull minde
With words of pure affect, his griefe to tell,
Instruct me now. Now *Colin* then goe on,
And I will follow thee, though farre behinde.
Colin. Phillisides is dead. O harmfull death,
O deadly harme. Vnhappie *Albion*[5]
When shalt thou see emong thy shepheards all,
Any so sage, so perfect? Whom vneath
Enuie could touch for vertuous life and skill;
Curteous, valiant, and liberall.
Behold the sacred *Pales*,[6] where with haire
Vntrust she sitts, in shade of yonder hill.
And her faire face bent sadly downe, doth send
A floud of teares to bathe the earth; and there
Doth call the heau'ns despightfull, enuious,
Cruell his fate, that made so short an end
Of that same life, well worthie to haue bene
Prolongd with many yeares, happie and famous.
The Nymphs and *Oreades*[7] her round about
Do sit lamenting on the grassie grene;
And with shrill cries, beating their whitest brests,
Accuse the direfull dart that death sent out

[5]England.
[6]A god of Roman shepherds.
[7]Nymphs of the hills; a species of nymph.

To giue the fatall stroke. The starres they blame,
That deafe or carelesse seeme at their request.
The pleasant shade of stately groues they shun;
They leaue their cristall springs, where they wont
    frame
Sweet bowres of Myrtel twigs and Lawrel faire,
To sport themselves free from the scorching Sun.
And now the hollow caues where horror darke
Doth dwell, whence banisht is the gladsome aire
They seeke; and there in mourning spend their time
With wailfull tunes, whiles wolues do howle and barke,
And seem to beare a bourdon to their plaint.
Lycon. Phillisides is dead. O dolefull ryme.
Why should my toong expresse thee? who is left
Now to vphold thy hopes, when they do faint,
Lycon vnfortunate? What spitefull fate,
What lucklesse destinie hath thee bereft
Of thy chief comfort; of thy onely stay?
Where is become thy wonted happie state,
(Alas) wherein through many a hill and dale,
Through pleasant woods, and many an vnknowne way,
Along the bankes of many siluer streames,
Thou with him yodest; and with him didst scale
The craggie rocks of th' Alpes and *Appenine*?[8]
Still with the *Muses* sporting, while those beames
Of vertue kindled in his noble brest,
Which after did so gloriously forth shine?
But (woe is me) they now yquenched are
All suddeinly, and death hath them opprest.

[8]Bryskett had accompanied Sidney on a continental tour, 1572–1575.

Loe father *Neptune*, with sad countenance,
How he sitts mourning on the strond now bare,
Yonder, where th' Ocean with his rolling waues
The white feete washeth (wailing this mischance)
Of *Douer* Cliffes. His sacred skirt about
The sea-gods all are set; from their moist caues
All for his comfort gathered there they be.
The *Thamis* rich, the *Humber* rough and stout,
The fruitfull *Seuerne*,[9] with the rest are come
To helpe their Lord to mourne, and eke to see
The dolefull sight, and sad pomp funerall
Of the dead corps passing through his kingdome.
And all their heads with Cypres gyrlonds crown'd
With wofull shrikes salute him great and small.
Eke wailfull *Eccho*, forgetting her deare
Narcissus, their last accents, doth resownd.
Colin. Phillisides is dead. O lucklesse age;
O widow world; O brookes and fountains cleere;
O hills, O dales, O woods that oft haue rong
With his sweet caroling, which could asswage
The fiercest wrath of Tygre or of Beare.
Ye Siluans, Fawnes, and Satyres, that emong
These thickets oft haue daunst after his pipe,
Ye Nymphs and *Nayades* with golden heare,
That oft haue left your purest cristall springs
To harken to his layes, that coulden wipe
Away all griefe and sorrow from your harts.
Alas who now is left that like him sings?
When shall you heare againe like harmonie?

[9]The Thames, Humber, and Severn are all rivers in England.

So sweet a sownd, who to you now imparts?
Loe where engraued by his hand yet liues
The name of *Stella*, in yonder bay tree.
Happie name, happie tree; faire may you grow,
And spred your sacred branch, which honor giues,
To famous Emperours, and Poets crowne.
Vnhappie flock that wander scattred now,
What maruell if through grief ye woxen leane,
Forsake your food, and hang your heads adowne?
For such a shepheard neuer shall you guide,
Whose parting, hath of weale bereft you cleane.
  Lycon. Phillisides is dead. O happie sprite,
That now in heau'n with blessed soules doest bide:
Looke down a while from where thou sitst aboue,
And see how busie shepheards be to endite
Sad songs of grief, their sorrowes to declare,
And gratefull memory of their kynd loue.
Behold my selfe with *Colin*, gentle swaine
(Whose lerned *Muse* thou cherisht most whyleare)
Where we thy name recording, seeke to ease
The inward torment and tormenting paine,
That thy departure to vs both hath bred;
Ne can each others sorrow yet appease.
Behold the fountaines now left desolate,
And withred grasse with cypres boughes be spred,
Behold these floures which on thy graue we strew;
Which faded, shew the giuers faded state,
(Though eke they shew their feruent zeale and pure)
Whose onely comfort on thy welfare grew.
Whose praiers importune shall the heau'ns for ay,
That to thy ashes, rest they may assure:

That learnedst shepheards honor may thy name
With yeerly praises, and the Nymphs alway
Thy tomb may deck with fresh and sweetest flowres;
And that for euer may endure thy fame.
　　Colin. The Sun (lo) hastned hath his face to steep
In western waues: and th' aire with stormy showres
Warnes vs to driue homewards our silly sheep,
Lycon, lett's rise, and take of them good keep.

aduance praise

affect feeling

albe albeit

algate nevertheless

als also

astert befall unawares

attone together

avail value, benefit

bale fatal influence

beare bier

bee (l. 26) by

bend band

besprint sprinkled

betight (were betight) had happened

bloncket liueries gray coates

bourdon burden, accompaniment (of a song)

brere briar

buskets branches of hawthorne

bynempt bequeathed

carefull sorrowful

carke care

cheare countenance

chiefe head, top

clouted clotted

colourable deceptive

complayne lament

conne can

consort harmony

contempt despised

corse corpse

cosset lamb reared without the clan

counterpoynt trick

couth knew how to

cracknell light biscuits

dight made, or decorate

dolors dint pang of grief

dreeriment 'dreery and heauy cheere'

drent drowned

eke also

embraue adorn

endite give a literary form to

enforce emphasize

expert experience

fallen happen to

faytours vagabonds

fondnesse folly

gawdy green yellowish green

girlonds garlands

gynnes begins

han be have been

hem them

heme home

herye praise

inly entirely

iolly gallant

iouisance mirth

launch pierce

lay song

lays leas

list wish

lust desire
lustihede lustfulness
make mate
maske disguise (herself), or (*May*, 2) dress
maugre in spite of
may maid
meint mingled
misgouernance tyranny
mizzle drizzle
nis is not
plesaunce joy
prunes preens
quaile wither, perish
queme please
relieue revive
remorse mitigation
rownd polished
rushrings rings of rush
scope target
sheen 'fayre and shining'
shrikes shrieks
sicker surely
sike such
skilfull thronge the crowd of skillful singers
slipper slippery
sollein sad
sopps in wine common garden pinks
souenance remembrance
sourse spring

stedde place
stownd tune
strayne put into verse
swincke toil
tabrere player on the tabor or drums
tene sorrow
thilke such a, this
turtle dove
vneath hardly
vnderfong undertake
vntil unto
vntrust unbound
vaine poetic vein
virelayes 'a light kind of song'
warke work
weale happiness
weene think
weete know
welked shortened, impaired, waned, withered
whilome formerly
whyleare formerly
wight person
woode mad
wote know
yerely occupying a year
ygoe (l. 77) gone
yode went
yougthes folke young people
younkers young men
ystabled stabled

The Theory of the Monody

JULIUS CAESAR SCALIGER

🌿 🌿 🌿

from THE POETICS[1]

1. A threnody [θρῆος] in Latin is called a lament [*luctus*], like the one in the Scriptures when the prophet weeps for the Holy City. They say that Linus was the first poet to write threnodies, though others seem to have come very close to it. Angry with Hercules because he was slow to learn, he was slain by his enraged and ungrateful pupil; the rest of his pupils mourned him in the song which they called *Aelinum*, from his name and the sound of wailing [*ai*! *ai*!], a word Theocritus also remembered in his grief.

*   *   *

It is fitting that the Elegy, too, was first spoken at funerals; that is what Ovid intimated at the funeral of Tibullus. Horace confessed he did not know the inventor of this form. Nevertheless they say a certain Theocles, whether it was he of Naxos, or of Eritrea, first poured forth elegies in inspired frenzy. Therefore they were by no means just a "constant babbling, compared to the silence of the dead," as the Grammarians ridiculously assert; but their origin was pity, ἔλεος λέγειν that is why Horace called Elegies pitiful (ἐλεὸς also means that nocturnal bird in Aristotle which we call Ulula, the screech-owl.) The word's origin, too, is more simple—εἴ εἴ λέγειν. For this is the same as the αἴ αἴ in Aelinum; both interjections are frequent in all the

---

[1]The first passage, on threnodies, is from Book I, Chapter i; the second, on monodies, from III, cxxii; and the third, on speeches of consolation, from III, cxxiii. *Poetices Libri Septem* appeared posthumously in 1561. For this translation the editor is very grateful to Rita Carey Guerlac. Milton made several references in his prose works to Scaliger's *Poetics*, though not specifically to these passages.

Tragedies. Didymus defined Elegy as "a dirge . . . on the flute";
for the flute is a plaintive instrument; but we can show, from the
Knights of Aristophanes, that ἐλεὸν had also another meaning in
its origin. Afterwards the use was changed to something far different, that is to say, to love songs, and yet not without reason. For
both constant complaint in love affairs and literal death are things
we foolishly endure for a most foolish and ungrateful sex. Then
the meaning was extended according to the poet who could master
it, as in Ovid: "Come, triumphal laurels, encircle my brow!"
But the accounts and inscriptions of funeral songs together with
their subjects were drawn from history and fable, those of Adonis,
Daphne, Lino, Hyla. Trypho the poet composed a song which he
called Erigone, for the maiden who hanged herself; in this poem
is frequent mention of rope. Thus Ialemos [half-brother of Orph-
eus] is mournful; and so is his idyll about the unhappy son of
Calliope. Such, too, the Calyca of Stesichorus, about a girl
desperately in love with the young Euathlon; for the sake of marriage to him she made vows to Venus; at last, rejected, she threw
herself from the Leucadian rock. The song is the modest prayer
of a maiden; she hopes for marriage, if it be permitted, but if not,
for death.

2.   Just as pictures of the dead were cherished at home, and
their statues in the forum and elsewhere, not only to honor in
everlasting memory the services of men and women to their
country, but also to inspire the minds of the citizens to emulate
their deeds, even so, their deeds which could not be represented
by any art were proclaimed in public orations.

When the oration was given at the tomb of those whom it honored, it was called an ἐπιτάφιος λόγος. It could also have been
called an ἐπιτύμβιου, but this usage was not accepted, as Venus
Epitumbia, whose statue, as Plutarch says, was worshipped by the
inhabitants of Delphi.

The ἐπιτάφιος therefore is the same as an ἐπικήδειος. Servius alone showed us the difference. . . . An epicedium is spoken only once [at the funeral], but epitaphiums can be delivered annually, just as they were at Athens. Pericles gave one, as we know from Thucydides; Plato did the same; and Aristides wrote three. Songs in honor of the dead, and Parentalia, in honor of deceased relatives, are of the same kind. But threnodies are more free in practice, and more copious; indeed, when states are overthrown the lamentation which is uttered is called a threnody. But *monody* must be understood in a quite different sense than is accepted by the learned, for it is not what they think it is. In fact, it took place as often as one man stepped forth from the Chorus to honor in mournful song the memory of the dead; he played this on the flute in the Lydian mode.

. . . The parts [of an epicedium] are: (1) The Praise, (2) the Narration, (3) the Lamentation, (4) the Consolation, and (5) the Exhortation. In the anniversary form [epigraph] these are all the same with the exception of the Lamentation; for no one bewails a man a year or two dead, much less if so much time has passed that neither his parents nor his children survive him. The treatment is different according to whether the song is for an emperor, for an army, for an urban magistrate, for a private citizen, a man, a woman, an adult, a child—each one of whom must be treated in the appropriate way. Sometimes the poem begins with a calm proem [in a moderate style] suitable for those who are sorrowful and even dazed with grief; sometimes with an exclamation or interrogation, as if we would question ourselves, as if searching our judgment for reasons: as how we must both speak and be silent, since grief prompts the one, duty the other, and the virtues of the dead man prompt them both. Then comes an explanation either of our role, or of the one who designated us—this cannot be omitted. [After the Proem, we begin; first comes the Praise:] praise not only of the dead, but also of his death, as my epitaph for those who died at Vienna in the Turkish War. The loss is described, first calmly, then with increasing excitement, in the

Narration, in which a dwelling on and an amplification of the theme increase the longing for the lost person. From this part [the Narration] naturally springs the Lamentation, for the Praise and the Narration are meant to lead to the Lamentation, as in my Royal Epicedium: "What will be my thoughts, seeing the realm so desolate and tearful at thy death; a realm once happy, preserved and restored to us by thy power." That is, after the loss of so bright a pledge of glory, there is nothing to do but mourn.

After this the Consolation must be begun. You may say that so grave a loss—say, the death of a king—can be alleviated by the virtues of his successor, whose praises you will set forth in a very ardent but brief account. If it is a loss of soldiers, it may be alleviated by the good fortune of their surviving comrades; and if the survivors are the audience, they are to be praised amply and at great length. The poem should close with the Exhortations: [e.g.,] to mourn them excessively would be to disparage the present felicity which has fallen to their survivors; rather their virtues, courage, and death are greatly to be desired for ourselves. We must so conduct ourselves in war that we purchase our life with valor and, if need be, protect the lives of others by our death.

3.   A discourse of consolation is one which restores the mind of the mourner to tranquility; but it can proceed only from a friend. For this reason the rule of the ancient writers was that the comforter also must show grief and must magnify the atrocity of the event; and yet they give no reason for this rule. I think they had observed the practice in some orator and misunderstood his purpose. Indeed I should have thought the reason was that we are better able to persuade a listener to quiet his grief if he sees us, too, bear it with equanimity. For from this he may know that we also share his sorrow, since we value the same object so highly. With good reason will a friend spurn the words of men who appear to hold in little value the person or the possession he has lost. And yet, while this is very pleasing, I do not think the consolation

must always be done in this manner. Let us discuss it, then, with better judgment, in this way.

The comforter is, with respect to his hearer, either greater, or less, or equal. By greatness I mean either greatness in power, or social rank, or wealth, or wisdom, or age. For Livia [the Empress] will console Naso [Ovid, the poet] in one way, Naso will comfort Livia in another; this with respect to power. But there can also be rank without power, as a father would console his son, or Pompey Cicero; in wealth, as if Crassus were to comfort some plebeian client of his; in wisdom, the manner in which Seneca would console Polybius, or would comfort his mother. Concerning age there is no want of examples. An older person will impose his authority, and may even chastise; a wise man may also make use of argument; for this maxims are abundant. The lesser person will show his sympathy; he has learned this from wiser men. An equal will give proof of his friendship, the equal right of kindness. . . .

There are also Consolations drawn from circumstances, in which different subjects must be expressly treated: parents, children, friends, country, authority, liberty, the sovereign—we can dismiss the others; from the variety of these also arose the various kinds of poetry. The emotions, then, must sometimes be aroused, sometimes quieted. Above all, the fears, hopes, and superstitions of the crowd must be rooted out. For not only must such feelings be increased by exaggeration, as the ancients intended, but sometimes they must also be weakened by diminution. . . .

GEORGE PUTTENHAM

꙲ ꙲ ꙲

from THE ARTE OF ENGLISH POESIE *(1589)*[1]

Of the shepheards or pastorall poesie called eglogue, and to what purpose it was first inuented and vsed.

Some be of opinion, and the chiefe of those who haue written in this Art among the Latines, that the pastorall Poesie which we commonly call by the name of *Eglogue* and *Bucolick*, a tearme brought in by the Sicilian Poets, should be the first of any other, and before the *Satyre*, *Comedie*, or *Tragedie*, because, say they, the shepheards and haywards assemblies & meetings when they kept their cattell and heards in the common fields and forests was the first familiar conuersation, and their babble and talk vnder bushes and shadie trees the first disputation and contentious reasoning, and their fleshly heates growing of ease the first idle wooings, and their songs made to their mates or paramours either vpon sorrow or iolity of courage the first amorous musicks; sometime also they sang and played on their pipes for wagers, striuing who should get the best game and be counted cunningest. All this I do agree vnto, for no doubt the shepheards life was the first example of honest felowship, their trade the first art of lawfull acquisition or purchase, for at those daies robbery was a manner of purchase. So saith *Aristotle* in his bookes of the Politiques; and that pasturage was before tillage, or fishing, or fowling, or any other predatory art or cheuisance. And all this may be true, for before there was a shepheard keeper of his owne or of some other bodies flocke, there was none owner in the

[1]Book I, Chapters xviii and xxiv.

world, quick cattel being the first property of any forreine possession. I say forreine, because alway men claimed property in
their apparell and armour, and other like things made by their
owne trauel and industry, nor thereby was there yet any good
towne, or city, or Kings palace, where pageants and pompes
might be shewed by Comedies or Tragedies. But for all this, I
do deny that the *Eglogue* should be the first and most auncient
forme of artificiall Poesie, being perswaded that the Poet deuised
the *Eglogue* long after the other *dramatick* poems, not of purpose
to counterfait or represent the rusticall manner of loues and com-
munication, but vnder the vaile of homely persons and in rude
speeches to insinuate and glaunce at greater matters, and such
as perchance had not bene safe to haue beene disclosed in any
other sort, which may be perceiued by the Eglogues of *Virgill*,
in which are treated by figure matters of greater importance then
the loues of *Titirus* and *Corydon*. These Eglogues came after to
containe and enforme morall discipline, for the amendment of
mans behauiour, as be those of *Mantuan* and other moderne Poets.

The forme of poeticall lamentations.

Lamenting is altogether contrary to reioising; euery man saith
so, and yet it is a peece of ioy to be able to lament with ease,
and freely to poure forth a mans inward sorrowes and the greefs
wherewith his minde is surcharged. This was a very necessary
deuise of the Poet and a fine, besides his poetrie to play also the
Phisitian, and not onely by applying a medicine to the ordinary
sicknes of mankind, but by making the very greef it selfe (in part)
cure of the disease. Nowe are the causes of mans sorrowes many:
the death of his parents, frends, allies, and children (though many
of the barbarous nations do reioyce at their burials and sorrow at
their birthes), the ouerthrowes and discomforts in battell, the
subuersions of townes and cities, the desolations of countreis, the
losse of goods and worldly promotions, honour and good renowne,
finally, the trauails and torments of loue forlorne or ill bestowed,

either by disgrace, deniall, delay, and twenty other wayes, that well experienced louers could recite. . . .

Therefore of death and burials, of th'aduersities by warres, and of true loue lost or ill bestowed, are th'onely sorrowes that the noble Poets sought by their arte to remoue or appease, not with any medicament of a contrary temper, as the *Galenistes* vse to cure [*contraria contrarijs*] but as the *Paracelsians*, who cure [*similia similibus*] making one dolour to expell another, and in this case, one short sorrowing the remedie of a long and grieuous sorrow. And the lamenting of deathes was chiefly at the very burialls of the dead, also at monethes mindes and longer times, by custome continued yearely, when as they vsed many offices of seruice and loue towardes the dead, and thereupon are called *Obsequies* in our vulgare, which was done not onely by cladding the mourners their friendes and seruauntes in blacke vestures, of shape dolefull and sad, but also by wofull countenaunces and voyces, and besides by Poeticall mournings in verse. Such funerall songs were called *Epicedia* if they were song by many, and *Monodia* if they were vttered by one alone, and this was vsed at the enterment of Princes and others of great accompt, and it was reckoned a great ciuilitie to vse such ceremonies, as at this day is also in some countrey vsed. . . .

Contemporary Elegies

THREE ELEGIES
ON THE
DEATH OF PRINCE HENRY, 1612

GILES FLETCHER[1]

Upon the Most Lamented Departure
of the
Right Hopefull, and Blessed
Prince Henrie, Prince of Wales.

The weeping time of Heav'n is now come in,
Kindely the season clowdes of sorrowe beares,
To smile, ô let it be a deadly sinne
And happy hee, his merry looks forswears,
See heav'n for us is melted into teares:
    O deerest Prince how many hearts wear knowne
    To save thy life, that would have lost their owne?

---

[1]This poem first appeared in *Epicedium Cantabrigiense; or Memoriæ Sacra Illustriss. Pontentiss. Principis Henrici Walliæ Principi, Ducis Cornubiae &c. Laudatis Funebris* (Cambridge, 1612); our text comes from *Giles and Phineas Fletcher: Poetical Works*, ed. Frederick S. Boas, 2 vols. (Cambridge, 1908), Vol. I, pp. 266–268.

When thou thy Countreys griefe, weart once her glory,
How was this blessed Isle crown'd with delight;
So long it never knew how to be sorry,
But anchor'd all her joyes upon thy sight;
The musique every whear did freely lite:
    The Sheapheards pip't, and countrey byrds did sing,
    The water-nymphs came dauncing from their spring.

It was the mother then of harmeles pleasure
The Queene of beawty all men came to see,
And poore it could not bee, thou weart her treasure,
Onely it was a little prowde of thee,
Aye mee, that ever so it might not bee!
    The Garden of the world, whear nothing wanted,
    Another Paradise, that God had planted.

Her happie fields wear dec'kt with every flowre,
That with her sweetest lookes Peace smil'd to see it:
Delight it selfe betwixt her breasts did bowre,
And oft her rustique Nymphs thy coach would meet,
And strow with flowers the way before thy feete.
    But now those flowers wee woont to strow before
        thee,
    Dead, in thy grave wee throw them to adore thee.

Sleepe softly, royall Ghost, in that cold bed,
Let deaths pale chambers give thee easie rest,
Whear all the Princely bones lie buried,
With guilded crowns and long white scepters drest.
Ah, little look't they thou shouldst be their guest!
    What makes the heav'ns proclaime such open warres?
    Wee did not owe thee so soone to the starres.

And yet our vowes doe not thy starres envie thee,
Bathe thee in joyes, wee in our teares will swim:
We doe not unto heav'n, or God denie thee,
Onely the Muses begge this leave of him,
To fill with teares their fountaine to the brim,
  And as thou sett'st emparadis'd above,
  To powre out to thee rivers of their love.

See how the yeare with thee is stricken dead,
And from her bosome all her flowers hath throwne,
With thee the trees their haires fling from their head,
And all the Sheapheards pipes are deadly blowne,
All musique now, and mirth is hatefull growne:
  Onely *Halcyons* sad lamenting pleases,
  And that Swans dirge, that, as hee sings, deceases.

Heav'n at thy death deni'd our world his light,
Ne suff'red one pale starre abroad to peepe,
And all about the world the winds have sigh'd,
Nor can the watrie-nymphs (so fast they weepe)
Within their banks their flouds of sorrow keepe.
  Suffer us, in this deluge of distresse,
  Thee, if not to enjoy, at least to blesse.

Bedded in all the roses of delight
Let thy engladded soule embalmed lie,
Imbrightned into that celestiall light,
Which all Gods saintly Lamps doth glorifie,
Thear boast thy kinred with the Deitie
  Whear God his Sonne, and Christ his Brother greet
   thee,
  And thy too little glorious Sisters meete thee.

But ô thou desert Island, that art found
Cast in the seas deepe bosome by mishap,
As if with our salt teares thou all weart drown'd,
And hadst from heav'n drop't into sorrowes lap;
Desolate house! what mantle now shall wrap
  Thy naked sides? poore widow, made to mourne,
  To whom wilt thou thy sad addresses tourne?

Alas, the silent Angels on his tombe
Can him no honour, thee no comfort sing,
Their pretie weeping lookes may well become
Themselves, but him to life can never bring.
Thee therefore, deerest Prince, from perishing
  Or yet alive wee in our hearts will save,
  Or dead with thee, our hearts shall be thy grave.

HENRIE farewell, heav'ns soone-restored Exile,
Immortall Garland of thy Fathers head,
Mantle of honour to this naked Isle,
Bright drop of heav'n, on whose wish't nuptiall bed
Now all our ripest hopes hung blossomed.
  Farewell, farewell; hearke how the Angels sing,
  On earth our Prince is now in Heav'n a King.

CYRIL TOURNEUR[2]

A Griefe on the Death of Prince Henrie, Expressed in a Broken Elegie, According to the Nature of Such a Sorrow

Good *Vertue* wipe thine eyes. Look vp and see!
And wonder to behold it. Some there be,
That weepe not; but are strangely merrie, dance,
And ruell. Can the losse of H I M aduance
The heart of any man to such a mirth?
Can H I S graue be the womb, from whence the birth
Of pleasure riseth? *Pity them. Their woe*
Distracts 'em, and they know not what they doe.
Yet note 'em better. Be they *wicked* men,
Their shew of *Ioy* is *voluntarie* then.
For now the *President* of *vertu's* dead.
Vice hopes to get her courses licenced.
Dead! T"is aboue my knowledge how we liue
To speake it. Is there any *Faith* to giue
The promises of *health* or *remedy?*
Or any *Meane* to be preserued by;
When *Temperance*, and *Exercise* of breath,
(Those best *Physitians*) could not keepe from death,

[2]This poem was first published in *Three Elegies on the most lamented Death of Prince Henrie* (London, 1613), and is reprinted in Ruth C. Wallerstein, *Studies in Seventeenth-Century Poetic* (Madison, 1950), pp. 353–357.

The strength of *Nature*? Was H E E temp'rate?
  whence
(Then) came H E E subiect to the violence
Of sicknesse? Rather was H E E not inclin'd
To *pleasures*? *Infinitely*; still H I S mind
Was on them; *Infinitely*; For H I S loue
No *Obiects* had, but those which were aboue
The causes of *vexation*; such, as *done*,
Repented not the pleasures they begun,
But made them endlesse: Nothing had the might
To dis-effect his *Actions* of delight.
No; nor H I S *suffrings*. For although H E E knew,
That sicknesse came from earth to claime her due;
And to depriue H I M of that fortunate
Succession to the greatnesse of the *State*,
Which H E E was borne to; *that* did likewise please,
And added nothing vnto H I S *disease*.
Of H I S *contentments* heere, that was the best.
Therefore the last; that it might crowne the rest.
But these are not the pleasures that decay
The body. How hath death (then) found a way
To O N E so able? H E E was *yong* and *strong*.
Vnguiltie of al *disorder* that could wrong
H I S *Constitution*. Doe no longer hide
It; t'was to vs a *plague* whereof H E E died.
A *plague* by much more common to vs, then
The last great sicknesses. Many more the men
Who suffer in it. That which now is gone,
Was but the *Figure*, of a greater One
To follow. Since the first that e'er was borne;
A fuller number was not knowne to mourne.

For all the *old Men* of the *Kingdomes* weepe,
Since H E that promis'd by H I S *strength* to keepe
Their *children* free from *others* violence;
And by *example* from their *owne* offence;
Is taken from 'em. And they would haue died
When H E did, but for tarying to prouide
A *second* care for that they would haue left
To H I M, of whose *protection* th' are bereft.
If we doe well consider their iust woes;
We must include our yong men too, in those:
And grieue for euer: For our old mens teares,
Are rather for the time *to come*, then theirs.
If they that shall not liue to suffer much
Vnder this cause of *sorrow*, vtter such
A passion for it; *more* it does belong
To *vs* that now are *growing* to it; *yong*;
As if our *generations* had intent,
We should be *borne* to feele the *punishment*.
Now let vs *willingly* giue griefe regard;
Least we be *forc'd* to doe it *afterward*,
By *Heauen's* iust anger. Stay a little. Why
Should yong men thinke the old shall sooner die?
H I S youths great broken promise wee complaine.
Yet none was greater. And are ours lesse vaine?
Mistake not. As *Humanitie* now goes;
H E E liu'd a *Man* as long as any does.
For (onelie) in those *Minutes* that wee giue
To *Vertue*, we are *Trulie* said to liue
Men, and no longer. If we recken then,
H I S good houres, with the good of other Men;
H I S Times whole added numbers will arise,

To his, that tels out foureskore ere he dies.
To prooue this, looke as low as ere you can;
And heare the words of the deiected Man;
The *Souldier* speakes them. *Honour! Now I see,*
There is no hope that any Age will be
So good and noble as the ancient were.
None so Heroique euer shall appeare.
For if that Fate, (which cannot be withstood)
Had not decreed, there should be none so good;
Shee would not haue neglected such a worth
As H I S *was, to haue brought that great worke forth.*
But hauing purpos'd it should neuer be;
And hearing every where by Fame, that H E E
Was making one; she kill'd H I M.—Marke his eye;
Hee weepes. *He* weepes; that can more easilie
Weepe *Bloud* then *Water*. Then I wonder, how
Or *He*, or anye other *Souldier*, now,
Can hold his *sword vnbroken*; since H E E was,
That gaue them *Count'nance*. That's the Cause
        (alas)
They doe not *breake* them; and a iust excuse.
They weare them *now*, to keepe them from *abuse*.
For that great *fauour* now has made an *end*;
That their despis'd conditions did *defend*.
Artes too, are so discourag'd by their harmes;
In losse of H I M, who lou'd both *them* and Armes;
That they would all leaue *studie* and decline
From Learning; if those *Naturall* and *Diuine*
Perswading *Contemplations*, did not leade
The *One* to *Heauen*; the other to the *dead*;
(Betweene whose *parts*, they haue diuided H I S;)

And promise, *so*, to bring them where H E E is.

But I would haue their *studies* neuer die;

For preseruation of H I S *Memorie.*

How can *that* perish? That will euer keepe;

Because th' impression of it is so deepe.

When any *Painter* to the *life*, that saw

H I S *presence* fullie, takes in hand to draw

An *Alexander*, or a *Cæsar*; his best

Imaginations will bee so possess't

With H I S *Remembrance*, that as H E E does limme,

Hee'l make that *Worthie's* picture like to H I M.

And then t'will be a *Piece* of such a *Grace*,

For *Height* and *Sweetnesse*; as that onely *Face*

Will make another *Painter*, that ne'er knew

H I M liuing, follow as the other drew.

How great a *Character* deserues H E E then,

Whose *Memorie* shall but expire with men?

When a Diuine, or Poet, sets downe right,

What other Princes should bee; Hee shall write

What T H I S *was.* That's H I S *Character*, which beares

My sorrow inward, to goe forth in teares.

Yet some of Ioy too, mix'd with those of Greefe;

That flow from apprehension of releefe.

I see H I S spirit turn'd into a *starre*;

Whose *influence* makes that H I S owne *Vertues* are

Succeeded iustlie; otherwise, the *worst*,

As at H I S *Funerall* should proceede the *first.*

H I S *Natiue goodnes*, followes in H I S *Roome*;

Else good Men would be buried in H I S *Tombe.*

> *O! suffer this to be a faithfull verse;*
> *To liue for euer, weeping o'er* H I S *Herse.*

JOHN DONNE[3]

ELEGIE UPON THE UNTIMELY DEATH
OF THE
INCOMPARABLE PRINCE HENRY

Looke to mee faith, and looke to my faith, God;
For both my centers feele this period.
Of waight one center, one of greatnesse is;
And Reason is that center, Faith is this;
For into'our reason flow, and there do end
All, that this naturall world doth comprehend:
Quotidian things, and equidistant hence,
Shut in, for man, in one circumference.
But for th'enormous greatnesses, which are
So disproportion'd, and so angulare,
As is Gods essence, place and providence,
Where, how, when, what soules do, departed
    hence,
These things (eccentrique else) on faith do strike;
Yet neither all, nor upon all, alike.
For reason, put to'her best extension,
Almost meetes faith, and makes both centers one.
And nothing ever came so neare to this,
As contemplation of that Prince, we misse.

[3]This poem was first published in *Lachrymæ Lachrymarum*, by Joshua Sylvester (London, 1613). Our text comes from *The Poems of John Donne*, ed. Sir Herbert Grierson, 2 vols. (Oxford, 1912), Vol. I, pp. 267–270.

126

For all that faith might credit mankinde could,
Reason still seconded, that this prince would.
If then least moving of the center, make
More, then if whole hell belch'd, the world to
    shake,
What must this do, centers distracted so,
That wee see not what to beleeve or know?
Was it not well beleev'd till now, that hee,
Whose reputation was an extasie
On neighbour States, which knew not why to
    wake,
Till hee discover'd what wayes he would take;
For whom, what Princes angled, when they
    tryed,
Met a *Torpedo*, and were stupified:
And others studies, how he would be bent;
Was his great fathers greatest instrument,
And activ'st spirit, to convey and tie
This soule of peace, through Christianity?
Was it not well beleev'd, that hee would make
This generall peace, th'Eternall overtake,
And that his times might have stretch'd out so
    farre,
As to touch those, of which they emblems are?
For to confirme this just beleefe, that now
The last dayes came, we saw heav'n did allow,
That, but from his aspect and exercise,
In peacefull times, Rumors of war did rise.
But now this faith is heresie: we must
Still stay, and vexe our great-grand-mother,
    Dust.

Oh, is God prodigall? hath he spent his store
Of plagues, on us; and onely now, when more
Would ease us much, doth he grudge misery;
And will not let's enjoy our curse; to dy?
As, for the earth throwne lowest downe of all,
T'were an ambition to desire to fall,
So God, in our desire to dye, doth know
Our plot for ease, in being wretched so.
Therefore we live; though such a life wee have,
As but so many mandrakes on his grave.
What had his growth, and generation done,
When, what we are, his putrefaction
Sustaines in us; Earth, which griefes animate?
Nor hath our world now, other Soule then that.
And could griefe get so high as heav'n, that
    Quire,
Forgetting this their new joy, would desire
(With griefe to see him) hee had staid below,
To rectifie our errours, They foreknow.
Is th'other center, Reason, faster then?
Where should we looke for that, now we'are not
    men?
For if our Reason be'our connexion
Of causes, now to us there can be none.
For, as, if all the substances were spent,
'Twere madnesse, to enquire of accident,
So is't to looke for reason, hee being gone,
The onely subject reason wrought upon.
If Fate have such a chaine, whose divers links
Industrious man discerneth, as hee thinks;
When miracle doth come, and so steale in

A new linke, man knowes not, where to begin:
At a much deader fault must reason bee,
Death having broke off such a link as hee.
But now, for us, with busie proofe to come,
That we'have no reason, would prove wee had
    some.
So would just lamentations: Therefore wee
May safelyer say, that we are dead, then hee.
So, if our griefs wee do not well declare,
We'have double excuse; he'is not dead; and we
    are.
Yet I would not dy yet; for though I bee
Too narrow, to thinke him, as hee is hee,
(Our Soules best baiting, and midd-period,
In her long journey, of considering God)
Yet, (no dishonour) I can reach him thus,
As he embrac'd the fires of love, with us.
Oh may I, (since I live) but see, or heare,
That she-Intelligence which mov'd this spheare,
I pardon Fate, my life: Who ere thou bee,
Which hast the noble conscience, thou art shee,
I conjure thee by all the charmes he spoke,
By th'oathes, which onely you two never broke,
By all the soules yee sigh'd that if you see
These lines, you wish, I knew your history.
So much, as you two mutuall heav'ns were here,
I were an Angell, singing what you were.

TWO ELEGIES
ON THE
DEATHS OF CLOSE FRIENDS

JOHN MILTON[1]

EPITAPHIUM DAMONIS[2]

O nymphs that haunt the old Sicilian stream,
Himera's stream, you that do still remember
Daphnis and Hylas, and the death of Bion
Lamented these long years,
Sing dirge beside these English river towns,
Sing by the Thames, as once in Sicily,
The low lament, the ceaseless bitter weeping
That broke the quiet of the caves,
River and forest ride and fleeting water,
Where Thyrsis went, bewailing his lost Damon,
Walking at dead of night in the silent places
Uncomforted, alone.

[1]In the Argument of the poem Milton said he and Charles Diodati were "inseparable friends." Milton received the news of Diodati's death while he was in Italy, and wrote the elegy on his return to England in 1640. As Milton described him, Diodati seems to have been "distinguished for his talents, learning, and all other notable virtues" (trans. Nelson McCrea).

[2]*Lament for Damon*, translated by Helen Waddell (London, 1943). Reprinted by permission of Constable & Co., Ltd.

It is the second year.
Twice has the green corn come to ear,
And twice the barns are filled with golden grain,
Since the ending day that took him to the shadows,
And I not there. I was in Tuscany,
Making my verses.
But now, my mind assuaged and the old task calling,
Now that I am come home,
Sitting again beneath the familiar elm,
Now, now, I know him gone,
And know how vast my grief.

Away, my lambs, unfed: your shepherd heeds you not.

O grief! what gods are there in heaven or earth
That I can cry to, since they've taken thee
In unrelenting death? O Damon, so to leave us,
And all thy valour pass, and no man name thee
In that dim fellowship of shades? Ah no!
Sure He whose golden bough divides men's souls
Shall lead thee to thy chosen company
And keep at bay the sluggish silent herd.

Away, my lambs, unfed: your shepherd heeds you not.

What e'er befall—unless the wolf first spy me—
Thou shalt not moulder in an unwept grave.
Thy honour shall abide, and have long life
Among the shepherds: thou wilt be remembered
When they remember Daphnis, after Daphnis
They'll fall to praising you, whilst the kind gods
Of field and fold still haunt the countryside:
If it be aught to have kept the ancient faith,
And loved the arts, and had a poet friend.

Away, my lambs, unfed: your shepherd heeds you not.

> These things are yours, O Damon, they are yours,
> And yours for ever:
> But Damon, Damon, what's to become of me?
> Who'll walk with me forever by my side,
> As you did, through the frost and through the mire,
> In the fierce sun, the thirsting dying grass?
> Or face the lion but a spear's cast off,
> Or scare the hungry wolves from the high folds?
> Or talking, singing, lull the day to sleep?

Away, my lambs, unfed: your shepherd heeds you not.

> To whom can I speak my heart? To whom shall I go
> To learn to master the dark thoughts that tear me,
> And cheat the night with talking, while the pears
> Are hissing on the fire and all the hearth
> Crackling with chestnuts, and the wind from the South
> Is wrecking all without, and overhead
> The elm tree cries and groans?

Away, my lambs, unfed: your shepherd heeds you not.

> Summer and noon, Pan sleeping under the oak,
> The nymphs all fled to their cool haunt under the waters,
> The shepherds gone to the shade and the swineherd
>   snoring—
> But who will bring me back that smiling enchantment,
> The Greek salt of your wit, and all your ways?

Away, my lambs, unfed: your shepherd heeds you not.

> Alone through the plough lands I go, alone through the
>   pasture,

Down where the branching trees grow thick in the valley,
There do I wait the night: above my head
Sadly the west wind sighs and the falling rain,
And sighs the shivering twilight of the trees.

Away, my lambs, unfed: your shepherd heeds you not.

The fields that once I ploughed are tangled with weeds,
Couch grass and bindweed: and the standing corn
Bows and rots where it grew: the virgin grape
Is shrivelling where it hangs on the unkempt vine.
I am sick of my sheep and the pitiful creatures bleat,
Crowding reproachful faces around their master.

Away, my lambs, unfed: your shepherd heeds you not.

One lad shouts from the hazels, and one from the rowans,
One is among the willows, and one by the river.
"Here's a spring well, and grass that is silky with moss,
A warm west wind and water lapping the branches"—
They cry to a deaf man. There's sanctuary in the forest.

Away, my lambs, unfed: your shepherd heeds you not. . . .[3]

O God, if one were a bullock!
All of them moving together roaming the field,
Any steer of the herd as good a friend as another.
The jackals crowd at their feasting, and the wild ass
Will rub his shaggy head against his neighbour
Indifferent of choice.
This too is the law of the sea: out on the desolate sands
Proteus calls, and the seals come to him in shoals.
Aye, even the lowly sparrow

[3]The translator omitted ll. 74–92 of the original.

Has never far to seek for company,
Cheerfully pecking his grain, flickering here and there,
Homing again at dusk to the familiar eaves:
Yet should Fate strike down his comrade,
Spitted on beak of hawk, or limed in a ditch,
Straight is he off again, the sociable creature,
To find another mate.
But what of men?
Men, the hard stock, schooled by grim destiny,
Alien, aloof in soul,
Discordant in their hearts?
Hardly in thousands may a man find one
That is his fellow.
And if at last Fate hath not proved unkind,
Hath given the heart's desire,
Comes stealthily the day you had not looked for,
The hour undreaded,
And snatches him, and leaves loss infinite,
For ever and for ever.

Away, my lambs, unfed: your shepherd heeds you not.

O grief! what craze for wandering captured me,
Drew me to unknown shores,
Climbing the sky-flung rocks, the Alps in snow?
Was it so great a thing to look on Rome,
Low in her grave—
Even had she been as when the Virgilian shepherd
Left his own flocks and herds to gaze on her—
When for her I must lack thy company
And set between us deep estranging seas,
Mountains and woods and rocks and sounding rivers?
O had it but been given me at the last

To touch thy hand in the still hour of dying,
And close those eyes beneath the carven brows,
And say "Farewell: go forth on thy high journey:
And still remember me."

Away, my lambs, unfed: your shepherd heeds you not.

God knows I do not grudge the memory
Of you, the men I found in Tuscany,
Poets and shepherds: Grace and Wit are there—
And Damon, Damon was himself a Tuscan,
His father's house from Lucca of the kings,
Etruscan kings and priests.
How high my heart was, stretched beside the Arno
Cool-fleeting past me, or in shadow of the poplars,
Where the grass is deeper, and violets to gather,
Myrtle to reach high for, listening to my poets
Arguing and versing: and sometimes, greatly daring,
I too made verses, that did not much displease.
Dati, Francini, I still have the gifts you gave me,
Fruit baskets, wine bowls, wax for my shepherd's flute.
Still I remember the song you made about us,
Singing under the beeches: lyric poets and scholars,
Both of you famous, both of Etruscan blood.

Away, my lambs, unfed: your shepherd heeds you not.

How would I dream there, at moonrise and dewfall,
Solitary, closing in the little tender goats,
How often said—and the earth dark above thee!—
"Damon will be singing now, or out to trap a hare,
Weaving his osiers for all his little contraptions!"
And so light-hearted, so sure was I of to-morrow,
I held it in my hand, the time to come.

Here! are you busy? If there is nothing you must do,
Shall we go and lie in the glancing quivering shade
Down by the Colne, or the fields above St. Albans,
And you can recite me all your herbs and simples,
Hellebore and iris and the saffron-crocus,
And the herbs in the marshland and all the arts of
      healing
—O perish all the herbs, and all the arts of healing,
Perish all the simples that could not save their master!
And I—more than a se'nnight gone—so grand, so grave
      a note
Rang from my pipe—I scarce had put my lips to it,
The reeds were new—and yet they leapt asunder,
Broke at the join, and that deep resonance
Could bear no more.
I fear I am too bold: yet let me speak,
Speak to the silent woods.

Away, my lambs, unfed: your shepherd heeds you not.

I shall sing of the Trojan prows
Cleaving the seas beneath the cliffs of Kent,
And the old Kingdom that was Imogen's,
And Arvirach, was son to Cymbeline,
And Bren and Belin, ancient British captains,
And the Breton coast brought under Britain's law,
And Igraine great with child that shall be Arthur,
And the false face of Uther that begat him,
Masking her husband's likeness and his armour,
Through Merlin's guile. O, if I live, yet live,
Thou shalt hang, my shepherd's pipe, on some ancient
      pine,
Remote, all but forgotten—

Unless thou change thy note
From the classic cadence to the harsher speech
Of the English tongue.
And then? What then?
It is not given to one man to have all things,
Or even to hope for all things.
Enough, enough for me, and grand the honour—
Although I be unknown in time to come,
Yea, be inglorious in the outer world—
If my own folk will chant me in the meadows
Beside the cowslip Ouse and the springs of Allen
And the swirling tides of the Severn, and wooded Trent,
And Thames—above all, my Thames—and Tamar
    tawny with ore,
And the far Orkneys in the furthest seas.

Away, my lambs, unfed: your shepherd heeds you not.

These songs I was keeping for thee, in the bark of the
    laurel:
These, and how many more!—and the goblets I was
    given
By Manso, glory of the Campanian shore,
Two chalices of marvellous workmanship
—Yet the old man no less marvellous than they—
Carved and inlaid with two-fold argument:
Here, the Red Sea, the long Arabian coast,
And fragrant-breathing spring and the woods of spice,
And in the midst of the Phœnix, the divine,
Sole in the earth, blazing with azure wings
Diversely bright, her eyes upon the dawn
That breaks above the green crystalline sea.
Obverse, the vast over-arching of the sky,

Height of Olympus,
And Love, aye, Love himself, against the clouds,
The dazzling bow, the torch, the arrows of fire.
No puny soul, no sordid breast his target.
Those burning eyes go seeking through the worlds
For the high heart, the proud undaunted spirit.
These, not the sprawling, are his arrows' mark,
The noblest minds, beauty as of the gods,
He kindles, and they burn.

And thou art with them, Damon, thou art there,
This is no cheating hope.
Thou too art there: where else should be
That holy sweet simplicity,
That radiant valiancy?
We did thee wrong to seek thee in the mirk
Of Lethe's waters.
No tears, no tears for thee, and no more wailing.
I'll weep no more. He hath his dwelling place
In that pure heaven,
He hath the power of the air, himself as pure.
His foot hath spurned the rainbow.
Among the souls of the heroes, the gods everlasting,
He drinks deep draughts of joy.

Thou hast the freedom of heaven: be with me now.
Canst hear me, Damon, come unto thy peace?
Art thou our Damon still,
Or do they call thee by thine other name,
The given of God, the name they knew in heaven,
But Damon in the woods.
Thine was untarnished youth, the flush of honour

Untouched by wantonness: and now to thee
The glories kept for virgin souls are given.
Upon thy radiant head a glittering crown,
And in thy hand the joyous green of the palm,
Thou goest deathless to the immortal feast,
Where the sound of the lyre and the voice of singing
Kindle and quicken the dancing feet,
Where the Bridegroom's feast is toward,
And the mystic wine is poured,
The madness and the ecstasy of Heaven.

ABRAHAM COWLEY

ON THE DEATH OF
MR. WILLIAM HERVEY [1]

Immodicis brevis est ætas, & rara Senectus.   *Mart.*

It was a dismal, and a fearful night,
Scarce could the Morn drive on th' unwilling Light,
When *Sleep, Deaths Image*, left my troubled brest,
      By something *liker Death* possest.
My eyes with Tears did uncommanded flow,
      And on my Soul hung the dull weight
      Of some *Intolerable Fate*.
What Bell was that? Ah me! Too much I know.

[1]Hervey was a close friend of the poet's at Cambridge, where they were fellow
students about the time Milton was writing "Lycidas." He died May 16, 1642.

My sweet *Companion*, and my gentle *Peere*,
Why hast thou left me thus unkindly here,
Thy *end* for ever, and my *Life* to moan;
 O thou hast left me all alone!
Thy *Soul* and *Body* when *Deaths Agonie*
 Besieg'd around thy noble heart,
 Did not with more reluctance part
Then *I*, my dearest *Friend*, do part from *Thee*.

My dearest *Friend*, would I had dy'd for thee!
Life and this *World* henceforth will tedious bee.
Nor shall I know hereafter what to do
 If once my *Griefs* prove tedious too.
Silent and sad I walk about all day,
 As sullen *Ghosts* stalk speechless by
 Where their hid Treasure ly;
Alas, my Treasures gone, why do I stay?

He was my *Friend*, the truest *Friend* on earth;
A strong and mighty *Influence* joyn'd our *Birth*.
Nor did we envy the most sounding *Name*
 By *Friendship* giv'n of old to *Fame*.
None but his *Brethren* he, and *Sisters* knew,
 Whom the kind youth preferr'd to Me;
 And ev'n in that we did agree,
For much above my self I lov'd them too.

Say, for you saw us, ye immortal *Lights*,
How oft unweari'd have we spent the Nights?
Till the *Ledæan Stars* so fam'd for *Love*,
 Wondred at us from above.
We spent them not in toys, in lusts, or wine;
 But search of deep *Philosophy*,

Wit, *Eloquence*, and *Poetry*,
Arts which I lov'd, for they, my *Friend*, were *Thine*.

Ye fields of *Cambridge*, our dear *Cambridge*, say,
Have ye not seen us walking every day?
Was there a *Tree* about which did not know
    The *Love* betwixt us two?
Henceforth, ye gentle *Trees*, for ever fade;
    Or your sad branches thicker joyn,
    And into darksome shades combine,
Dark as the *Grave* wherein my *Friend* is laid.

Henceforth no learned *Youths* beneath you sing,
Till all the tuneful *Birds* to' your boughs they
    bring;
No tuneful *Birds* play with their wonted chear,
    And call the learned *Youths* to hear,
No whistling *Winds* through the glad branches fly,
    But all with sad solemnitie,
    Mute and unmoved be,
Mute as the *Grave* wherein my *Friend* does ly.

To him my *Muse* made haste with every strain
Whilst it was new, and *warm* yet from the *Brain*.
He lov'd my worthless *Rhimes*, and like a *Friend*
    Would find out something to *commend*.
Hence now, my *Muse*, thou canst not me delight;
    Be this my latest verse
    With which I now adorn his *Herse*,
And this my *Grief*, without *thy* help shall write.

Had I a wreath of *Bays* about my brow,
I should condemn that flourishing honor now,

Condemn it to the *Fire*, and joy to hear
    It rage and crackle there.
Instead of *Bays*, crown with sad *Cypress* me;
    Cypress which *Tombs* does beautifie;
    Not *Phœbus* griev'd so much as I
For him, who first was made that mournful *Tree*.

Large was his *Soul*; as large a *Soul* as ere
Submitted to *inform* a *Body* here.
High as the Place 'twas shortly 'in *Heav'n* to have,
    But low, and humble as his *Grave*.
So *high* that all the *Virtues* there did come
    As to their chiefest seat
    Conspicuous, and great;
So *low* that for *Me* too it made a room.

He scorn'd this busie world below, and all
That we, *Mistaken Mortals*, Pleasure call;
Was fill'd with inn'ocent *Gallantry* and *Truth*,
    Triumphant ore the sins of *Youth*.
He like the *Stars*, to which he now is gone,
    That shine with beams like *Flame*,
    Yet burn not with the same,
Had all the *Light* of *Youth*, of the Fire none.

Knowledge he only sought, and so soon caught,
As if for him *Knowledge* had rather *sought*.
Nor did more *Learning* ever crowded lie
    In such a short *Mortalitie*.
When ere the skilful *Youth* discourst or writ,
    Still did the *Notions* throng
    About his eloquent Tongue,
Nor could his *Ink* flow faster then his *Wit*.

So strong a *Wit* did *Nature* to him frame,
As all things but his *Judgement* overcame;
His *Judgement* like the heav'nly *Moon* did show,
    Temp'ring that mighty *Sea* below.
Oh had he liv'd in *Learnings World*, what bound
      Would have been able to controul
      His over-powering Soul?
We' have lost in him *Arts* that not yet are *found*.

His *Mirth* was the pure *Spirits* of various Wit,
Yet never did his *God* or *Friends* forget.
And when deep talk and wisdom came in view,
    Retir'd and gave to them their due.
For the rich help of *Books* he always took,
      Though his own searching mind before
      Was so with *Notions* written ore
As if wise *Nature* had made that her *Book*.

So many *Virtues* joyn'd in him, as we
Can scarce pick here and there in *Historie*.
More then old *Writers Practice* ere could reach,
    As much as they could ever *teach*.
These did *Religion*, *Queen* of Virtues sway,
    And all their sacred *Motions* steare,
      Just like the First and *Highest Sphere*
Which wheels about, and turns all *Heav'n* one way.

With as much Zeal, Devotion, Pietie,
He always *Liv'd*, as other Saints do *Dye*.
Still with his soul severe account he kept,
    Weeping all *Debts* out ere he slept.
Then down in peace and innocence he lay,
    Like the *Suns* laborious light,

Which still in Water sets at Night,
Unsullied with his *Journey* of the *Day*.

Wondrous young Man, why wert thou made so
    good,
To be snatcht hence ere better *understood*?
Snatcht before half of thee enough was seen!
    Thou Ripe, and yet thy *Life* but *Green*!
Nor could thy Friends take their last sad Farewel,
        But Danger and *Infectious Death*
        Malitiously seiz'd on that Breath
Where *Life*, *Spirit*, *Pleasure* always us'd to dwell.

But happy Thou, ta'ne from this frantick age,
Where *Igno'rance* and *Hypocrisie* does rage!
A fitter *time* for Heav'n no soul ere chose,
        The place now onely free from those.
There 'mong the *Blest* thou dost for ever shine,
        And wheresoere thou casts thy view
        Upon that white and radiant crew,
See'st not a *Soul* cloath'd with more *Light* then
        Thine.

And if the glorious *Saints* cease not to know
Their wretched Friends who *fight* with *Life* below;
Thy Flame to *Me* does still the same abide,
        Onely more pure and rarifi'd.
There whilst immortal Hymns thou dost reherse,
        Thou dost with holy pity see
        Our dull and earthly *Poesie*,
Where *Grief* and *Mis'ery* can be join'd with *Verse*.

Justa Edovardo King

EDWARD KING

All that is known about the composition and publication of "Lycidas" is that it was written in November, 1637, and appeared in 1638 as the final selection in a little volume of thirty-six poems commemorating the death of Edward King. Beyond Milton's own statement, prefixed to "Lycidas" when it appeared seven years later in the first collection of Milton's poems, we know little about the manner of King's death or the nature of his and Milton's friendship.[1]

"Unfortunately drown'd in his passage from Chester on the Irish Seas, 1637," is all Milton thought necessary, but a Latin paragraph prefacing the commemorative volume gives us a few details:

P.M.S.—Edward King, son of John (Knight and Privy Councillor for the Kingdom of Ireland to their majesties, Elizabeth, James, and Charles), Fellow of Christ's College in the University of Cambridge, happy in the consciousness and in the fame of piety and erudition, and one in whom there was nothing immature except his age, was on his voyage to Ireland, drawn by natural affection to visit his country, his relatives and his friends—chiefly, his brother Sir Robert King, Knight, a most distinguished man; his sisters, most excellent women, Anne, wife of Lord G. Caulfield, Baron Charlemont, and Margaret, wife of Lord G. Loder, Chief Justice of Ireland; the venerable prelate Edward King, Bishop of Elphin, his godfather; and the most reverend and learned William Chappell, Dean of

[1]Edward Phillips, Milton's nephew and biographer, writing long after the poet's death, of a period in the poet's life antedating Phillips' maturity, and in a biography containing several errors, said that among Milton's friends at Cambridge was "a Young Gentleman, one Mr. *King*, with whom, for his great Learning and Parts, he had contracted a particular Friendship and Intimacy; whose death (for he was drown'd on the *Irish* Seas in his passage from *Chester* to *Ireland*) he bewails in that most excellent Monody in his forementioned Poems, Intituled *Lycidas*." *The Early Lives of Milton*, ed. Helen Darbishire, (London, 1932), p. 54. The sentence sounds suspiciously like an inference from Milton's own statement.

Cashel and Provost of Trinity College, Dublin, whose hearer and pupil he had been in the University—when, the ship in which he was having struck on a rock not far from the British shore and been ruptured by the shock, he, while the other passengers were fruitlessly busy about their mortal lives, having fallen forward upon his knees, and breathing a life which was immortal, in the act of prayer going down with the vessel, rendered up his soul to God, Aug. 10, 1637, aged 25.[2]

Of the detail about King's decision to pray first and man the boats later some editors have been skeptical; but as Verity points out, since several of the contributors mention it, Milton's failure to make any use of it may have been due to his lack of a complete account of the diasaster. On the other hand, Milton may have thought the episode inappropriate to "Lycidas". Only one factual point in the account has importance for the student of "Lycidas": Milton had Hippotades defend the winds by saying

> That not a blast was from his dungeon strayed,
> The air was calm, and on the level brine
> Sleek Panope with all her sisters played.

From this statement the uncouth swain concludes that a failure in the structure of the ship was to blame. Nothing in Milton's brief allusion to the event conflicts with the statement in the preface to the volume. Since a light breeze, a sharp rock, and a poor pilot could together sink a ship built and rigged under the most benign influence, there is no need to assume that a storm made a fatal contribution. But Henry King, Edward's brother, in his poem twice uses metaphors implying that a storm drove the ship on the rocks.[3] In any event, there seems to be little reason for

[2]Translated by David Masson, who says his translation is "not more clumsy than the original." *The Life of John Milton*, (London, 1881), I, 651.

[3]Verity says of Milton's version: "As to the fair weather, it was, very likely, a mere fiction, happy enough artistically since it heightens the pathos of the scene, but assumed by Milton because the episode fell at the beginning of August when in theory the sea ought to have been calm, whatever it was in fact." Milton's *Ode on the Morning of Christ's Nativity, etc.* (Cambridge, 1924), p. xlii.

supposing that Milton would have heard the story in detail, or that if he had, he would have felt bound by it.

In his two-sentence argument, or preface, to the poem Milton refers to King simply as "a learned Friend"; he says nothing about the extent of their friendship or about King's ability as a poet. All we know is that King entered Christ's College, at the age of fourteen, in 1626, when Milton was seventeen and in his second year. In 1630 King was awarded a fellowship, an honor for which King and Milton may have been equally well qualified but to which King was helped by influential connections. Two years later Milton left Cambridge. King held his fellowship until his death. Among Milton's familiar letters are two written to his close friend Charles Diodati from London on September 2 and September 23, 1637, by which time, if King had been an intimate friend, Milton would have heard of his death; the letters make no mention of it.

In the years after 1633, when King became Master of Arts, he continued his preparation for the ministry, served his college as tutor and praelector, and contributed Latin verses to seven volumes published by the University, six of them commemorating such events as the birth of a princess, the King's recovery from smallpox, and the safe return of the king from a journey to Scotland. Of their quality Masson says:

> On the whole, there is nothing in any of these performances that would impress one now, if one came upon them unawares, with the notion of superior genius in the writer. There is little poetry in the thought; and the obstetric plainness of phrase in each of the birthday pieces, though excusable perhaps in verse made by the dictionary, is what the taste of a true son of the muses would certainly have avoided. The verses, however, are not below the average of most of those that accompany them, and one can well understand that they do not reveal all the author's ability.[4]

[4]Op. cit. I., 649–650.

SELECTIONS FROM
JUSTA EDOVARDO KING

This small volume of sixty-one pages appeared in 1638, in Cambridge, entitled *Justa Edovardo King naufrago ab amicis mœrentibus, amoris et* μνείας χάριν ("Obsequies by mourning friends, in loving memory of Edward King, drowned"). The title is followed by a motto from Petronius Arbiter: "Si recte calculum ponas, ubique naufragium est" ("If you reckon correctly, there are shipwrecks everywhere"). The first part of the volume consists of twenty Latin poems and three Greek, by various contributors; the second part, introduced by an English title page ("Obsequies to the memorie of Mr. Edward King, Anno Dom. 1638"), consists of thirteen English poems, the last of which, signed simply "J. M.," is "Lycidas."

Such commemorative volumes were not uncommon in the early part of the seventeenth century; both Oxford and Cambridge produced collections to which King himself had contributed. Oxford, especially, had memorialized in this manner the deaths of certain of her alumni. The sponsor of the volume to King is unknown, but it may have been his brother Henry.

The following six poems, selected from those preceding Milton's, are good examples of the poetic style most popular among Milton's collegiate contemporaries. A facsimile of *Justa Edovardo King* has been published for the Facsimile Text Society by Columbia University Press (New York, 1939).

OBSEQUIES TO THE MEMORIE OF MR. EDWARD KING

No Death! I'le not examine Gods decree,
Nor question providence, in chiding thee:
Discreet Religion binds us to admire
The wayes of providence, and not enquire.
My grief is sober, and my faith knows thee
To b'executioner to destinie;
Brought in by sinne, which still maintains thee here,
As famines, earthquakes, and diseases were,
Poore mans tormentours, with this mischief more,
More grievous farre, his losse whom we deplore;
His, whose perfections had that Atheist seen,
That held souls mortall, he would straight have been
In t' other extreme, and thought his body had
Neen as immortall, as his soul was made.
Whose active spirit so swift and clearly wrought
Free from all dregs of earth, that you'd have thought
His body were assum'd, and did disguise
Some one of the celestiall Hierarchies.
Whose reason quite outstript our faith, and knew
What we are bound but to beleeve is true;
Religion was but the position
Of his own judgement, truth to him alone

Stood nak'd; he strung th' arts chain, and knit the
       ends,
And made divine and humane learning friends;
Of which he was the best edition,
Not stuft with doubts, but all decision;
Conjecture, wonder, probabilitie,
Were terms of weaknesse; nothing bound his eye
With fold or knot, but the earths globe did seem
Full as transparent as the aire to him.
He drest the Muses in the brav'st attire
That e're they wore, and taught them a strain higher,
And farre beyond their winged horses flight.
But oh! the charming tempest, and his might
Of eloquence, able to Christianize
India, or reconcile Antipathies!
He—but his flight is past my reach, and I
May wrong his worth with too much pietie:
I will not lessen then each single part
Of goodness, by commending; (for the art
Of serverall pens would soon be at a losse)
But take him whole, and praise him in the grosse,
And say that goodnesse, learning, vertue, all
Strive to recover him from the first great fall;
Had not that sad irrevocable breath
Resisted them, which curst us all to death.

[Fourteen lines omitted]

Mean while let me poore, senselesse, dead,
       alone
Sit and expect my resurrection,
To follow him; two sorrows sure will do,

That he is dead, that I am not dead too.
Yet dead I'm once already: for in him
I lost my best life, which I did esteem
Farre beyond nature's, reputation
And credit, which the mere reflection
Of his worth, like a twilight cast on me,
And fix'd me as it were i' the Galaxie:
But now my stock is shipwreck't all, and lost,
Quite bankrupt, all my hopes and fortunes crost.

[Twenty-four lines omitted]

    Curst element, whose nature ever vies
With fire in mischiefs, as in qualities!
Thou sav'dst but little more in the whole ark,
Then thou hast swallow'd now in this small bark;
As if it strove the last fire to outrunne,
And antedate the worlds destruction.
    But we have sinn'd, and now must bear the
        curse,
    Even that is our worst plague, which is our
        nurse:
(Though drowning but a second baptisme was,
T'admit him to the other Churches place)
My griefs eternall hate! hence I'le not own
One drop on't in my composition,
But throw't away in tears. And sad sea, thou,
Thou, whose black crime, though the dry sun should
        now
Drink all thy waters into clouds, and rain
Them on the deserts down in tears again,
Yet could not expiate; may the memorie
Of this be thy perpetuall infamie;

May that hid cause that rocks thee, now be still;
And may thy guilty waters turn as ill
As the dead sea, that it may ne're be said
That any thing lives there, where he lies dead.
Who though he want an Epitaph yet they
That henceforth crosse those seas, shall use to say,
   Here lyes one buried in a heap of land,
   Whom this sea drown'd, whose death hath
     drown'd the land.

HEN. KING

Whiles Phebus shines within our Hemisphere,
There are no starres, or at least none appear:
Did not the sunne go hence, we should not know
Whether there were a night and starres, or no.
Till thou ly'dst down upon thy western bed,
Not one Poetick starre durst shew his head;
Athenian owls fear'd to come forth in verse,
Untill thy fall darkned the Universe:
Thy death makes Poets: Mine eyes flow for thee,
And every tear speaks a dumbe elegie.
Now the proud sea grown richer then the land,
Doth strive for place, and claim the upper hand:
And yet an equall losse the sea sustains,
If it lose alwayes so much as it gains.
Yet we who had the happinesse to know
Thee what thou wast, (oh were it with us so!)
Enjoy thee still, and use thy precious name
As a perfume to sweeten our own fame.
And lest the body should corrupt by death,
To Thetis we our brinish tears bequeath.

As night, close mourner for the setting sunne,
Bedews her cheeks with tears when he is gone
To th' other world: so we lament and weep
Thy sad untimely fall, who by the deep
Didst climbe to th' highest heav'ns: Where being
    crown'd
A King, in after-times 'twill scarce be found,
Whether (thy life and death being without taint)
Thou wert Edward the Confessour, or the Saint.

                          [ANONYMOUS]

I like not tears in tune: nor will I prise
His artificiall grief, that scannes his eyes:
Mine weep down pious beads: but why should I
Confine them to the Muses Rosarie?
I am no Poet here; my penne's the spout
Where the rain-water of my eyes runs out
In pitie of that name, whose fate we see
Thus copi'd out in griefs Hydrographie.
The Muses are not Mayr-maids; though upon
His death the Ocean might turn Helicon.
The sea's too rough for verse; who rhymes upon't,
With Xerxes strives to fetter th' Hellespont.
My tears will keep no chanell, know no laws
To guide their streams; but like the waves, their
    cause,
Run with disturbance, till they swallow me
As a description of his miserie.
But can his spacious vertue find a grave
Within th' impostum'd buble of a wave?
Whose learning if we sound, we must confesse

The sea but shallow, and him bottomlesse.
Could not the winds to countermand thy death,
With their whole card of lungs redeem thy breath?
Or some new Iland in thy rescue peep,
To heave thy resurrection from the deep?
That so the world might see thy safety wrought
With no lesse miracle then thy self was thought.
The famous Stagirite, who in his life
Had Nature as familiar as his wife,
Bequeath'd his widow to survive with thee
Queen Dowager of all Philosophie.
An ominous legacie, that did portend
Thy fate, and Predecessours second end!
Some have affirm'd, that what on earth we find,
The sea can parallel for shape and kind:
Books, arts, and tongues were wanting; but in thee
Neptune hath got an Universitie.

　　　We'll dive no more for pearls. The hope to see
Thy sacred reliques of mortalitie
Shall welcome storms, and make the sea-man prize
His shipwrack now more than his merchandise.
He shall embrace the waves, and to thy tombe
(As to a Royaller Exchange) shall come.
What can we now expect? Water and Fire
Both elements our ruine do conspire;
And that dissolves us, which doth us compound:
One Vatican was burnt, another drown'd.
We of the Gown our libraries must tosse,
To understand the greatnesse of our losse,
Be Pupills to our grief, and so much grow
In learning, as our sorrows overflow.
When we have fill'd the rundlets of our eyes,

We'll issue 't forth, and vent such elegies,
As that our tears shall seem the Irish seas,
We floating Ilands, living Hebrides.

J. CLEVELAND

I do not come like one affrighted, from
The shades infernall, or some troubled tombe;
Nor like the first sad messenger, to wound
Your hearts, by telling how and who was drown'd.
I have no startled hairs; nor their eyes, who
See all things double, and report them so.
My grief is great, but sober; thought upon
Long since; and reason now, not Passion.
Nor do I like their pietie, who sound
His depth of learning, where they feel no ground,
Strain till they lose their own; then think to ease
The losse of both, by cursing guiltlesse seas.
I never yet could so farre dote upon
His rare prodigious lifes perfection,
As not to think his best Philosophie
Was this, his *skill in knowing how to die.*
No, no, they wrong his memorie, that tell
His life alone, who liv'd and di'd so well.
I have compar'd them both, and think heavens were
No more unjust in this, then partiall there.
Canst thou believe their paradox, that say
The way to purchase is to give away?
This was that Merchants faith, who took the seas
At all adventures with such hopes as these.
Which makes me think his thoughts diviner, and
That he was bound for heaven, not Ireland.

Tell me no more of Stoicks: Canst thou tell
Who 'twas, that when the waves began to swell,
The ship to sink, sad passengers to call,
Master we perish, slept secure of all?
Remember this, and him that waking kept
A mind as constant, as he did that slept.
Canst thou give credit to his zeal and love,
That went to heav'n and to those fires above
Rapt in a fierie chariot? Since I heard
Who 'twas that on his knees the vessel steer'd
With hands bolt up to heaven, and since I see
As yet no signe of his mortalitie;
Pardon me, Reader, if I say he's gone
The self-same journey in a watry one.

W. MORE

Pardon, blest soul, the slow pac'd Elegies
Of sad survivers: they have pregnant eyes
For vulgar griefs. Our sorrows find a tongue,
Where verse may not the losse or metir wrong:
But an amazed silence might become
Thy obsequies, as fate deni'd a tombe.
Poetick measures have not learn'd to bound
Unruly sorrows: shallow streams may sound,
And with their forward murmures chide the sea,
While deepest griefs a silent tribute pay.

[Twenty-four lines omitted]

Heav'n would (it seems) no common grave
    intrust,
Nor bury such a Jewel in the dust.

The fatall barks dark cabbin must inshrine
That precious dust, which fate would not confine
To vulgar coffins. Marble is not fit
T' inclose rich jewels, but a cabinet.
Corruption there shall slowly seise its prize,
Which thus embalm'd in brinie casket lies.
The saucy worm which doth inhabit here
In earthly graves, and quickly domineer
In stateliest marbles, shall not there assail
The treasure hidden in that watry vale.

[Twelve lines omitted]

Grieving survivers, did they know thy grave,
Would there dissolve, and death a labour save
By voluntarie melting into tears:
To spare them, fate to interre thee forbears.
Thus doth the setting sunne his evening light
Hide in the Ocean, when he makes it night;
The world benighted knows not where he lies,
Till with new beams from seas he seems to rise:
So did thy light, fair soul, it self withdraw
To no dark tombe by natures common law,
But set in waves, when we thought it noon,
And thence shall rise more glorious then the
      sunne.

                                        W. HALL

What water now shall vertue have again
(As once) to purge? The Ocean't self's a stain:
And at this mourning, weeping eyes do fear
They sinne against thee, when a pious tear

Steals from our cheeks. Go, go you waters back
So foully tainted: all the Muses black
Came from your surges. Had the Thebane Swan
Who lov'd his Dirce (while it proudly ran
Swell'd by his lyre) now liv'd, he would repent
The solemn praises he on Water spent.
Why did not some officious dolphine hie
To be his ship and pilot through the frie
Of wondring Nymphs; and having passes o're,
Would have given more then Tagus to his shore?
Be this excuse; Since first the waters gave
A blessing to him which the soul could save,
They lov'd the holy body still too much,
And would regain some vertue from a touch:
They clung too fast; great Amphitrite so
Embraces th' earth, and will not let it go.
So seem'd his soul the struggling surge to greet,
As when two mighty seas encountring meet:
For what a sea of arts in him was spent,
Mightier then that above the firmament?
As Achelous with his silver fleet
Runnes through salt Doris purely, so to meet
His Arethusa; the Sicanian maid
Admires his sweetnesse by no wave decai'd:
So should he, so have cut the Irish strand,
And like a lustie bridgroom leapt to land;
Or else (like Peter) trode the waves: but he
Then stood most upright, when he bent his knee.

ISAAC OLIVIER

John Milton

MILTON'S LIFE
FROM 1608 TO 1637

Almost from the time of his birth, in 1608, John Milton was destined by his father to a life of study. Long before he went to St. Paul's School, in his native city of London, Milton was given daily instruction by private tutors, and at his graduation from St. Paul's he had mastered Greek and Latin, had read many of the classic texts (in addition to much in English), and could probably read French, Italian, and Hebrew. At Christ's College, Cambridge, where he matriculated in 1625, he continued his "labor and intent study" for seven years. Some time before he finished at Cambridge, he decided against entering the ministry, the profession most attractive to a student with his interests and training. In his own words: "Comming to some maturity of yeers and perceaving what tyranny had invaded the Church, that he who would take Orders must subscribe slave, and take an oath withall, which unlesse he took with a conscience that would retch, he must either strait perjure, or split his faith, I thought it better to preferre a blamelesse silence before the sacred office of speaking bought and begun with servitude and forswearing."[1]

Of the poems written during these years at Cambridge forty were later published: seven Latin elegies (so-called because they were written in the elegiac meter); ten other Latin poems on subjects such as the death of the Bishop of Ely, Guy Fawkes' Day, That Nature is Not Subject to Old Age, and the Platonic Idea as Understood by Aristotle; five Italian sonnets and one canzone; and seventeen English poems, including two sonnets ("O Nightingale" and "How Soon Hath Time") and longer poems, such as

---

[1] *The Reason of Church Government*, Columbia *Milton*, Vol. III, pt. i, p. 241.

"On the Death of a Fair Infant Dying of a Cough," "On the Morning of Christ's Nativity," "On Shakespeare," and perhaps "L'-Allegro" and "Il Penseroso." Nine of the forty commemorated deaths, but none of the dead had been a close friend of Milton's.

In 1632 Milton's only brother had married, and his father (rather well-to-do and nearly seventy) and mother had retired to spend their last years in the little village of Horton, eighteen miles west of London. Having completed the M.A., Milton decided to retire to Horton, where in the rural quiet he could pursue a course of study which he had outlined for himself. His own brief description of the period follows:

> At my father's country house, to which he had retired to pass the remainder of his days, being perfectly at my ease, I gave myself up entirely to reading the Greek and Latin writers, exchanging, however, sometimes, the country for the town, either for the purchase of books or to learn something new in mathematics or in music, which at that time furnished the sources of my amusement.[2]

How conscientiously Milton stuck to his books is shown by a passage in a letter written near the end (1637) of his five-year program in the country to his old schoolmate Charles Diodati, then a practicing physician:

> You shall also have information respecting my studies. I have by continuous reading brought down the affairs of the Greeks as far as to the time when they ceased to be Greeks. I have been long engaged in the obscure business of the state of the Italians under the Longobards, the Franks, and the Germans, down to the time when liberty was granted them by Rodolph, King of Germany: from that period it will be better to read separately what each city did by its own wars. . . . Meanwhile, if it can be done without trouble to you, I beg you to send me Justiniani, the historian of the Venetians. I will, on my word, see that he is well kept against your arrival, or, if you prefer it, that he is sent back to you not very long after the receipt.[3]

[2]*Second Defense*, trans. George Burnett, Columbia *Milton*, Vol. VII, p. 121.
[3]Trans. David Masson, Columbia *Milton*, Vol. XII, p. 29.

"Lycidas" was written a few months before the end of Milton's stay in Horton: in April of 1638 he left for a year of travel abroad. During the five years of retirement he apparently wrote little poetry, but among the poems he did write was *Comus*, a masque presented in 1634 as part of the celebration marking the installation of the Earl of Bridgewater as Lord President of Wales. Two years before, he had written a short masque, *Arcades*, which had been presented to honor the Countess Dowager of Derby. He wrote it, presumably, at the invitation of Henry Lawes, one of the leading composers in London and probably an old friend. Since the Earl of Bridgewater was the stepson of the Countess Dowager of Derby, it seems likely that the success of *Arcades* as well as the influence of Lawes (who composed the music for *Comus*, also) led to the invitation to write a longer and more elaborate masque.

To be sure, Milton's reputation as a poet in Christ's College was probably great enough to insure his being asked to contribute to such a volume as was proposed by King's brother, but if it had not been, the publication of *Comus* in the very month of King's death would certainly have led to an invitation. During the three years after the presentation of the masque, Henry Lawes had been so often asked for copies of the poem that with Milton's permission he finally published it. With the exception of his poem on Shakespeare, which appeared in the second edition of Shakespeare's collected works (1632) signed J. M., this was the first of Milton's poems to be published. "Lycidas" was the third.

During 1637 Milton had several unusual reasons for contemplating the mystery of death. The plague which had been virulent in London the year before, reached Horton in the spring of 1637, and the fatal disease that moved invisibly and struck so finally made death part of the milieu in which the poem grew. Of more importance to Milton, perhaps, was the death of Ben Jonson (in the same month as King's drowning—August). To a young man who planned seriously to devote his life to poetry, the death of the poet laureate would be a natural occasion for him to consider the question of the value of any poet's effort to achieve worldly fame (though Jonson, unlike King, had reached sixty-three and a grave in Westminster Abbey) Jonson was not only the supreme authority among poets—he was also a man whose learning Milton respected. When the contributors to a volume marking Jonson's death were selected, the young J. M., whose praise of Shakespeare had appeared five years before but who in his *Comus* showed little affinity for the style of Ben and his tribe, was not included. Was Milton therefore more ready to use the death of King, a poet only in name, as an opportunity to express thoughts inspired by other occasions?

Seven months before he wrote "Lycidas", Milton's mother died. For five years she, her husband, and their son, in his twenties, had lived together. Though details concerning Milton's life during 1637 are slight, the poem itself is proof that "Lycidas" was produced by a mind filled with poetry and a sensitivity kindled by recent contacts with the doubts and despair inherent in experience with death.

MILTON'S OWN ACCOUNT
OF HIS EARLY TRAINING
AND ASPIRATIONS

🌿 🌿 🌿

from AN APOLOGY FOR SMECTYMNUUS[1]

I had my time Readers, as others have, who have good learning
bestow'd upon them, to be sent to those places, where the opinion
was it might be soonest attain'd: and as the manner is, was not
unstudied in those authors which are most commended; whereof
some were grave Orators & Historians; whose matter me thought
I lov'd indeed, but as my age then was, so I understood them;
others were the smooth Elegiack Poets, whereof the Schooles are
not scarce. Whom both for the pleasing sound of thier numerous
writing, which in imitation I found most easie; and most agreeable
to natures part in me, and for their matter which what it is, there
be few who know not, I was so allur'd to read, that no recreation
came to me better welcome. For that it was then those years with
me which are excus'd though they be least severe, I may be sav'd
the labour to remember ye. Whence having observ'd them to

[1]Soon after his return from Italy Milton began to write pamphlets supporting
the Puritans' attack on the Established Church. The pamphleteers on both
sides in this polemical warfare slipped easily into calumny, and in the pamphlet from which this passage is taken (published in 1642), Milton digressed
to defend himself against the charge that he had lived a dissolute life. The
text is that of the Columbia *Milton*, Vol. III, pt. i, pp. 302–306.

account it the chiefe glory of their wit, in that they were ablest to judge, to praise, and by that could esteeme themselves worthiest to love those high perfections which under one or other name they took to celebrate, I thought with my selfe by every instinct and presage of nature which is not wont to be false, that what imboldn'd them to this task might with such diligence as they us'd imbolden me, and that what judgement, wit, or elegance was my share, would herein best appeare, and best value it selfe, by how much more wisely, and with more love of vertue I should choose (let rude eares be absent) the object of not unlike praises. For albeit these thoughts to some will seeme vertuous and commendable, to others only pardonable, to a third sort perhaps idle, yet the mentioning of them now will end in serious. Nor blame it Readers, in those yeares to propose to themselves such a reward, as the noblest dispositions above other things in this life have sometimes preferr'd. Whereof not to be sensible, when good and faire in one person meet, argues both a grosse and shallow judgement, and withall an ungentle, and swainish brest. For by the firme setling of these perswasions I became, to my best memory, so much a proficient, that if I found those authors any where speaking unworthy things of themselves; or unchaste of those names which before they had extoll'd, this effect it wrought with me, from that time forward their art I still applauded, but the men I deplor'd; and above them all preferr'd the two famous renowners of *Beatrice* and *Laura* who never write but honour of them to whom they devote their verse, displaying sublime and pure thoughts, without transgression. And long it was not after, when I was confirm'd in this opinion, that he who would not be frustrate of his hope to write well hereafter in laudable things, ought him selfe to bee a true Poem, that is, a composition, and patterne of the best and honourablest things; not presuming to sing high praises of heroick men, or famous Cities, unlesse he have in himselfe the experience and the practice of all that which is praise-worthy. These reasonings, together with a certaine nicenesse of nature, an honest haughtinesse, and self-esteem either of what I was, or what I might be, (which let envie call pride) and lastly that modesty, whereof though not in the Title page yet here I may be excus'd to make some beseeming profession, all these uniting the supply of their naturall aide together, kept me still above those low descents of minde, beneath which he must deject and plunge himself, that can agree to salable and unlawfull prostitutions. Next, (for heare me out now Readers) that I may tell ye whether my younger feet wander'd; I betook me among those lofty Fables and Romances, which recount in solemne canto's the deeds of Knighthood founded by our victorious Kings; & from hence had in renowne over all Christendome. There I read it in the oath of every Knight, that he should defend to the expence of his best blood, or of his life, if it so befell him, the honour and chastity of Virgin or Matron. From whence even then I learnt what a noble vertue chastity sure must be, to the defence of which so many worthies by such a deare adventure of themselves had sworne. And if I found in the story afterward any of them by word or deed breaking that oath, I judg'd it the same fault of the Poet, as that which is attributed to *Homer*; to have written undecent things of the gods. Only this my minde gave me that every free and gentle spirit without that oath ought to be borne a Knight, nor needed to expect the guilt spurre, or the laying of a sword upon his shoulder to stirre him up both by his counsell, and his arme to secure and protect the weaknesse of any attempted chastity. So that even those books which to many others have bin the fuell of wantonnesse and loose living, I cannot thinke how unlesse by divine indulgence prov'd to me so many incitements as you have heard, to the love and stedfast observation of that vertue which abhorres the society of Bordello's. Thus from the Laureat fraternity of Poets, riper yeares, and the ceaseless round of study and reading led me to the shady spaces of philosophy, but chiefly to the divine volumes of *Plato*, and his equall *Xenophon*. Where if I should tell ye what I learnt, of chastity and love, I meane that which is truly so, whose charming cup is only vertue which she bears in her hand to those who are worthy. The rest are cheated with a thick intoxicating potion which a certaine Sorceresse the abuser of loves name carries about; and how the first and chiefest office of love, begins and ends in the soule, producing those happy twins of her divine generation knowledge and vertue, with such abstracted sublimities as these, it might be worth your listning, Readers, as I may one day hope to have ye in a still time, when there shall be no chiding; not in these noises, the adversary as ye know, barking at the doore; or searching for me at the Burdello's where it may be he has lost himselfe, and raps up without pitty the sage and rheumatick old *Prelatesse* with all her young *Corinthian Laity* to inquire for such a one. Last of all not in time, but as perfection is last, that care was ever had of me, with my earliest capacity not to be negligently train'd in the precepts of Christian Religion: This that I have hitherto related, hath bin to shew, that though Christianity had bin but slightly taught me, yet a certain reserv'dnesse of naturall disposition, and morall discipline learnt out of the noblest Philosophy was anough to keep me in disdain of farre lesse incontinences then this of the Burdello.

⚜ ⚜ ⚜

from *A REVISED DRAFT OF A LETTER TO A FRIEND*[1]

Sir, besides that in sundry other respects I must acknowledge me to proffit by you when ever wee meet, you are often to me,

---

[1]In the Cambridge Manuscript this revision and its original are undated, but their contents indicate that they were written sometime during Milton's stay at Horton. Columbia *Milton*, Vol. XII, pp. 322–324.

& were yesterday especially, as a good watch man to admonish that the howres of the night passe on (for so I call my life as yet obscure, & unserviceable to mankind) & that the day with me is at hand wherin Christ commands all to labour while there is light. which because I am persuaded you doe to no other purpose then out of a true desire that god should be honourd in every one; I therfore thinke my selfe bound though unask't, to give you account, as oft as occasion is, of this my tardie moving; according to the præcept of my conscience, which I firmely trust is not without god. yet now I will not streine for any set apologie, but only referre my selfe to what my mynd shall have at any tyme to declare her selfe at her best ease. But if you thinke, as you said, that too much love of Learning is in fault, & that I have given up my selfe to dreame away my yeares in the armes of studious retirement like Endymion with the Moone as the tale of Latmus goes, yet consider that if it were no more but the meere love of learning, whether it proceed from a principle bad, good, or naturall it could not have held out thus long against so strong opposition on the other side of every kind, for if it be bad why should not all the fond hopes that forward Youth & Vanitie are fledge with together with Gaine, pride, & ambition call me forward more powerfully, then a poore regardlesse & unprofitable sin of curiosity should be able to withhold me, wherby a man cutts him selfe off from all action & becomes the most helplesse, pusilanimous & unweapon'd creature in the word, the most unfit & unable to doe that which all mortals most aspire to either to defend & be usefull to his freinds, or to offend his enimies. Or if it be to be thought an naturall pronenesse there is against that a much more potent inclination & inbred which about this tyme of a mans life sollicits most, the desire of house & family of his owne to which nothing is esteemed more helpefull then the early entring into credible employment, & nothing more hindering then this affected solitarinesse and though this were anough yet there is to this another act if not of pure yet of refined nature no lesse available to dissuade prolonged obscurity, a desire of honour & repute & immortall fame seated in the brest of every true scholar which all make hast to by the readiest ways of publishing & divulging conceived merits as well those that shall as those that never shall obtaine it, nature therfore would præsently worke the more prævalent way if there were nothing but this inferiour bent of her selfe to restraine her. Lastly if the Love of Learning as it is be the persuit of somthing good, it would sooner follow the more excellent & supreme good knowne & præsented and so be quickly diverted from the emptie & fantastick chase of shadows & notions to the solid good flowing from due & tymely obedience to that command in the gospell set out by the terrible seasing of him that hid the talent. it is more probable therfore that not the endlesse delight of speculation but this very consideration of that great commandment does not presse forward as soone as may be to undergoe but keeps off with a sacred reverence, & religious advisement how best to undergoe not taking thought of beeing late so it give advantage to be more fit, for those that were latest lost nothing when the maister of the vinyard came to give each one his hire. & heere I am come to a streame head copious enough to disburden it selfe like Nilus at seven mouthes into an ocean, but then I should also run into a reciprocall contradiction of ebbing & flowing at once & doe that which I excuse my selfe for not doing preach & not preach. yet that you may see that I am something suspicious of my selfe, & doe take notice of a certaine belatednesse in me I am the bolder to send you some of my nightward thoughts some while since because they com in not altogether unfitly, made up in a Petrarchian stanza which I told you of

> How soone hath Time the suttle theefe of Youth
>   stolne on his wing my three and twentith yeere
>   my hasting days fly on with full careere
>   but my late spring no bud or blossome shew'th
> Perhapps my semblance might deceave the truth

that I to manhood am arriv'd so neere
& inward ripenesse doth much lesse appeare
that some more timely-happie spirits indu'th
Yet be it lesse or more, or soone or slow
it shall be still in strictest measure even
to that same lot however meane or high
toward which Tyme leads me, & the will of heaven
all is if I have grace to use it so
as ever in my great task-maisters eye

〆 〆 〆

from *A LETTER TO CHARLES DIODATI*[1]

For, lest you should threaten too much, know that it is impossible for me not to love men like you. What besides God has resolved concerning me I know not, but this at least: He has instilled into me, if into anyone, a vehement love of the beautiful. Not with so much labour, as the fables have it, is Ceres said to have sought her daughter Proserpina as it is my habit day and night to seek for this idea of the beautiful, as for a certain image of supreme beauty, through all the forms and faces of things (for many are the shapes of things divine) and to follow it as it leads me on by some sure traces which I seem to recognize. Hence it is that, when anyone scorns what the vulgar opine in their depraved estimation of things, and dares to feel and speak and be that which

[1]Written in Latin, September 27, 1637 (trans. David Masson), Columbia *Milton*, Vol. XII, pp. 25–27.

the highest wisdom throughout all ages has taught to be best, to
that man I attach myself forthwith by a kind of real necessity,
wherever I find him. If, whether by nature or by my fate, I am so
circumstanced that by no effort and labour of mine can I myself
rise to such an honour and elevation, yet that I should always
worship and look up to those who have attained that glory, or
happily aspire to it, neither gods nor men, I reckon, have bidden
nay.

But now I know you wish to have your curiosity satisfied. You
make many anxious inquiries, even as to what I am at present thinking of. Hearken, Theodotus, but let it be in your private ear,
lest I blush; and allow me for a little to use big language with
you. You ask what I am thinking of? So may the good Deity help
me, of immortality! And what am I doing? Growing my wings
and meditating flight; but as yet our Pegasus raises himself on
very tender pinions. Let us be lowly wise!

⚜ ⚜ ⚜

from THE REASON OF CHURCH GOVERNMENT URGED AGAINST PRELATY[1]

I must say therefore that after I had from my first yeeres by the
ceaselesse diligence and care of my father, whom God recompence,
bin exercis'd to the tongues, and some sciences, as my age would
suffer, by sundry masters and teachers both at home and at the

[1]In this pamphlet, written in 1642, as in *An Apology for Smectymnuus*
(written in the same year), Milton speaks at some length of himself. The text
is from the Columbia *Milton*, Vol. III, pt. i, pp. 235–236.

schools, it was found that whether ought was impos'd me by them
that had the overlooking, or betak'n to of mine own choise in
English, or other tongue, prosing or versing, but chiefly this latter,
the stile by certain vital signes it had, was likely to live. But much
latelier in the privat Academies of *Italy*, whither I was favor'd to
resort, perceiving that some trifles which I had in memory,
compos'd at under twenty or thereabout (for the manner is that
every one must give some proof of his wit and reading there) met
with acceptance above what was lookt for, and other things which
I had shifted in scarsity of books and conveniences to patch up
amongst them, were receiv'd with written Encomiums, which the
Italian is not forward to bestow on men of this side the *Alps*, I
began thus farre to assent both to them and divers of my friends
here at home, and not lesse to an inward prompting which now
grew daily upon me, that by labour and intent study (which I take
to be my portion in this life) joyn'd with the strong propensity of
nature, I might perhaps leave something so written to aftertimes,
as they should not willingly let it die.

England in 1637

TREVELYAN

※ ※ ※

from ENGLAND UNDER THE STUARTS[1]

During the decade when Government policy at home and abroad
continued in exact contradiction to the general sentiment, the
absence of all forms of agitation is most remarkable, if we consider
the violence of the storm when once it broke. A hundred years
back such discontent would have caused armed risings like the
Pilgrimage of Grace or Wyatt's rebellion. But the Tudor peace
had done its work. The inhabitants of an island where there was
neither an army nor a police force capable of quelling a single mob,
were now, by custom, civil and obedient to law. Until Parliament
met again, and again gave the semblance of authority to the
national cause, there seems to have been no rioting against the
unpopular taxation and the yet more unpopular ecclesiastical
courts. And when Parliament was not sitting, there was no method
of constitutional protest possible, except the merely passive
resistance of Hampden. There was no party organisation, no right
of public meeting, no freedom of the press. If meetings had been
held, they would have been suppressed as seditious riots; when
political writings by chance escaped the censor, their authors were
punished for libel. Words against the royal policy spoken at the
ale-house, the market-place or the dinner-table would be punished
if spies reported them at Whitehall; the only practical safeguard
for private conversation was that the hand of the central Government was short, and that the local magistrates were unwilling to

[1]From G. M. Trevelyan, *England Under the Stuarts* (London, 1904),
pp. 163–182.
Reprinted by permission.

179

become busybodies on its behalf. Since the last of the fighting Barons had perished, no subject who happened to disagree with his King had the right of free speech, either in theory or in custom. Liberty of speech within the walls of Parliament, unknown in other countries and now violated here by the imprisonment of Eliot, was the limit of an Englishman's right to talk against his rulers. The methods of espionage and repression, to which Pitt reverted at the height of the anti-Jacobin panic, were indisputable Government rights in the time of Charles, and were frequently exercised against individuals without causing general surprise or offence. For example, when Buckingham returned with his routed army from the Isle of Rhé and the whole nation was seething with suppressed rage at the disaster, a grocer's prentice was laid by the heels for having in his pocket a "Prophecy of Evil to befal the Kingdom," and a woman for saying that the Isle of Rhé was now the Isle of Rue.

This state of things, which would now seem quite intolerable, would probably never have been altered if the people as a whole had not quarrelled with the Government on general policy. Until that quarrel came to a head under King Charles, there was no personal sympathy for the victims of authority, unless they were champions of the popular cause. Even in much later times it has been shown how little freedom of speech, in press and person, is valued, in cases where popular opinion is on the side of central power. In time of excitement there are few who will go about to defend the rights of political opponents. It is therefore highly probable that, if Parliament had peacefully and imperceptibly succeeded to the functions of the Crown, the Parliamentary leaders would have inherited from the King the customary ideas of administrative rights in these matters, and might even have continued the Star Chamber as the weapon of the national will. It was during the eleven years of unparliamentary government that this famous tribunal and the whole system of repression connected with it, came, fortunately for the progress of the world, into conflict with popular feeling.

The Petition of Right had not aimed at securing freedom of speech, nor succeeded in securing freedom of person. The royal Judges could still use the ordinary courts to condemn the King's opponents; while the Star Chamber was an engine even more expressly fashioned and more formidably armed for the same purpose. That court consisted of the whole body of Privy Councillors, aided by the two Chief Justices; they had the power to summon before them any subject whom they chose, and to judge him without observing the rules of procedure and evidence which protected the prisoner in ordinary courts; their punishments were fine, imprisonment or mutilation, without any reference to customary or statutory limitations. The very men in whom the political power of the State resided, sat as judges and gave decisions solely by their own sense of what was just and expedient. So powerful a court could not fail to do great good or great harm. It sat in two capacities, practically though not technically distinct: as a high-handed court of equity, and as the sword of political power. In Tudor times it had been indispensable in both capacities. As a court supervising all other tribunals, it had made law and justice strong in an age of social disruption, and had tamed the manners of quasi-military barbarism. As the Revolutionary Tribunal of royalty, it had again and again saved the tottering State from murderous plots and armed rebels.

In the reign of Charles I. society had changed, but the Star Chamber had not moved with the times. As a court of equity it was still useful but no longer indispensable. The ordinary tribunals were now strong enough to execute justice, so far as any court was capable of so doing when there was no detective force and no understanding of the laws of evidence. Juries were no longer overawed, or corrupted wholesale by great lords. Judges no longer sat in fear of riot or resistance. Indeed, throughout the seventeenth century, the courts erred much more on the side of bureaucratic tyranny than of subservience to local interests. The Star Chamber of the Tudors had secured respect for the Assize

Court of the Stuarts. A careful study of the non-political cases in the Star Chamber in the time of Charles I. shows good work being done by an unnecessarily powerful instrument of State. We do not find cases of the defiance of ordinary justice, nor generally of violence, and scarcely ever of such violence as the ordinary tribunals would have feared to correct; the Star Chamber in its latter years dealt principally with libel actions, challenges and poaching disputes between silly gentlemen, forgery, perjury, fraud in commercial or domestic life, petty acts of malice or violence among the middle orders of society.[2] If there was little reason why such a jurisdiction should be abolished, there was less why it should be prolonged.

The Star Chamber fell, not because of its work as a court of equity, in which nine-tenths of its time was engaged, but because of its more rarely exercised but far more important political func-

---

[2] *E.g.*, among the thirty-one cases that came before the Star Chamber from the Easter Term, 1631, to the Trinity Term, 1632, as many as twenty-nine could clearly have been left to the ordinary courts of the land. In only two cases is there any question of force or influence such as might have intimidated or corrupted the Judge and Jury. One concerns the riotous resistance of the fen population to the draining of the fens. The other case, where Lord Saville with a great company and drawn swords interrupted the sport of Sir John Jackson on land where the Free Warren was in dispute, is the only case which approaches to the violence of an armed and riotous aristocrat. Nor is it by any means certain that the ordinary courts could not have dealt even with this case (see *Cases in the Courts of Star Chamber and High Commission* (Camden Soc., 1886)).

The exception that proves the rule is the necessary and warrantable interference of the Star Chamber in the ordinary course of Irish justice; in Ireland society still resembled English society in the fifteenth century, and the courts were subject to violence and corruption (see Rushworth, ii., pp. 203, 204).

tions, the abolition of which was the first step towards free speech. There could indeed be no more complete and dangerous example of merging the judiciary with the executive. The Privy Councillors were themselves the judges of their political antagonists. Such a jurisdiction becomes hurtful the moment it ceases to be indispensable. Yet the English were so well accustomed to the control of the Government over the expression of political views, that the Star Chamber would quite possibly have survived the Great Rebellion, if it had not interfered in ecclesiastical matters, and become the instrument of the Erastian Bishops for the punishment of their libellers, at a moment when all England would have been glad to have a hand in the libels.

To all ephemeral discontents, popular humours, and infant aspirations towards political liberty, was added the grand passion without which all other desires corrupt, and liberty itself proves vain—the passion of freedom of conscience. That which revealed by fire the hidden treasures of the nation, which called the high-minded into the public ways and the contemplative into the world of action, which made Cromwell a soldier and Milton a pamphleteer, was not the intrigue of greedy priests to gain some petty advantage over other creeds, but the last struggle of the individual to maintain his own spiritual existence, and to prevent the extinction upon earth of the lights by which he reads her meaning. This passion, the only one that ever drove the English into the paths of revolution was aroused by William Laud.

During the years when his opinions and character were formed, Laud's experience of life was confined to a University, and all his knowledge of religion was gathered from theologians. In the narrow hot-bed of college personalities he learned to hate a set of men who were not improbably odious—the Puritan divines then dominant in Oxford. For many years they tried to suppress him; but in 1611 he rose in spite of them to be the President of St. John's. A reaction set in, and he was able to purify Oxford, largely by the help of that college discipline and influence, which had, two hundred years before, weeded out Lollardry from its ancient home. A few colleges alone retained their Puritan character; in the cloisters and river walks of Magdalen, Hampden and his Buckinghamshire neighbours imbibed those principles which they afterwards maintained in arms, when they held the Chiltern Hills as the outwork of London against the Oxford Cavaliers.

As a middle-aged man Laud was called into a larger sphere to take part in the government of Church and State; and when at last he became Primate in 1633, he still conceived that all Puritans were like the clerical pedants over whom his first victory had been won. England was to him another Oxford, a place whence Puritanism, at first blustering and assertive, could soon be driven out by methodical application of college discipline.

Discipline indeed and order were to him not only a large part of the essence of religion, but the only means by which it could outwardly be expressed. Thus because he did not find "order" in the churches on his northern journey, he concluded that there was "no religion" among the Scots, and proceeded to manufacture one for the use of that nation. The religion that dictated every action of his own modest, unselfish and conscientious life, was genuine, but cold, orderly and formal.

> If he is called upon (writes Gardiner) to defend his practice of bowing towards the altar upon entering a church, he founds his arguments not on any high religious theme, but upon the custom of the Order of the Garter. To him a church was not so much the Temple of a living Spirit, as the palace of an invisible King.

The spirit that cries and tears itself and goes out into the wilderness to pray; the mind that, rapt and silent under the sense of the eternal mystery, rejects as trivial impertinences all forms and shows of worship; the free, strong, self-dependent and self-controlling life of a practical and simple religion, were all alike to be "harried out of the land" by this excellent man.

Laud was not cruel. He put no one to death, and corporal punishment was not his favourite method. Systematic and universal inquiry, deprivation, exile, imprisonment, were his regular weapons; and they would have been used with equal readiness by most of the Puritans. But Laud and not his enemies had the power to put an end to that comprehension which had so long held English Protestants together in one Church. And he, more than any other Anglican leader of that day, was ready to use the power to the full. By strict inquiry and coercion he abolished a working system of local variations in religion and imposed the will of the Bishop on that of the congregation. But neither he nor the bitter generation of enemies whom persecution raised up to defy him, could perceive that if there is no comprehension within the Church there must be toleration without. Though many would have wished to continue the practice of comprehension, no one even stated the theory of toleration: that great doctrine, in which expediency and mercy triumph over logic and passion, was taught to England, during fifty years of war and faction and terror, by the scourge with which the justice of events so often bleeds and tames the stupid intolerance of creed or race.

The plan adopted by Laud was to stop up every hole through which Puritan feeling could find vent in the press, the pulpit, the influence of the clergyman, the legal services of the Church, or the illegal worship of conventicles. He was able almost single-handed to accomplish his work of universal repression, because of the prestige he enjoyed and the fear he inspired as the King's confidant; and because the parish system and the Church Courts gave the Primate much more authority to interfere in local religion than the King possessed in local government. But no other one of the High Churchmen of that day would have been at the pains to use those powers with such unwonted stringency. His two chief instruments were the High Commission Court and the Metropolitical Visitation.

The Court of High Commission was a mixed body of clergy and laity to whom the King delegated the ecclesiastical power of the Crown. Though the bishops swayed its decisions, it was Erastian not only in origin but in spirit. Its members were in close touch with the politicians and the Court. It had long been well and deservedly hated. Even under Elizabeth it "savoured of the Roman Inquisition," as the sage and moderate Burghley declared. Under James, Coke questioned the legality of its jurisdiction, and Parliament exposed its abuses. The unpopularity of the Star Chamber was a late reflex of this old-established feeling against the High Commission. The secular tribunal only fell into disgrace under Charles, and then chiefly because it undertook the rough work of the ecclesiastical court by punishing the Bishops' libellers. The Star Chamber seldom dealt with political cases, but the High Commission in its ordinary daily work dealt with matters in the highest degree controversial. Authors and printers, lecturers and clergymen, congregations of churches and conventicles, were coerced or punished at its bar. The trials were often cut short by the refusal of the prisoners to take the "*ex officio* oath," by which the court compelled its victim to bear witness against himself. This odious power with which the royal prerogative had endowed the Commission, was resented not only by individual prisoners, but by the lawyers of the lay courts and by all Englishmen.

The other chief weapon of Laud's reform, the Metropolitical Visitation, was of his own device. He revived a claim of his mediæval predecessors to visit, in person or by deputy, every parish not only in the diocese, but in the whole province, of Canterbury. He thus established his personal authority through-out the greater part of England, and was enabled to make his in-quiries, and to enforce his own rules, in the territories of less busy Bishops. Nothing could now escape the eye of the master. A supervisory system, such as the State could not boast, was estab-lished for the Church by this Richelieu of religion.

Armed with these powerful weapons, the fearless and energetic man set to work to silence the religious voices of England. As early as 1628 men had been forbidden to discuss Free Will and Predestination. Free Will had not yet enough supporters, even among the Anglicans, to claim the monopoly in a Church whose Thirty-nine Articles had been drawn up by men of the opposite party. But Laud, who had a natural antipathy to speculation, had seized on the plan which James had initiated, of prohibiting the whole discussion. The Predestinarians, as had been declared on their behalf by the House of Commons, wished to close the mouths of their adversaries; Laud imposed silence on both sides. It is difficult to say which plan would have proved most fatal to free-thought.

But on other matters, for which they cared far more than for dogmatic speculation, the Anglicans were encouraged to talk, while the Puritans were silenced. The censorship of the press was then not in civil, but in episcopal hands. A decree of the Star Chamber in Elizabeth's reign had decided that no book might be printed without the leave of an Archbishop or of the Bishop of London. Under this rule Laud diligently prevented the Puritans from speaking in print. The High Commission maintained the rights of episcopal censorship by severe punishments, and even prevented the importation of Calvinist theology from abroad. In proportion as open controversy was suppressed, the libels put secretly into circulation grew more violent, and at the same time more popular with an angry people. The channels of genuine political and religious speculation were choked, until the Great Rebellion loosed the pent flood of books and pamphlets which covered the land for twenty years, cutting far and wide new river-beds in which the thought and practice of our own day now run, and leaving when it subsided not a little of pure gold on the sands of the spent deluge. Laud's system of episcopal censorship would, if it had survived to afflict later ages, have distorted the development of English literature and poetry, of which one essential excellence lies in the profundity and freedom of treatment given to historical, speculative and spiritual truth.

In those times the press was scarcely of greater importance than the pulpit. The Sunday sermon, afterwards the chief means of

Tory propaganda, was in the days of the first Charles used with most vigour by the Puritans. Those Anglican clergy who were genuine disciples of Laud and Andrewes, preferred catechising to preaching, and ritual to dogmatics; while the great body of indifferent and old-fashioned parsons, with whom Laud was forced to be content for want of better, the "blind mouths" of Milton's *Lycidas*, could only spell out the Prayer-book service, and then dismiss their congregations to keep Sunday round the May-pole. The English Bishops, in their jealousy of Puritan influence, had even in the reign of Elizabeth been anxious to restrain long and frequent sermons, not considering how necessary it was to preach, if a Catholic population was to be converted to a vital and intelligent Protestantism. But it was only under Laud's primacy that this long meditated design was put into effect. Deprivations of the clergy for Puritanism had been few since the great "outing of the ministers" in 1604. In 1633 King James's *Book of Sports* was reissued, and on this occasion the clergy who refused to read it were turned out of their livings. Thus a manifesto which under James had been an act of toleration for the laity, became under Charles a persecution of the clergy. Others, challenged on points of ritual or of teaching, were forced to choose between ruin or submission. In the Eastern Counties, Wren, Bishop of Norwich, carried on a vigorous campaign of visitations and suspensions, independent of Laud's activity. On one charge or another, some of the most enthusiastic preachers were either deprived or put to silence. The great majority, against whom no proceedings were taken, dared no longer preach freely for fear of some inquiry by their Bishop, a visitation of their parish, or a summons before the High Commission.

In trading and market towns, when the incumbent was unwilling to preach or his Puritan audience to listen, the municipality hired unbeneficed clergymen to "lecture" after the service had been read. The profession of lecturer, though practised within the walls of the church, was a near approach to Nonconformity;

but when powerful classes were unanimous, such a plan was the only alternative to disruption. Gentlemen often employed private chaplains for a similar purpose. But Laud now made it almost impossible for corporations to engage Puritan "lecturers," and forbade private gentlemen to keep chaplains at all. Two proud classes were wounded in their liberties and self-respect, and all strong Protestants saw disappear the last means by which their religious feelings could find expression within the pale of the Church, which thereby lost for one eventful generation the loyalty of moderate men.

The manner in which the Prayer-book services were conducted was also made the subject of inquiry in every parish. The table was moved into the east end and treated as an altar, often against the expressed wishes of the people. The Puritan clergy were being gradually superseded by ardent ritualists, or by time-servers who took the ritual path to promotion. The worst grievance was not that in a few churches a native ceremonialism sprouted into gorgeous excess, but that in many churches a moderate ceremonial was being forced on unwilling congregations, who were not permitted to meet for worship elsewhere. The only legal form of worship, beautiful and orderly as it had now become, appeared an intolerable triviality to many of the most imaginative and intellectual, and as it proved the most forcible men of every class. Such conditions were, in the phrase of the day, "too hot to last".

On these terms the service to which, ever since the accession of Elizabeth, the Government had succeeded in driving four-fifths of the nation, became in many parishes as unedifying to Protestants as it had long been to Catholics. Many indeed who afterwards attested their Puritanism in council and in war, continued to attend church in sullen discontent. Some twenty thousand fled to America. Others met secretly in woods and in garrets to preach and pray. The frequenters of these conventicles were men of mean station; for the Puritan squires and merchants before the Civil War preferred either to conform or to leave England altogether.

The trials for active dissent under Laud are the records of the poor, seized at their worship and confronted with the might of Church and State in the High Commission. Their love of English liberty and their steadfast adherence to the light within them, more than atone for the want of that learning which had never been within their reach. Men and women such as these—more than Bastwick, Burton and Prynne, more than Hampden himself —are worthy to stand with Eliot as pure confessors of liberty and religion. The apologists of Laud argue now, as the Bishops urged then, that persons so poor and ignorant as the conventiclers could have had no real capacity to make religion for themselves. Even if such an argument could ever be true, it was certainly false when applied to men of that period, when the lower classes of society had high imagination and opportunity for the noblest spiritual life. The meanest of English trades then produced John Bunyan; and George Fox was a shoemaker's man. But if Laud's war on Puritanism as the religion of the poor and ignorant had met with success, the tinker could never have given his *Pilgrim's Progress* to the world; and the founder of the Friends could never have left his master's shop to revive in the most spiritual of its thousand forms the religion of the Carpenter's Son.

*   *   *

Religious persecution was not the only means by which Laud contributed to his master's downfall. Immersed in mediæval precedents and in Canon Law, regarding the Tudor reform not as the Creation but only as the Deluge, the successor of Anselm and Becket ignored the social and political revolution of Henry VIII., and attempted to revive the power of the priest over laymen. A return to clerical government in society and politics alienated some who regarded alteration in doctrine and worship with indifference.

The Church courts, which had for a hundred years been cowed

by fear of the emancipated laity and the prospect of further confiscations, were inspired once more with a conceit of their authority and traditions. Laud, who feared the anger of the rich as little as he respected the feelings of the poor, used the same tribunals which punished the conventiclers to chastise the adultery of influential men, who might otherwise have been his powerful friends. The Church courts still retained the power to punish sin. In the last two centuries of Catholicism this jurisdiction had been odious and venal; under the Tudors the terrified clergy had let it fall into abeyance; and now a few honest men tried to revive what no large body of people were willing again to tolerate. The only result was to unite the loose-liver with the precisian in common hatred of the ecclesiastical courts; until, on the eve of the Civil War, fear of the approaching rule of the saints drove back Comus and his crew into the arms of mother Church. Both religious parties in this epoch made a fearless effort to put down immorality by force, and both paid dearly for the error. But whereas the rule of the saints was an inquisition of laymen over laymen through the agency of Puritan magistrates, Laud's method was the jurisdiction of the priest.

*   *   *

By every form of patronage and encouragement Laud brought to the front a small school of ritualists, who in zeal and learning were very different from the old-fashioned Anglican incumbent. The new Laudian clergy had high notions of the respect due to them and of the powers which they ought to enjoy in the parish; but these the gentry were unwilling to concede. Previously to the rise in the value of tithe in the eighteenth century, the clergyman was often of a lower class, a fact which even a higher education could not always efface. The squire was thus accustomed to admit no copartner in his rule, and had not yet formed with the parson the

Holy Alliance against Dissent, which ever since the Restoration has been the one almost certain factor in English politics. The village quarrel, which in ever-fresh forms of class rivalry or personal pique, has been going on in almost every English hamlet since *Domesday Book* was compiled, often assumed under Laud the form of bad blood between parson and squire; the landlord, constrained by fear of the ecclesiastical courts to dissemble his anger for years together, was heartily willing to vote for Mr. Pym's friend at the elections of 1640; and two years later it was lucky if he did not turn the unhappy clergyman out of the vicarage, and arm his serving-men for the Parliament, under the curious delusion that he had adopted Presbyterian principles.

While the parson was driving the squire to radicalism, the Bishops were performing the same office for the lawyers. The increasing pretensions of the Church courts, no less than the absolutist doctrines of the High Church party, aroused the jealousy of a profession which always loves the laws, though not always the liberties of England. The rising generation at the Temple, nursed on the principles and precedents of Coke, were observed to be growing steadily more hostile to the royal prerogative. Their resistance to the Ship Money, and the vigour with which they threw themselves into popular politics after the Long Parliament met, was due in part to the jealousy which they felt as lay lawyers to the revived activity of clerical jurisdiction.

Fears that priestly power would recover its old position in society and in law, were borne out by the sudden elevation of Bishops to leadership of the Privy Council and to high secular offices, which their order had not enjoyed since the breach with Rome. When in 1636 Juxon, Bishop of London, was put at the head of the Treasury, Laud noted in his diary that no churchman had held the post since the days of Henry VII. The Archbishop himself had his hand deep in the details of secular administration, and more than any other Councillor, could influence Charles on the larger questions of State. The laity were alarmed at this revival of priestly rule; while lords-in-waiting and would-be successors of Buckingham murmured that the avenues of promotion were choked up by lawn-sleeves.

The King's party was neither intelligent, zealous, nor united. Although the patron of Rubens and Vandyke made the Court, for the last time in English history, a true school for the nation in art, culture and manners, he took no better pains than his father that it should be "replenished with choice of excellent men." While he saw nothing of the future Roundheads, he did not introduce into his Council the better sort of Royalists. His Cottingtons, Westons and Windebanks were an ignoble tribe, very different from the Hydes and Falklands, the Verneys and Langdales who rallied in the hour of danger to a cause of which they only half approved. When Laud wrote to Wentworth in Ireland, "I am alone in those things that draw not profit after them," he was scarcely exaggerating the truth; and the old Oxford tutor had not the courtier's art to conceal from his selfish and venal coadjutors his dislike of their proceedings. Laud and Wentworth were almost the only honest men at the head of affairs, though they were also the two most earnest contrivers of despotism in Church and State. The courtiers hated them for their virtues, and the people for their faults. They had no party. They held their ground only by the King's favour. This they were able to enjoy, but were compelled to share it with men and women who were not of their confidence.

Laud did nothing to secure himself by feminine influence against masculine dislike. In personal intercourse he was unable and unwilling to please. His religion, calculated rather to control Protestant than to stimulate Catholic ardour, was too little imaginative to become the inspiration of England, too little sensational to become the toy of Whitehall. Throughout the country the women of England, whether Puritan or Anglican, were Protestant and not Ritualist. The ladies of the Palace were given over to frivolity, and those who wanted ritual as a pastime, went straight to the more splendid and ancient source of those delights. In his dealings with the strong Roman Catholic ring at Court, Laud came to grief, because his influence over Charles, greater than that of any other man, was incomplete. Henrietta Maria was against him.

Since the death of Buckingham, Charles had fallen in love with his Catholic Queen. He now treated her as much too well as he had formerly treated her too ill. In 1626 he had destroyed his foreign policy by the fatal French war, because he chose, in violation of his marriage treaty, to persecute his Catholic subjects; after 1629 he destroyed his home policy, because he chose to please his wife by showing those subjects dangerous favour. The period of the Spanish match seemed to have returned. Again in the country the Penal Laws fell into general, though never into complete, disuse; again at the Palace Catholicism became the fashionable if not the dominant creed. Residence under his uncle's roof had the effect of very nearly making the young Prince Rupert a Catholic, to the intense indignation of his mother, the Electress Palatine. Such was the atmosphere of the house from which England was governed. Papal legates came over, were received with every mark of welcome, and concluded from what met their eyes at Court that the country was on the way back to Rome.

Laud was in a difficult position. He had no antipathy to Roman Catholics, whose company he sought while he avoided that of Puritans. Both parties misconstrued this simple preference. When he became Primate, the Pope seriously offered him a Cardinal's hat; when he persecuted conventiclers, his victims supposed that their sacrifice was designed to prepare the Roman triumph. Indeed, when avowed conversions became numerous, especially among the rich and most of all among the courtiers, and when the strongest Protestants were sailing in thousands for America, the danger was not fanciful that the Catholics might regain social and political power. If the Elizabethan settlement was to be maintained, either the Puritans must be tolerated, or the statutes against the Romanists must be enforced. In 1637 Laud made an honest but insufficient effort to enforce the Penal Laws. The Queen was too strong for him and he gave up the attempt. He had not the wisdom to see that he must therefore give up that other part of his policy which drove the chief opponents of Catholicism across the sea.

As Laud was known to be the King's adviser in the treatment of the Puritans, it was naturally supposed that he was equally responsible for the treatment of the Catholics. All men saw that the enemies of Rome were being crushed, and that her friends were daily growing in wealth, power and self-assertion. Though his contemporaries were in part mistaken as to the motives of Laud's policy, they were by no means mistaken as to the results that must have ensued from its indefinite continuance.

In August, 1636, Charles I. held high festival at Oxford. It was the culminating triumph of Laud, who received his royal friends, as Chancellor of the University which he had conquered and reformed. Lords and Ladies partook of magnificent feasts in the college halls; they admired in the chapels the new decorations, and in the gardens the new architecture, which were in no small degree the work of Laud. A new play was given in Christ Church Hall, where the Puritan with his short cloak, and Prynne with his short ears, were caricatured on the boards before the rulers of England. That was how the King knew the Puritans. If he had had eyes for men in the flesh half so keen as for men on canvas, he would have looked first at the real Puritans, in the streets even of loyal Oxford, through which he had just passed without a cheer; he would have seen the sad faces and closed lips of many who were neither cowards nor hypocrites. That autumn festival was the last careless hour of the old English monarchy. The troubles began before another year was out. Seven times the trees were to bud on the banks of Cherwell, and again these Lords and Ladies would inhabit these same colleges of Oxford, acting plays, composing sonnets, aiming epigrams, fighting duels and making love. But in 1643 the Puritans were no longer the fools upon the stage, but myriads of armed and angry men weaving far and wide over England the net of destruction for Oxford and its inhabitants.

The year 1637 is the first of the revolutionary epoch. The demonstrations round the pillory in Palace Yard, the universal interest in Hampden's Ship Money case, and the rising of Scotland against the Prayer-book, form in an ascending scale of importance the first three steps of the popular movement which brought Charles to the scaffold.

Prynne a lawyer, Burton a clergyman, and Bastwick a doctor, had composed and secretly put into circulation violent attacks on the Bishops. They were condemned by the Star Chamber to be pilloried, to lose their ears, and to suffer solitary confinement for life. The cruel mangling and branding, which idle crowds watched with cheerful interest when inflicted on cheating tradesmen or sturdy beggars, were on this occasion resented as an indecent outrage on the three liberal professions to which the victims belonged. Prynne, indeed, had once before bled unpitied in the pillory for a fanatical attack on stage plays called *Histriomastix*; but three years had passed since then, and the libeller of Laud was now the hero of the nation. London poured out to Palace Yard, and held round the scaffold a monster reform meeting which Government had no soldiers to disperse. The orators, with their heads through the pillory, spoke much of their faith in Jesus, of legal precedents, and of the ancient liberties of Englishmen. In the great crowd below many wept aloud, and the rudest were ennobled by that good English mood of hoarse anger at cruelty inflicted on the brave. When the hangman sawed off Prynne's ears, a yell arose to which Charles should have listened in Whitehall, while yet it was heard there for the first time. It was a new sound even in old riotous England, for it was not the ancient voice of faction or of plunder, but the cry of deeper mutiny from brain and heart. Often in the coming years that sound would roll through the trembling Palace, across galleries where courtiers stood in silent groups, and secret chambers where ladies knelt in terror before the crucifix.

It was many years since a political demonstration had been held, and it is for this reason that the story of these libellers is great in history. The incident must be read not as the cause, but as the result, of the unpopularity of the Church.

The State, too, met its Prynne in the more attractive personality of John Lilburne. "Freeborn John" now began at about the age of twenty-one his life-long confession of liberty; before he died in the last years of the Protectorate, he had defied, in the same interest of English law and personal freedom, four arbitrary Governments of widely different political complexions. But the first was the most cruel. Six months after Prynne's sentence, he refused, as a prisoner before the Star Chamber, to take the oath to answer all questions put to him by the court. For this offence, though he was a gentleman born, Lilburne was whipped at the cart's tail from the Fleet to Palace Yard, pilloried, gagged, and deliberately starved almost to death in prison. Again, men observed with indignation that classes hitherto exempt from corporal punishment were being degraded by a jealous absolutism. Peers and apprentices alike felt, not that democracy was being vindicated by even justice, but that honourable custom was being trodden in the mud by an encroaching and un-English tyranny.

WILLIAM PRYNNE

from

A Breviate of the Prelates intollerable usurpations, both upon the Kings Prerogative Royall, and the Subjects Liberties.

Ezechiel. 34. 2. *to* 11.

Thus saith the Lord God unto the Shepheards of Israell that doe feed themselves: Should not the Shepheards feede the Flock?

Yee eate the fat, and yee cloath you with the wooll, yee kill them that are fed, yee feede not the Flocke. The diseased have yee not strengthned, neither have yee healed that which was sicke, neither have yee bound up that which was broken, neither have yee brought againe that which was driven away, neither have yee sought that which was lost, but with force & with cruelty have you ruled them, &c. Therefore, O yee Shepheards, heare the word of the Lord. Thus saith the Lord God, Behold I am against the Shepheards, and will require my Flocke at their hand, and cause them to cease from feeding the Flocks, neither shall the Shepheards, feede themselves any more, for I will deliver my

Flock from their mouth, that they may not be meat
for them.

Published by W. Huntley, Esquier.[1]

In the Yeare 1637.

To the high and mighty Prince, *Charles*, by the grace of God, of *England*, *Scotland*, *France*, and *Ireland*, *King*; Defender of the Faith, &c.

MOST gracious Soveraigne, meeting with this compendious *Remonstrance of the Prelates late daingerous encrochments, both upon your owne Prerogative Royall, and your Subjects Liberties*, compiled by a late learned Gentleman, out of a Zeale to your Majesties service and your peoples good: I could doe no lesse in point of allegiance to your Highnes, and true affection to my Countries weale, then prostrate it in all humility, at your Royall feete, imploring your Princely acceptation of it. The rather because it was originally destinated to your Majesty by the author; whom I heard oft complaining, that it was the infelicity, sometimes, of the best Princes (by reson of the unfaithfulnesse and misrepresenta-

[1]Pseudonym for William Prynne. *Edition 3. much enlarged.*

tions of those State-agents whom they most imployed, and least suspected,) to be utterly ignorant of the true estate both of their owne and the Republikes affaires . . . The consideration whereof, as it instigated the Author originally to compile, so it hath animated mee to enlarge this *Breviate* (with the addition onely of some late occurrences;) and to present this third Impression of it to your Highnes veiw, (though perchance with some hazard to my person and estate, by reason of the Prelates great swaying power and implacable malice:) wherein as in a Christall glasse, your Majesty may eft soone discerne the insufferable usurpations of your ungratefull Bishops, upon your owne Royall Preheminences and your Subjects Liberties: (contrary to all Law and Justice,) in their true naked coulors, uncased of all such false varnishes, and specious glosses which themselves have cast upon them, to cover their deformity, and delude your Majesties senses, who suspect no such blacke workes of darknes under their pure white Rochets.

* * *

Yea they [the Prelates] are now so strangly audacious, as without any Letters, Patents from your Majesty, to keepe Consistory Courts, visitations, Synods in their owne names and rights: to make out Citations, processe, excommunications, Letters of Administration, Licenses for Marying without banes &c. in their owne stiles, names, and with their owne Seales alone; to institute and prescribe new Articles, Constitutions, Ordinances, Ceremonies, Lawes, Rites, formes of Oathes &c. and impose them on your Subjects, publishing them in print in their owne names, and swearing Churchwardens, Sidemen, with other your Majesties Subjects, to execute, and submit unto them, contrary to their owne *12. Canon,* (as if they were absolute Popes, Kings, and Lawgivers,) without your Majesties privity and the Parliaments approbation: of which exorbitances they are so farre from being ashamed, that in a late Latine Pamphlet, licensed by the *Archbishop of Canterbury*

his Chaplaine, that now is, and dedicated to his Grace, by one
Chownæus, they stick not to proclaime; *that your Majestie and
other Princes Ecclesiasticall Lawes, receive both their vitality and
vivacity, from the Bishops, as from the* HEART AND HEAD: yea
Doctor Wien Bishop of Norwich (no more a *Regulus*, but a *Rex*,) in
his late presumptuous *Visitation Articles*, printed at *London*, 1636.
in his owne name (worthy your Majesties consideration) makes
not onely the *Archbishop of Canterbury, and his Vicar generall and
Visitors Ecclesiasticall Lawgivers, and their Injunctions, Oracles,
and Lawes to be diligently observed and inquired of upon Oath*: but
himselfe most presumptuously takes upon him like an absolute
King or Pope, to prescribe new Lawes, Canons, Injunctions,
Articles, Orders in his owne name and right without any Commission from your Majesty, or your Royall privity or assent,
*contrary to your Lawes, and your owne late Royall Declaration before
the 39. Articles*; suspending no lesse then 30. Ministers of best
note and quality in his late Visitation, (though every way confirm-
able to the Doctrine and Discipline, by Law established in the
Church of England, and so reputed in his predecessors times)
onely for refusing to conforme against their consciences, duties, and
allegiance to those grosse Innovations, which hee would obtrude
upon them, contrary to your Royall Lawes and *Declarations
against such Innovations*. Which Tyranny of his, as it hath produced
a *great famine of Gods word* in those parts, and bread in your Subjects hearts a great murmuring, discontent and feare of alteration of
Religion; so it hath caused many to forsake the Realme, and will
no doubt *draw downe Gods Plagues and Vengeance on it*, who since
this Bishops late Visitation, hath visited many places of the Realme,
with Plague and Pestilence, and threatneth even a famine of bread
unto it, to recompence that famine of his word, which hee and
other Bishops have everywhere made; who neither preach themselves, and inhibit others from preaching, upon no just occasion
who else would gladly doe it.

*   *   *

Master William Tyndall *Martyr, writes* thus: Let Kings rule
their Realmes themselves, with the helpe of Laymen that are sage,
wise, learned and expert. Is it not a shame above all shames and a
monstrous thing, that no man should be found able to governe a
wordly Kingdome save Bishops and Prelates that have forsaken
the world, and are taken out of the world, and appointed to preach
the Kingdome of God; Christ saith, that the Kingdome is not of
this world, *John. 18. and Luk. 19.* Unto the young man that desired
him, to bid his brother to give him part of the inheritance, hee
answered; who made me a judge or a devider over you: No man
that layeth his hand to the plowe and looketh back, is fit for the
Kingdome of heaven, *Luke 9.* No man can serve two Maisters,
for hee must despise the one. *Matth 6.* To preach Gods word, is to
much for halfe a man: and to minister a temporall Kingdome, is
to much for halfe a man. Either other requireth an whole man.
One therefore cannot well doe both. The Bishops after they had
put Christ out of his roome, they gate themselves to the Emperors
and Kings, and so long ministred their busines, till they have also
put them out of their roomes, and have get their authorities from
them, and raigne also in their steed: So that the Emperour and
Kings are but vaine names, and shadowes, as Christ is, having
nothing to doe in the world. Thus raigne they in steed of God and
man, and have all power under them, and doe what they list.
What names have they? My Lord Bishop, my Lord Archbishop,
if it please your fatherhood, if it please your Lordship, if it please
your Grace, if it please your holines, and innummerable such like.
Behold, how they are esteemed, and how they are crept up above
all, not into wordly seates onely, but into the seate of God, the
hearts of men, where they sit above God himselfe. For, both they,
and whatsoever they make of their owne heades, is more feared and
dread, then God and his Commandements. Antichrists Bishops
preach not, because they have no leisure for their lust and pleasures, and aboundance of all things, and for the combrance that
they have in Kings matters; and busines of the Realme. One
keepeth the privy Seale, another the great Seale, the third is

Confessor, that is to say a privy traitor, and a secret Judas, hee is President of the Kings Counsell, hee is an Ambassadour, another sort of the Kings secret Counsell. Wo is unto the Realmes where they are of the Counsell, as profitable are the Prelacy, unto the Realmes with their Counsell, as the Wolves unto the Sheep, or the Foxes unto the Geese.

*   *   *

For as the body wasteth and consumeth away for lacke of bodily meate; so doth the soule pine away for want of ghostly meate. And as diligently as the husbandman plougheth for the sustentation of the body; so diligently must the Prelates and Ministers labour for the feeding of the soule; both the ploughes must still be going as most necessary for man. They have great labors, and therefore they ought to have good livings, that they may commodiously feed their flock; for the preaching of the word of God is called meate. Scripture calleth it meate, not strawberies, that come but once a yeare, and tarry not long, but are sone gone; but it is meate, it is no dainties. The people must have meate that must be familiar, AND CONTINUALL, *and* DAYLY GIVEN UNTO THEM TO FEED ON, *&c.*

*   *   *

It being now more safe to be a Jesuite, or Traytor to your Majesty, then an enemy to your Bishops disloyall proceedings, so are you [the King] every way meetest, both in respect of your Soveraigue power, and authority to rescue your poore oppressed wooried Subjects from these ravenous *Wolves*, under whose cruelty, injustice, and manifold exactions, they now grone and

languish, a short view whereof the second part of this *Breviate*
will represent unto your Hignes.

*   *   *

Sixtly, They [the Prelates] fine, imprison, suspend, deprive,
outlaw, exile, condemne, destroy his Majesties Subjects, and put
them from their free-holds, callings, not onely without, and besides, but directly against the Law (to wit, the Common Law,) of
the Land, upon Articles, Canons, Constitutions, Ceremonies of
their owne making, (which are *no Law of the Land unles confirmed
by Act of Parliament*) and for matters no way criminall by any Law
or Canon. To instance in some particulars, by what Law of the
Land, I pray, was *Master Peter Smart* a reverend Prebend and
Minister of Durham, fined, imprisoned, and deprived, An. 1629.
by the High-Commissioners of Yorke, both of his Prebendary and
living onely, for preaching against *the setting up of Images, Altars,
bowing to them, and placing them at the East end of the Church*;
directly contrary to the *booke of Common Prayer*, and the *Homily
against the Perill of Idolatry.* confirmed by *Act of Parliament*, to
which *all Ministers and Bishops subscribe*? By what Law of the Land
was *Master George Huntly*, not longe since fined, imprisoned,
deprived of his living, and degraded of his Ministry, *for refusing
to preach a Visitation Sermon upon the Archdeacons warning, though
hee were then sickly and unable to preach, and sent xx s to him to
procure another to preach for him*; there being no Canon Law or
Statute extant, enjoyning Ministers to preach at Visitation; but
*many prescribing the Bishops and Archdeacons, who visit to preach
themselves in person.* By what Law of the Land was one *Master
Crowder*, Vicar of *Vell*, neare Nonesuch about 6. yeares since,
committed close prisoner to New-gate, 16. weekes together, by the
now Archbishops of Canterbury and Yorke, under pretence of
some treasonable words, delivered in the Pulpit; (but in truth,

because hee preached conscionably twice a day *neare the Court*, and would not resigne his Vicaridge;) and after that deprived, both of his Vicaridge and Ministry in the High-Commission, without any Articles at all exhibited, or witnesses examined against him, or any proofe, confession or conviction of any crime, under this pretext, that the matters against him were so foule, as they weare not fit to be Articled or prooved in Court against him, nor yet to be notified to himselfe, that hee might either defend or justify himselfe if innocent, or confesse and amend if peccarit? A proceeding so desperatly, transcendently injust, and yet most true, that no age, no Court of justice whatsoever can parralell it, in the most barbarous tyrannicall places or ages of the world? By what Law of the Land, I pray, was *Master John Hayden*, a poore Devonshire Minister, about 7. yeares since, *for preaching a Sermon at Norwich, wherein hee let fall some passages against setting up of Images in Churches* (contrary to the *Homily of the perill of the Idolatry*) and *bowing at the name of Jesus*, apprehended like a traytor, with Constables, Bills, Halberts, by Doctor Harsnet, then Bishop of Norwich, and brought manacled to him like a fellon; and for this offence onely committed by him close prisoner to the Common-goale at Norwich for 13. weekes space or more; where hee was like to starve, the Bishop taking away from him both his money, papers, horse; and when the Justices of peace at their quarter-sessions upon his petition would have bayld him; By what Law did the Bishop, to prevent his bayling, tell them, that hee would lay high-treason to his charge; and after that send him up to London by an High-Commission Pursevant, under whose custody hee was kept without bayle or mainprise for two whole Termes or more, till his cause came to hearing before the High-Commissioners in the Consistory of Pauls, onely upon these two points? or by what Law did the High-Commissioners then & there censure him to be imprisoned, deprived of his Ministry, orders, and to pay a fine besides, meerely *for preaching against Images, and this superstitious Ceremony*? Or by what Law did the

Commissioners since that time, imprison him in the Gatehouse Common Dungeon, and the now Archbishop of Canterbury send him from thence to Bridewell to be whipped, and there keepe him all the last extreame cold winter in a cold darke Dungeon, without fire or candle-light, chained to a post in the midst of a roome, with heavy Irons on his hands and feete, allowing him onely bread and water, and a Pad of straw to lye on: and since upon his release, cause him to take an Oath, and give bond to preach no more, and to depart the Kingdome within 3. weekes or a moneths space, and not to return; and all this onely for preaching againe after his first unjust deprivation, though no exception was taken against his Doctrine?

*   *   *

To the [assertion that] the Starchamber examines men upon Oath against themselves, and fines, and imprisons men: *Ergo*, the High-Commissioners may doe it.

I answer, *First*, That the Argument is a meere *Nonsequitur*: the one Court being Civill, the other Ecclesiasticall, both in respect of causes and proceedings, the one kept onely by an arbitrary Commission; the other absolute by *Act of Parliament*. And if this be a good argument, I know no reason, but every Bishop may inferre as well: The Starchamber can fine, imprison, examine men upon Oath, in criminall causes: Therefore wee may doe it in our Consistories and Visitations, which Conclusion is both false and absurd. And the High-Commissioners may as well argue, that the Star chamber adjudgeth men to *the Pillary, to loose their eares, and the like; and may punish all forjuries, perjuries, routs, riots, conspiracies, trespasses in parkes, subornation of perjury, and the like*: Therefore the High-Commissioners may doe it. I am sure, they dare not argue thus; The Kings Bench can hold plea of Trespasse, Debt, Felonies, Murthers, Treasons, and adjudge men to death for the same; *Ergo*, the Ecclesiasticall Commissioners may doe it: This were but a frenticke consequent: Why not then the other? Shall the Lords of the Starchamber argue thus? The High-Commissioners may hold plea of all Ecclesiasticall offences, and punish men by excommunication, degradation, sequestration, and other Ecclesiasticall Censures; *Ergo*, we may much more doe it? If the Prelates will not grant this consequence, as I presume they dare not: I must by the same, or farre better reason deny to grant the other.

*   *   *

[Prynne quotes from "Rescuing of the Romish Fox," by William Wraughton:]

Wherefore to open the Conclusion of this litle lamentation, if yee will banish for ever the Antichrist the Pope out of this Realme, yee must fell downe to the ground those rotten posts, the Bishops, which be cloudes without moisture, and utterly abandon all and every of his ungodly Lawes, Traditions, and Ceremonies.

[Prynne quotes from *Henry Stalbridge his Exhortatory Epistle, to his dearely beloved Countrey of England, against the pompous Popish Bishops thereof, as yet the true members of their filthy Father the great Antichrist of Rome, printed at Basil, in King Henry the 8. his dayes:*]

Who seeth not that in these days your bloody Bishops of England, Italy, Cycell, France, Spaine, Portingale, Scotland and Ireland, be the ground and originall fondation of all controversies, Schismes, variances and warres betwixt Realme and Realme at this present, &c. Consider your beginning. Never came yee in with your Miters, Robes, and Rings by the doore, as did the poore Apostles, but by the window unrequired, like robbers, theeves and manquellers with Simon Magus,

Marcion and Menander. Never was your proud Pontificall power of the heavenly Fathers planting, and therefore it must at the last up by the rootes, ye must in the end be destroyed without handes, Dan. 8. &c.

🌿 🌿 🌿

from

A Briefe
Relation

Of certain speciall and most material passages, and speeches in the Starre-Chamber, occasioned and delivered June the 14th. 1637. at the censure of those three worthy Gentlemen, Dr. Bastwicke, Mr. Burton and Mr. Prynne, as it hath beene truely and faithfully gathered from their owne mouthes by one present at the sayd Censure.

Printed in the yeere 1637.

The Execution of the Lods Censure in Starre-Chamber upon Dr. Bastwicke, Mr. Prynne, and Mr. Burton, in the Pallace-yard at Westminster, the 30th. day of June last 1637. at the spectation whereof the number of people was so great (the place being very large) that it caused admiration in all that beheld them; who came with tender affections to behold those three renowned Souldiers

and Servants of Jesus Christ, who came with most undaunted and
magnanimous courage thereunto, having their way strawed with
sweet hearbes from the house out of which they came to the
Pillary, with all the honour that could be done unto them.

Dr. Bastwicke and Mr. Burton meeting, they did close one in the
others armes three times, with as much expressions of love as
might be, rejoycing that they mett at such a place, upon such an
occasion, and that God had so highly honoured them, as to call
them forth to suffer for his glorious Truth.

Then immediately after, Mr. Prynne came, the Dr. and hee
saluting each other, as Mr. Burton and hee did before. The Dr.
then went up first on the Scaffold, and his wife immediately
following came up to him, and like a loving Spouse saluted each
eare with a kisse, and then his mouth; whose tender love, boldnes,
and cheerefullnes so wrought upon the peoples affections, that
they gave a marvailous great showte, for joy to behold it. Her
husband desired her not to be in the least maner dismay'd at his
sufferings: And so for a while they parted, she using these words:
Farewell my Deerest, be of good comfort, I am nothing dismay'd.
And then the Dr. began to speake these words.

There are many that are this day Spectators of our standing
here, as Delinquents, though not Delinquents, we blesse God for
it. I am not conscious to my self wherein I have committed the
least trespasse (to take this outward shame) either against my God,
or my King. And I doe the rather speake it, that you that are now
beholders, may take notice, how farre Innocency will preserve
you in such a day as this is; for wee come here in the strength of
our God, who hath mightily supported us, and filled our hearts
with greater comfort then our shame or contempt can be. The first
occasion of my trouble was by the Prelates, for writing a Booke
against the Pope, and the Pope of Canterbury sayd I wrote against
him, and therefore questioned mee: But if the Presses were as
open to us, as formerly they have beene, we would shatter his
Kingdome about his eares: But be yee not deterred by their power,

neither be affrighted at our sufferings; Let none determine to turne from the wayes of the Lord, but goe on, fight couragiously against Gog and Magog. I know there be many here who have set many dayes apart for our behalfe, (let the Prelates take notice of it) and they have sent up strong prayers to heaven for us, wee feele the strength and benefit of them at this time; I would have you to take notice of it; wee have felt the strength and benefit of your prayers all along this cause. In a word, so farre I am from base feare, or caring for any thing they can doe, or cast upon mee, that had I as much blood as would swell the Theames, I whould shedd it every droppe in this cause. Therefore be not any of you discouraged, be not daunted at their power, ever labouring to preserve Innocency, and keep peace within, goe on in the strength of your God, and he will never fayle you, in such a day as this; As I sayd before, so I say againe; Had I as many lives as I have heires on my head, or dropps of blood in my veynes, I would give them up all for this cause. This plot offending us to those remote places, was first consulted and agitated by the Jesuites, as I can make it plainely appeare. O see what times wee are fallen into, that the Lords must sit to act the Jesuites plots! For our owne parts wee owe no malice to the persons of any of the Prelates, but would lay our necks under their feet to doe them good as they are men, but aginst the usurpation of their power, as they are Bishops, wee doe professe ourselves enemies till doomes day.

> Mr. Prynne shaking the Dr. by the hand, desired him that hee might speake a word or two. With all my heart, sayd the Doctor.

The cause (sayd Mr. Prynne) of my standing here, is for not bringing in my Answer, for which my cause is taken *pro confesso* against mee. What endeavours I used for the bringing in thereof that, God and my owne conscience, and my Counsell, knowes, whose cowardise stands upon Record to all ages. For rather then I will have my cause a leading cause, to deprive the Subjects of that liberty which I seeke to maintaine, I rather expose my person to a leading example, to beare this punishment: And I beseech you all to take notice of their proceedings in this cause. When I was served with a Subpoena into this Court, I was shut up close prisoner, that I could have no accesse to Counsell, nor admitted pen, inke or paper to draw up my Answer by my Instuctions, for which I feed them twice (though to no purpose) yet when all was done, my Answer would not be accepted into the Court, though I tendered it upon my oath. I appeale to all the world, if this were a legall or just proceeding. Our accusation is in point of Libell (but supposedly) against the Prelates. To cleare this now, I will give you a little light, what the Law is in point of Libell (of which profession I have sometimes beene, and still professe my selfe to have some knowledge in) you shall finde in case of Libell, two Statutes: The one in the second of Queen Mary; The other in the seaventh of Queen Elizabeth. That in the second of Queen Mary, the extremity and heighth of it runs thus: That if a Libeller doth goe so farre and so high as to Libell against King or Queen by denomination, the higth and extremity of the Law is, that they lay no greater fine on him then an hundred pounds, with a moneths imprisonment; and no corporall punishment, except he doe refuse to pay his fine; and then to inflict some punishment in liewe of that fine at the moneths end; Neither was this Censure to be passed on him, except it were fully prooved by two witnesses, who were to produce a certificat of their good demeanor for the credit of their report, or else confessed by the Libeller. You shall finde in that Statute 7. Eliz. some further addition to the former of 2. Mariae, and that onely in point of fine and punishment; and it must still reach as high as the person of King and Queen. Here this Statute doth set a fine of two hundred pounds; the other, but one: This sets three moneths imprisonment; the former but one: So that therein onely they differ. But in this they both agree, namely, at the end of his imprisonment to pay his fine, and so to goe free without any further questioning: But if hee refuse to pay his fine, then the Court is to inflict some punishment on him correspondent to his fine. Now see the dis-

parity betweene those times of theirs, and ours. A Libeller in
Queen Maries time was fined but an hundred pounds, in Queen
Elizabeths time two hundred: In Queen Maries dayes but a moneths
imprisonment; in Queen Elizabeths three moneths; and not so
great a fine, if they libelled not against King or Queen. Formerly
the greatest fine was but two hundred pounds, though against
King or Queen; Now five thousand pounds, though but against the
Prelates, and that but supposedly, which cannot be prooved:
Formerly, but three moneths imprisonment; Now perpetuall
imprisonment: Then, upon paying the fine, no corporall punishment was to be inflicted: But now, infamous punishment with the
losse of blood and all other circumstances that may aggravate it.
See now what times wee are fallen into, when that Libelling (if it
were so) against Prelates onely, shall fall higher, then if it touched
Kings and Princes.

That which I have to speake of next, is this: The Prelates find
themselves exceedingly agrieved and vexed against what wee have
written concerning the usurpation of their calling, where indeed
wee declare their calling not to be *Jure Divino*. I make no doubt,
but there are some Intelligencers or Abbettors within the hearing,
whom I would have well to know and take notice of what I now
say. I here in this place make this offer to them, That if I may be
admitted a fayre dispute, on fayre termes, for my cause; that I will
maintaine, and doe here make the challenge against all the Prelates
in the Kings Dominions, and against all the Prelates in Christendome, (let them take in the Pope, and all to help them) that their
calling is not *Jure Divino*. I will speake it againe; I make the
challeng against all the Prelates in the Kings Dominions, and all
Christendome to maintaine, that their calling is not *Jure Divino*.
If I make it not good, let me be hanged up at the Hall-Gate:
Whereupon the people gave a great shout.

The next thing that I am to speake of, is this: The Prelates find
themselves exceedingly agrieved and vext against what I have
written in point of Law, concerning their Writs and Proces, That

the sending forth of Writs and Proces in their owne name, is against all Law and Justice, and doth entrench on his Majesties Prerogative Royall, and the Subjects Liberties. And here now I make a second challeng against all the Lawyers in the Kingdome in way of fayre Dispute, That I will maintaine, the Prelates sending forth of Writs and Proces in their owne names, to be against all Law and Justice, and entrencheth on his Majesties Prerogative Royall, and Subjects Liberty. Least it should be forgotten, I speake it againe, I here challeng all the whole Society of the Law upon a fayre Dispute to maintaine, That the sending forth of Writs and Proces in the Prelates owne names, to be against all Law and Justice, and entrencheth on the Kings Prerogative Royall, and the Subjects Liberty. If I be not able to make it good, let me be put to the tormentingest death they can devise.

Wee prayse the Lord, wee feare none but God and the King: Had wee respected our Liberties, wee had not stood here at this time: it was for the generall good and Liberties of you all that wee have now thus farre engaged our owne Liberties in this cause. For did you know, how deeply they have entrenched on your Liberties in point of Popery; If you knew but into what times you are cast, it would make you looke about you: And if you did but see what changes and revolutions of persons, causes and actions, have beene made by one man, you would more narrowly looke into your Previledges, and see how farre your Liberty did Lawfully extend, and so maintaine it.

*   *   *

Alas poore England, what will become of thee, if thou looke not the sooner into thine owne Previledge, and maintainest not thine owne lawfull Liberty? Christian people; I beseech you all, stand firme, and be zealous for the Cause of God, and his true Religion, to the shedding of your dearest blood, otherwise you will bring your selves, & all your posterities, into perpetuall bondage and slavery.

Now the Executioner being come, to seare him and cut off his eares, Mr. Prynne spake these word to him: Come friend, Come burne mee, cut mee, I feare it not. I have learn'd to feare the fire of Hell, and not what man can doe unto mee: Come seare mee, seare mee, I shall beare in my body the markes of the Lord Jesus: Which the bloody Executioner performed with extraordinary cruelty, heating his Iron twice to burne one Cheeke: And cut one of his eares so close, that hee cut off a peice of his Cheeke. At which exquisit torture hee never mooved with his body, or so much as changed his countenance, but still lookt up as well as he could towards heaven, with a smiling countenance, even to the astonishment of all the beholders. And uttering (as soone as the Executioner had done) this heavenly sentence: *The more I am beate downe, the more am I lift up.* And returning from the execution in a boate made (as I heare) these two verses by the way on the Two Characters branded on his Cheekes.

S. L. STIGMATA LAVDIS.

STIGMATA maxillis bajulans insignia Lavdis
Exultans remeo, victima grata deo.

Which one since thus Englished.

S. L. LAVDS SCARS.

Triumphant I returne, my face descries,
Lavds scorching Scars, Gods greatefull
Sacrifice. . . .

*   *   *

Mr. Burtons heavenly and most comfortable Speech, which hee made at the time of his suffering, both before, and while hee stood in the Pillary, which was set something distant from the other double Pillary, wherein *Dr. Bastwicke* and *Mr. Prynne* stood.

The night before his suffering, about eight a clocke, when he first had certaine notice thereof, upon occasion of his wives going to aske the Warden, whither her husband should suffer the next day, immediately he felt his spirits to be raysed to a farre higher pitch of resolution and courage to undergoe his sufferings, then formerly he did, so as hee intreated the Lord to hold up his spirits at that height all the next day in his sufferings, that hee might not flagg nor faint, least any dishonour might come to his Majestie or the cause: And the Lord heard him: For all the next day in suffering (both before and after) his spirits were carried aloft as it were upon Eagles wings (as himself sayd) farre above all apprehension of shame or paine.

The next morning (being the day of his sufferings) hee was brought to Westminster, and with much cheerefullnes being brought into the Pallace-yard unto a Chamber that looked into the Yard, where hee viewed three Pillaries there set up: Me thinkes (sayd hee) I see Mount Calvery, where the three Crosses (one for Christ, and the other two for the two theives) were pitched: And if Christ were numbred among theives, shall a Christian (for Christs cause) thinke much to be numbred among Rogues, such as wee are condemned to be? Surely if I be a Rogue, I am Christs Rogue, and no mans. And a little after, looking out at the casement towards the Pillary, hee sayd: I see no difference betweene looking out of this square window and yonder round hole, (poynting towards the Pillary) hee sayd: It is no matter, of difference to an honest man. And a little after that, looking somewhat wisely upon his wife, to see how shee did take it; shee seemed to him to be something sadd; to whom hee thus spake: Wife, why are thou so sadd? To whom shee made answer; Sweet-heart, I am not sadd: No sayd hee? See thou be not, for I would not have thee to dishonour the day, by shedding one teare, or fetching one sigh: for

behold there for thy comfort my triumphant Chariot, on the which
I must ride for the honour of my Lord and Master: And never
was my wedding day so wellcome, and joyfull a day, as this day is;
and so much the more, because I have such a noble Captaine and
Leader, who hath gonne before mee with such undauntednes of
spirit, that hee sayth of himselfe, I gave my backe to the smiters,
my cheekes to the nippers, they pluckt off the haire, I hidd not my
face, from shame and spitting, for the Lord God will help mee,
therefore shall I not be confounded, therefore have I set my faee
like a flint, and I know I shall not be ashamed. At length being
carried toward the Pillary, hee mett Dr. Bastwicke at the foot of
the Pillary, where they lovingly saluted and embraced each other;
and parting a little from him, hee returned (such was the ardency
of his affection) and most affectionately embraced him the second
time, being heartily sorry hee missed Mr. Prynne, who was not
yet come before hee was gonne up to his Pillary, which stood
alone next the Starre-Chamber, and about halfe a stones cast from
the other double Pillary, wherein the other two stood: so as all
their faces looked Southward, the bright Sunne all the while for the
space of two howers shining upon them: Being ready to be put into
the Pillary, standing upon the Scaffold, hee spied Mr. Prynne new
come to the Pillary, and Dr. Bastwicke in the Pillary, who then
hasted of his band, and called for a Handkercher, saying, What,
shall I be last? or shall I be ashamed of a Pillary for Christ, who was
not ashamed of a Crosse for mee? Then being put into the Pillary,
hee sayd: Good people, I am brought hither to be a spectacle to
the world, to Angells, and men; And howsoever I stand here to
undergoe the punishment of a Rogue, yet except to be a faithful
Servant to Christ, and a loyall Subject to the King, be the property
of a Rogue, I am no Rogue. But yet if to be Christs faithful Servant,
and the Kings loyall Subject, deserve the punishment of a Rogue,
I glory in it, and I blesse my God, my conscience is cleare, and is
not stained with the guilt of any such crime, as I have beene
charged with, though otherwise I confesse my self to be a man

subject to many frailties and humane infirmities. Indeed that Booke intiteled, An Apology of an Appeale with sundry Epistles, and two Sermons, for God and the King, charged against me in information, I have and doe acknowledge (the misprinting excepted) to be mine, and will by Gods grace never disclayme it whilst I have breath within mee. After a while, hee having a Nosegay in his hand, a Bee came and pitched on the Nosegay, and began to suck the flowers very savourly, which hee beholding and well observing sayd, Doe yee not see this poore Bee? She hath found out this very place to suck sweetnes from these flowers; And cannot I suck sweetnes in this very place from Christ? The Bee sucking all this while and so took her flight. By and by hee tooke occasion from the shining of the Sunne, to say, You see how the Sunne shines upon us, but that shines as well upon the evill as the good, upon the just and unjust, but the Sonne of righteousnes (Jesus Christ, who hath healing under his winges) shines upon the soules and consciences of every true beleever onely, and no clowd can hide him from us, to make him ashamed of us, no not of our most shamefull sufferings for his sake: And why should wee be ashamed to suffer for his sake, who hath suffered for us? All our sufferings be but fleabitings to that hee endured, hee endured the Crosse, and despised the shame and is set on the right hand of God: Hee is a most excellent patterne for us to looke upon, that treading his stepps, and suffering with him, wee may be glorified with him. And what can we suffer, wherein hee hath not gonne before us, even in the same kinde? Was hee not degraded, when they scornefully put on him a purple Robe, a Reed into his hand, a thorny Crowne upon his head, saluting him with Hayle King of the Jewes, and so disrobed him againe? Was not hee deprived, when they smote the Shepherd, and the Sheepe were scattered? Was not violence offered to his sacred person, when hee was buffited, and scourged, his hands and his feet peirced, his head pricked with thornes, his side goared with a Speare &c.? Was not the Crosse more shamefull, yea and more painfull then a Pillary? Was not hee stript of all hee had, when hee was left starke naked upon the Crosse, the Souldiers dividing his garments, and casting lots upon his vesture? And was hee not confin'd to perpetuall close imprisonment in mans imagination, when his body was layd in a Tombe, and Tombe sealed, least hee should breake prison, or his Disciples steale him away? And yet did hee not rise againe, and thereby brought deliverance and victory to us all, so as wee are more than Conquerors through him that loved us? Here then wee have an excellent Patterne indeed. And all this hee uttered (and whatsoever else hee spake) with marvailous alacrity. . . .

By and by after, some of them offering him a cup of wine; Hee thanked them, telling them hee had the wine of consolation within him, and the joyes of Christ in possession, which the world could not take away from him, neither could it give them vnto him. Then he looked towards the other Pillary, and making a signe with his hand, cheerefully called to Dr. Bastwicke, and Mr. Prynne, asking them how they did. Who answered, Very well. A woman sayd unto him, Sr. every Christian is not worthy this honor, which the Lord hath cast upon you this day. Alas (sayd hee) who is worthy of the least mercy? But it is his gracious favour and free gift, to account us worthy in the behalf of Christ to suffer any thing for his sake? Another woman sayd, There are many hundreds which by Gods assistance would willingly suffer, for the cause you suffer for this day. To whom he sayd, Christ exalts all of us that are ready to suffer afflictions for his Name with meekenes and patience: But Christs military discipline in the use of his spirituall warfare in point of suffering, is quite forgotten, and wee have in a manner lost the power of Religion, in not denying our selves and following Christ as well in suffering, as in doing. After a while Mr. Burton calling to one of his freinds for a Handkercher, returned it againe, saying it is hott, but Christ bore the burthen in the heate of the day; Let us alwayes labour to approove our selves to God in all things, and unto Christ, for therein stands our happines, come of it what will in this world. . . .

In conclusion, some told him of the approach of the Executioner, and prayed God to strengthen him. Hee sayd, I trust he will, why should I feare to follow my Master Christ, who sayd, I gave my backe to the smitters, and my chekes to the nippers, that plucked off my haire, I hidd not my face from shame and spitting, for the Lord God will help mee, therefore shall I not be confounded, therfore have I set my face like a flint, and I know that I shall not be ashamed.

When the Executioner had cut off one eare, which hee had cut deepe and close to the head in an extraordinary cruell manner: Yet this Champion of Christ never once mooved or stirred for it, though hee had cut the veyne, so as the blood rann streaming downe upon the Scaffold, which divers persons standing about the Pillary seeing, dipped their handkerchers in, as a thing most precious, the people giving a mournefull shout, and crying for the Chirurgeon, whom the crowd and other impediments for a time kept off, so that hee could not come to stopp the blood: This Patient all the while held up his hands, and sayd, Be content, it is well, blessed be God. The other eare being cut no lesse deepe, hee then was freed from the Pillary, and come downe, where the Chirurgeon waiting for him, presently applyed remedy for stopping the blood after a large effusion thereof, yet for all this hee faynted not, in the least manner, though through expense of much blood hee waxed pale. And one offering him a little wormewood water; hee sayd, it needs not, yet through importunity hee onely tasted of it, and no more, saying, his Master Christ was not so well used, for they gave him gall and viniger, but you give me good strong water to refresh me, blessed be God. His head being bound up, two Freinds, ledd him away to an house provided for him in Kings Street, where being set downe, and bidd to speake little, yet hee sayd after a pawse, This is too hott to hold long: Now lest they in the roome, or his wife should mis-take, and thinke hee spake of himself concerning his paine, hee sayd, I speake not this of my self: for that which I have suffered is nothing to that my Saviour suffered for mee, who had his hands and feete nayled to the Crosse: And lying still a while, hee tooke Mr. Prynnes sufferings much to heart, and asked the people how hee did, for (sayd hee) his sufferings have beene great. Hee asked also how Dr. Bastwicke did, with much compassion and grief, that hee (being the first that was executed) could not stay to see how they two fayred after him. His wife being brought to him, behaved herself very graciously towards him, saying,

Wellcome Sweet heart, wellcome home. Hee was often heard to repeate these words: The Lord keepe us that wee doe not dishonour him in any thing.

AMEN.

THUS Christian Readers, you have heard the Relation of such a Censure (and the Execution thereof) as I dare say, all circumstances layd together, cannot be paralleld in any age of man throughout the Christian world, and I thinke I may take in even the world of Pagans and Heathens to it. Which though it be not drawen up in so elegant a straine as it was delivered and deserved, nor all the Heavenly words and eloquent speeches recorded, which were uttered by these Three Worthies of the Lord, both in the presence of the Lords themselves at their Censure, and also at the place of Execution: Yet I earnestly beseech you in the bowels of Jesus Christ, that you doe not in the least manner under-value the glory and dignity, either of the persons, or the cause, but rather lay the blame upon the rudenes and meane capacity of the Composer, who is an unfeyned Well-wisher to them both.

JOHN MILTON

⚜ ⚜ ⚜

from

Of Reformation Touching Church-Discipline in England and the Causes that hitherto have hindered it[1]

Let us not be so overcredulous, unlesse God hath blinded us, as to trust our deer Soules into the hands of men that beg so devoutly for the pride, and gluttony of their owne backs, and bellies, that sue and sollicite so eagerly, not for the saving of Soules, the consideration of which can have heer no place at all, but for their Bishopricks, Deaneries, Prebends, and Chanonies; how can these men not be corrupt, whose very cause is the bribe of their own pleading; whose mouths cannot open without the strong breath, and loud stench of avarice, Simony, and Sacrilege, embezling the treasury of the Church on painted, and guilded walles of Temples wherein God hath testified to have no delight, warming their Palace Kitchins, and from thence their unctuous, and epicurean paunches, with the almes of the blind, the lame, the impotent, the aged, the orfan, the widow, for with these the treasury of Christ ought to be, here must be his jewels bestow'd, his rich Cabinet must be emptied heer; as the constant martyr Saint *Laurence* taught the *Roman Prætor*. Sir would you know what the remonstrance of these men would have, what their Petition imply's? They intreate us that we would not be weary of those insupportable

<hr />

[1]This passage is the conclusion of Milton's first pamphlet, written in 1641, a little over three years after "Lycidas." The text is from the Columbia *Milton*, Vol. III, pt. i, pp. 73–79.

greevances that our shoulders have hitherto crackt under, they
beseech us that we would think 'em fit to be our Justices of peace,
our Lords, our highest officers of State, though they come furnish't
with no more experience then they learnt betweene the *Cook*, and
the *manciple*, or more profoundly at the Colledge *audit*, or the *regent
house*, or to come to their deepest insight, at their *Patrons Table*;
they would request us to indure still the russling of their Silken
Cassocks, and that we would burst our *midriffes* rather then laugh
to see them under Sayl in all their Lawn, and Sarcenet, their
shrouds, and tackle, with a *geometricall rhomboides* upon their heads:
they would bear us in hand that we must of duty still appear before
them once a year in *Jerusalem* like good circumcizd *males*, and
Females to be taxt by the poul, to be scons't our head money, our
tuppences in their Chaunlerly Shop-book of *Easter*. They pray us
that it would please us to let them still hale us, and worrey us with
their band-dogs, and Pursivants; and that it would please the
Parliament that they may yet have the whipping, fleecing, and
fleaing of us in their diabolical Courts to tear the flesh from our
bones, and into our wide wounds instead of balm, to power in the
oil of Tartar, vitriol, and mercury; Surely a right reasonable,
innocent, and soft-hearted Petition. O the relenting bowels of the
Fathers. Can this bee granted them unlesse God have smitten us
with frensie from above, and with a dazling giddinesse at noon
day? Should not those men rather be heard that come to plead
against their owne preferments, their worldly advantages, their
owne abundance; for honour, and obedience to *Gods word*, the
conversion of Soules, the *Christian peace* of the Land, and *union*
of the reformed *Catholick Church*, the *unappropriating*, and *un-
monopolizing* the rewards of *learning* and *industry*, from the greasie
clutch of ignorance, and high feeding. We have tri'd already, &
miserably felt what *ambition worldly glory & immoderat wealth*
can do, what the boisterous & contradictional hand of a temporall,
earthly, and corporeall Spiritualty can availe to the edifying of
Christs holy *Church*; were it such a desperate hazard to put to the

venture the universall Votes of *Christs* Congregation, the fellowly and friendly yoke of a teaching and laborious Ministery, the Pastorlike and Apostolick imitation of meeke and unlordly Discipline, the gentle and benevolent mediocritie of Church-maintenance, without the ignoble Hucsterage of pidling *Tithes*? Were it such an incurable mischiefe to make a little triall, what all this would doe to the flourishing and growing up of *Christs* mysticall body? As rather to use every poore shift, and if that serve not, to threaten uproare and combustion, and shake the brand of Civill Discord?

O Sir, I doe now feele my selfe inwrapt on the sodaine into those mazes and *Labyrinths* of dreadfull and hideous thoughts, that which way to get out, or which way to end I know not, unlesse I turne mine eyes, and with your help lift up my hands to that Eternall and Propitious *Throne*, where nothing is readier then *grace* and *refuge* to the distresses of mortall Suppliants: and it were a shame to leave these serious thoughts lesse piously then the Heathen were wont to conclude their graver discourses.

Thou therefore that sits't in light & glory unapprochable, *Parent* of *Angels* and *Men*! next thee I implore Omnipotent King, Redeemer of that lost remnant whose nature thou didst assume, ineffable and everlasting *Love*! And thou the third subsistence of Divine Infinitude, *illumining Spirit*, the joy and solace of created *Things*! one *Tri-personall* Godhead! looke upon this thy poore and almost spent, and expiring *Church*, leave her not thus a prey to these importunate *Wolves*, that wait and thinke long till they devoure thy tender *Flock*, these wilde *Boares* that have broke into thy *Vineyard*, and left the print of thir polluting hoofs on the Soules of thy Servants. O let them not bring about their damned *designes* that stand now at the entrance of the bottomlesse pit expecting the Watch-word to open and let out those dreadfull *Locusts* and *Scorpions*, to *re-involve* us in that pitchy *Cloud* of infernall darknes, where we shall never more see the *Sunne* of thy *Truth* againe, never hope for the cheerfull dawne, never more heare the *Bird* of *Morning* sing. Be mov'd with pitty at the afflicted state of this our shaken

Monarchy, that now lies labouring under her throwes, and struggling against the grudges of more dreaded Calamities.

O thou that after the impetuous rage of five bloody Inundations,
and the succeeding Sword of intestine *Warre*, soaking the Land
in her owne gore, didst pitty the sad and ceasles revolution of our
swift and thick-comming sorrowes when wee were quite breath-
lesse, of thy *free grace* didst motion *Peace*, and termes of Cov'nant
with us, & having first welnigh freed us from *Antichristian* thral-
dome, didst build up this *Britannick Empire* to a glorious and
enviable heighth with all her Daughter Ilands about her, stay us
in this felicitie, let not the obstinacy of our halfe Obedience and
will-Worship bring forth that *Viper* of *Sedition*, that for these
Fourescore Yeares hath been breeding to eat through the entrals of
our *Peace;* but let her cast her Abortive Spawne without the danger
of this travailling & throbbing *Kingdome*. That we may still remember in our *solemne Thanksgivings*, how for us the *Northern
Ocean* even to the frozen *Thule* was scatter'd with the proud Ship-
wracks of the *Spanish Armado*, and the very maw of Hell ransack't,
and made to give up her conceal'd destruction, ere shee could vent
it in that horrible and damned blast.

O how much more glorious will those former Deliverances
appeare, when we shall know them not onely to have sav'd us from
greatest miseries past, but to have reserv'd us for greatest happinesse
to come. Hitherto thou hast but freed us, and that not fully, from
the unjust and Tyrannous Claime of thy Foes, now unite us intirely,
and appropriate us to thy selfe, tie us everlastingly in willing
Homage to the *Prerogative* of thy eternall *Throne*.

And now wee knowe, O thou our most certain hope and defence,
that thine enemies have been consulting all the Sorceries of the
great Whore, and have joyn'd their Plots with that sad Intelligencing
Tyrant that mischiefes the World with his Mines of *Ophir*, and
lies thirsting to revenge his Navall ruines that have larded our
Seas; but let them all take Counsell together, and let it come to
nought, let them Decree, and doe thou Cancell it, let them gather

themselves, and bee scatter'd, let them embattell themselves and bee broken, let them imbattell, and be broken, for thou art with us.

Then amidst the *Hymns*, and *Halleluiahs* of *Saints* some one may perhaps bee heard offering at high *strains* in new and lofty *Measures* to sing and celebrate thy *divine Mercies*, and *marvelous Judgements* in this Land throughout all Ages; whereby this great and Warlike Nation instructed and inur'd to the fervent and continuall practice of *Truth* and *Righteousnesse*, and casting farre from her the *rags* of her old *vices* may presse on hard to that *high* and *happy* emulation to be found the *soberest, wisest,* and *most Christian People* at that day when thou the Eternall and shortly-expected King shalt open the Clouds to judge the severall Kingdomes of the World, and distributing *Nationall Honours* and *Rewards* to Religious and just *Common-wealths*, shalt put an end to all Earthly *Tyrannies*, proclaiming thy universal and milde *Monarchy* through Heaven and Earth. Where they undoubtedly that by their *Labours, Counsels,* and *Prayers* have been earnest for the *Common good* of *Religion* and their *Countrey*, shall receive, above the inferiour *Orders* of the *Blessed*, the *Regall* addition of *Principalities, Legions,* and *Thrones* into their glorious Titles, and in supereminence of *beatifick Vision* progressing the *datelesse* and *irrevoluble* Circle of *Eternity* shall clasp inseparable Hands with *joy*, and *blisse* in over measure for ever.

But they contrary that by the impairing and diminution of the true *Faith*, the distresses and servitude of their *Countrey* aspire to high *Dignity, Rule* and *Promotion* here, after a shamefull end in this *Life* (which *God* grant them) shall be thrown downe eternally into the *darkest* and *deepest Gulfe* of Hell, where under the *despightfull controule*, the trample and spurne of all the other *Damned*, that in the anguish of their *Torture* shall have no other ease then to exercise a *Raving* and *Bestiall Tyranny* over them as their *Slaves* and *Negro's*, they shall remaine in that plight for ever, the *basest*, the *lowermost*, the *most dejected*, most *underfoot* and *downetrodden Vassals* of *Perdition*.

Commentaries and Notes

COMMENTARY ON "LYCIDAS"[1]

Addison says that he who desires to know whether he has a true taste for history or not should consider whether he is pleased with Livy's manner of telling a story; so, perhaps it may be said that he who wishes to know whether he has a true taste for poetry or not should consider whether he is highly delighted or not with the perusal of Milton's "Lycidas." If I might venture to place Milton's works according to their degrees of poetic excellence, it should be perhaps in the following order: *Paradise Lost, Comus, Samson Agonistes*, "Lycidas," "L'Allegro," "Il Penseroso." The three last are in such an exquisite strain, says Fenton, that though he had left no other monuments of his genius behind him, his name had been immortal.

JOSEPH WARTON[2]

I will conclude my remarks upon this poem with the just observation of Mr. Thyer. The particular beauties of this charming pastoral are too striking to need much descanting upon; but what gives the greatest grace to the whole is that natural and agreeable wildness and irregularity which runs quite through it, than which nothing could be better suited to express the warm affection which Milton had for his friend and the extreme grief he was in for the loss of him. Grief is eloquent, but not formal.

THOMAS NEWTON[3]

I see no extraordinary "wildness" and "irregularity," according to Doctor Newton, in the conduct of this little poem. It is true there is

---

[1]C. A. Patrides's *Milton's Lycidas: The Tradition and the Poem* is an excellent anthology of twentieth-century essays on *Lycidas*.
[2]Quoted by Thomas Warton in his edition of Milton's minor poems.
[3]In his edition of Milton's minor poems, 1752.

227

a very original air in it, although it be full of classical imitations; but this I think is owing, not to any disorder in the plan, nor entirely to the vigor and luster of the expression, but, in a good degree, to the looseness and variety of the meter. Milton's ear was a good second to his imagination.

RICHARD HURD[4]

In the examination of Milton's poetical works, I shall pay so much regard to time as to begin with his juvenile productions. For his early pieces he seems to have had a degree of fondness not very laudable: what he has once written he resolves to preserve, and gives to the publick an unfinished poem, which he broke off because he was *nothing satisfied with what he had done*, supposing his readers less nice than himself. These preludes to his future labours are in Italian, Latin, and English. Of the Italian I cannot pretend to speak as a critick; but I have heard them commended by a man well qualified to decide their merit. The Latin pieces are lusciously elegant; but the delight which they afford is rather by the exquisite imitation of the ancient writers, by the purity of the diction, and the harmony of the numbers, than by any power of invention, or vigour of sentiment. They are not all of equal value; the elegies excell the odes; and some of the exercises on Gunpowder Treason might have been spared.

The English poems, though they make no promises of *Paradise Lost*, have this evidence of genius, that they have a cast original and unborrowed. But their peculiarity is not excellence: if they differ from verses of others, they differ for the worse; for they are too often distinguished by repulsive harshness; the combination of words are new, but they are not pleasing; the rhymes and epithets seem to be laboriously sought, and violently applied.

That in the early parts of his life he wrote with much care appears from his manuscripts, happily preserved at Cambridge, in which many of his smaller works are found as they were first written, with the subsequent corrections. Such reliques shew how excellence is required; what we hope ever to do with ease, we may learn first to do with diligence.

[4]In Warton's edition.

Those who admire the beauties of this great poet, sometimes force their own judgement into false approbation of his little pieces, and prevail upon themselves to think that admirable which is only singular. All that short compositions can commonly attain is neatness and elegance. Milton never learned the art of doing little things with grace; he overlooked the milder excellence of suavity and softness; he was a *Lion* that had no skill in *dandling the Kid*.

One of the poems on which much praise has been bestowed is *Lycidas*; of which the diction is harsh, the rhymes uncertain, and the numbers unpleasing. What beauty there is, we must therefore seek in the sentiments and images. It is not to be considered as the effusion of real passion; for passion runs not after remote allusions and obscure opinions. Passion plucks no berries from the myrtle and ivy, nor calls upon Arethuse and Mincius, nor tells of rough *satyrs* and *fauns with cloven heel*. Where there is leisure for fiction there is little grief.

In this poem there is no nature, for there is no truth; there is no art, for there is nothing new. Its form is that of a pastoral, easy, vulgar, and therefore disgusting: whatever images it can supply, are long ago exhausted; and its inherent improbability always forces dissatisfaction on the mind. When Cowley tells of Hervey that they studied together, it is easy to suppose how much he must miss the companion of his labours, and the partner of his discoveries; but what image of tenderness can be excited by these lines!

> We drove a field, and both together heard
> What time the grey fly winds her sultry horn,
> Battening our flocks with the fresh dews of night.

We know that they never drove a field, and that they had no flocks to batten; and though it be allowed that the representation may be allegorical, the true meaning is so uncertain and remote, that it is never sought because it cannot be known when it is found.

Among the flocks, and copses, and flowers, appear the heathen deities; Jove and Phoebus, Neptune and Aeolus, with a long train of mythological imagery, such as a College easily supplies. Nothing can less display knowledge, or less exercise invention, than to tell how a shepherd has lost his companion, and must now feed his flocks alone, without any judge of his skill in piping; and how one god asks another god what is become of Lycidas, and now neither god can tell. He who thus grieves will excite no sympathy; he who thus praises will confer no honour.

This poem has yet a grosser fault. With these trifling fictions are mingled the most awful and sacred truths, such as ought never to be polluted with such irreverent combinations. The shepherd likewise is now a feeder of sheep, and afterwards an ecclesiastical pastor, a super-intendent of a Christian flock. Such equivocations are always unskilful; but here they are indecent, and at least approach to impiety, of which, however, I believe the writer not to have been conscious.

Such is the power of reputation justly acquired, that its blaze drives away the eye from nice examination. Surely no man could have fancied that he read *Lycidas* with pleasure, had he not known its author.

SAMUEL JOHNSON[5]

Doctor Johnson observes, that *Lycidas* is filled with the heathen deities; and a long train of mythological imagery, such as a College easily supplies. But it is such also, as even the Court itself could now have easily supplied. The public diversions, and books of all sorts and from all sorts of writers, more especially compositions in poetry, were at this time over-run with classical pedantries. But what writer, of the same period, has made these obsolete fictions the vehicle of so much fancy and poetical description? How beautifully has he applied this sort of allusion, to the Druidical rocks of Denbighshire, to Mona, and the fabulous banks of Deva! It is objected, that its pastoral form is disgusting. But this was the age of pastoral: and yet *Lycidas* has but little of the bucolic cant, now so fashionable. The Satyrs and Fauns are but just mentioned. If any trite rural topics occur, how are they heightened!

> Together both, ere the high lawns appear'd
> Under the opening eye-lids of the morn,
> We drove afield, and both together heard
> What time the gray-fly winds her sultry horn,
> Batt'ning our flocks with the fresh dews of night.

Here the day-break is described by the faint appearance of the upland lawns under the first gleams of light: the sunset, by the buzzing of the

[5] From his *Life of Milton*, 1779.

chaffer: and the night sheds her *fresh dews* on their flocks. We cannot blame pastoral imagery, and pastoral allegory, which carry with them so much natural painting. In this piece there is perhaps more poetry than sorrow. But let us read it for its poetry. It is true, that passion plucks no berries from the myrtle and ivy, nor calls upon Arethuse and Mincius, nor tells of *rough Satyrs with cloven heel.* But poetry does this; and in the hands of Milton, does it with a peculiar and irresistible charm. Subordinate poets exercise no invention, when they tell how a shepherd has lost his companion, and must feed his flocks alone without any judge of his skill in piping: but Milton dignifies and adorns these common artificial incidents with unexpected touches of picturesque beauty, with the graces of sentiment, and with the novelties of original genius. It is said "here is no art, for there is nothing new." But this objection will vanish, if we consider the imagery which Milton has raised from local circumstances. Not to repeat the use he has made of the mountains of Wales, the isle of Man, and the river Dee, near which Lycidas was shipwrecked; let us recollect the introduction of the romantic superstition of Saint Michael's Mount in Cornwall, which overlooks the Irish seas, the fatal scene of his friend's disaster. But the poetry is not always unconnected with passion. The poet lavishly describes an antient sepulchral rite, but it is made preparatory to a stroke of tenderness. He calls for a variety of flowers to decorate his friend's hearse, supposing that his body was present, and forgetting for a while that it was floating far off in the ocean. If he was drowned, it was some consolation that he was to receive the decencies of burial. This is a pleasing deception: it is natural and pathetic. But the real catastrophe recurs. And this circumstance again opens a new vein of imagination.

Our author has been censured for mixing religious disputes with pagan and pastoral ideas. But he had the authority of Mantuan and Spenser, now considered as models in this way of writing. Let me add, that our poetry was not yet purged from its Gothic combinations; nor had legitimate notions of discrimination and propriety so far prevailed, as sufficiently to influence the growing improvements of English composition. These irregularities and incongruities must not be tried by modern criticism.

THOMAS WARTON[6]

[6]From his edition of Milton's minor poems, 1791.

Of all Milton's smaller poems, *Lycidas* is the greatest favourite with us. We cannot agree to the charge which Dr. Johnson has brought against it, of pedantry and want of feeling. It is the fine emanation of classical sentiment in a youthful scholar—"most musical, most melancholy." A certain tender gloom overspreads it, a wayward abstraction, a forgetfulness of his subject in the serious reflections that arise out of it. The gusts of passion come and go like the sounds of music borne on the wind. The loss of the friend whose death he laments seems to have recalled, with double force, the reality of those speculations which they had indulged together; we are transported to classic ground, and a mysterious strain steals responsive on the ear while we listen to the poet,

> With eager thought warbling his Doric lay.

We shall proceed to give a few passages at length in support of our opinion. The first we shall quote is as remarkable for the truth and sweetness of the natural descriptions as for the characteristic elegance of the allusions:

[Lines 25–49]

After the fine apostrophe on Fame which Phœbus is invoked to utter, the poet proceeds:

[Lines 85–99]

If this is art, it is perfect art; nor do we wish for anything better. The measure of the verse, the very sound of the names, would almost produce the effect here described. To ask the poet not to make use of such allusions as these, is to ask the painter not to dip in the colours of the rainbow, if he could. In fact, it is the common cant of criticism to consider every allusion to the classics, and particularly in a mind like Milton's, as pedantry and affectation. Habit is a second nature; and, in this sense, the pedantry (if it is to be called so) of the scholastic enthusiast, who is constantly referring to images of which his mind is full, is as graceful as it is natural. It is not affectation in him to recur to ideas and modes of expression, with which he has the strongest associations, and in which he takes the greatest delight. Milton was as conversant with the world of genius before him as with the world of nature about him; the fables of the ancient mythology were as familiar to him as his dreams. To be a pedant, is to see neither the beauties of nature nor of art. Milton saw both; and he made use of the one only to adorn and give new interest to the other. He was a passionate admirer of nature; and, in a single couplet of his, describing the moon,—

> Like one that had been led astray
> Through the heaven's wide pathless way,—

there is more intense observation, and intense feeling of nature (as if he had gazed himself blind in looking at her), than in twenty volumes of descriptive poetry. But he added to his own observation of nature the splendid fictions of ancient genius, enshrined her in the mysteries of ancient religion, and celebrated her with the pomp of ancient names.

> Next Camus, reverend sire, went footing slow,
> His mantle hairy and his bonnet sedge,
> Inwrought with figures dim, and on the edge
> Like to that sanguine flower inscrib'd with woe.
> Oh! who hath reft (quoth he) my dearest pledge?
> Last came, and last did go,
> The pilot of the Galilean lake.

There is a wonderful correspondence in the rhythm of these lines to the idea which they convey. This passage, which alludes to the clerical character of *Lycidas*, has been found fault with, as combining the truths of the Christian religion with the fictions of the heathen mythology. We conceive there is very little foundation for this objection, either in reason or good taste. We will not go so far as to defend Camoens, who, in his *Lusiad*, makes Jupiter send Mercury with a dream to propagate the Catholic religion; nor do we know that it is generally proper to introduce the two things in the same poem, though we see no objection to it here; but of this we are quite sure, that there is no inconsistency or natural repugnance between this poetical and religious faith in the same mind. To the understanding, the belief of the one is incompatible with that of the other; but in the imagination, they not only may, but do constantly co-exist. We will venture to go farther, and maintain, that every classical scholar, however orthodox a Christian he may be, is an honest Heathen at heart. This requires explanation. Whoever, then, attaches a reality to any idea beyond the mere name, has, to a certain extent, (though not an abstract), an habitual and practical belief in it. Now, to any one familiar with the names of the personages of the Heathen mythology, they convey a positive identity beyond the mere name. We refer them to something out of ourselves. It is only by an effort of abstraction that we divest ourselves of the idea of their reality; all our involuntary prejudices are on their side. This is enough for the poet. They impose on the imagination by all the attractions of beauty and grandeur. They come down to us in sculpture and in song. We have the same associations with them, as if they had really been; for the belief of the fiction in ancient times has produced all the same effects as the reality could have done. It was a reality to the minds of the ancient Greeks and Romans, and through them it is reflected to us. And, as we shape towers, and men, and armed steeds, out of the broken clouds that glitter in the distant horizon, so, throned above the ruins of the ancient world, Jupiter still nods sublime on the top of blue Olympus, Hercules leans upon his club, Apollo has not laid aside his bow, nor Neptune his trident; the sea-gods ride upon the sounding waves, the long procession of heroes and demi-gods passes in endless review before us, and still we hear

—The Muses in a ring
Aye round about Jove's altar sing:

. . .

Have sight of Proteus coming from the sea,
And hear old Triton blow his wreathed horn.

If all these mighty fictions had really existed, they could have done no more for us! We shall only give one other passage from *Lycidas*; but we flatter ourselves that it will be a treat to our readers, if they are not already familiar with it. It is the passage which contains that exquisite description of the flowers:

[Lines 132–164]

Dr. Johnson is very much offended at the introduction of these Dolphins; and indeed, if he had had to guide them through the waves, he would have made much the same figure as his old friend Dr. Burney does, swimming in the *Thames* with his wig on, with the water-nymphs, in the picture by Barry at the Adelphi. . . .

Dr. Johnson's general remark, that Milton's genius had not room to show itself in his smaller pieces, is not well-founded. Not to mention *Lycidas*, the *Allegro*, and *Penseroso*, it proceeds on a false estimate of the merits of his great work, which is not more distinguished by strength and sublimity than by tenderness and beauty. The last were as essential qualities of Milton's mind as the first. The battle of the angels, which has been commonly considered as the best part of the *Paradise Lost*, is the worst.

WILLIAM HAZLITT[7]

It has been said, I think very fairly, that Lycidas is a good test of a real feeling for what is peculiarly called poetry. Many, or perhaps we might say, most readers, do not taste its excellence; nor does it follow that they may not greatly admire Pope and Dryden, or even Virgil and Homer. It is, however, somewhat remarkable that Johnson, who has committed his critical reputation by the most contemptuous depreciation of this poem, had in an earlier part of his life selected the tenth eclogue of Virgil for peculiar praise; the tenth eclogue, which, beautiful as it is, belongs to the same class of pastoral and personal allegory, and requires the same sacrifice of reasoning criticism as the Lycidas itself. In the age of Milton the poetical world had been accustomed by the Italian and Spanish writers to a more abundant use of allegory than has been pleasing to their posterity; but Lycidas is not so much in the nature of an allegory as of a masque: the characters pass before our eyes in imagination, as on the stage; they are chiefly mythological, but not creations of the poet. Our sympathy with the fate of Lycidas may not be

[7]From *The Round Table*, 1815.

much stronger than for the desertion of Gallus by his mistress; but many poems will yield an exquisite pleasure to the imagination that produce no emotion in the heart; or none at least except through associations independent of the subject.

. . . The introduction of St. Peter after the fabulous deities of the sea has appeared an incongruity deserving of censure to some admirers of this poem. It would be very reluctantly that we could abandon to this criticism the most splendid passage it presents. But the censure rests, as I think, on too narrow a principle. In narrative or dramatic poetry, where something like illusion or momentary belief is to be produced, the mind requires an objective possibility, a capacity of real existence, not only in all the separate portions of the imagined story, but in their coherency and relation to a common whole. Whatever is obviously incongruous, whatever shocks our previous knowledge of possibility, destroys to a certain extent that acquiescence in the fiction, which it is the true business of the fiction to produce. But the case is not the same in such poems as Lycidas. They pretend to no credibility, they aim at no illusion; they are read with the willing abandonment of the imagination to a waking dream, and require only that general possibility, that combination of images which common experience does not reject as incompatible, without which the fancy of the poet would be only like that of the lunatic. And it had been so usual to blend sacred with mythological personages in allegory, that no one probably in Milton's age would have been struck by the objection.

HENRY HALLAM[8]

As for the versification of "Lycidas," it was of course disagreeable to the ear of Johnson, which could relish nothing but tame regularity, "the right butter-woman's rank to market," as Touchstone terms it. The verse is of Milton's own formation, in this, as in most of his other poems. From Tasso and Guarini he adopted the practice of mingling three-foot lines with the regular verses of five feet, and of adding occasionally the ornament of rime. In this he did not follow any rule but that of his own ear, and they therefore can only be perfectly enjoyed

[8]From his *Introduction to the Literature of Europe*, 1854.

by those few whose ear, like his own, is fully attuned to the variety of poetic melody. It has not, we believe, been observed by any critic that the last eight lines of "Lycidas" form a perfect stanza in *ottava rima*. As they stand detached, such was probably the poet's design; but we meet with eight other lines (124–131) which, though they terminate a paragraph, are united with what precedes more closely than is ever the case in the Italian poets. Whether this was accidental or not, we are unable to determine. He had, it is true, the authority of Fairfax (see *Godfrey of Bullogne*, XIX, 3, 4) for such a structure; but we are inclined to think it casual, as in another place (165–172) by merely transposing two lines we should have a perfect stanza, and a third (111–118), by altering a single line.

THOMAS KEIGHTLY[9]

Now, in order to deal with words rightly, this is the habit you must form. Nearly every word in your language has been first a word of some other language—of Saxon, German, French, Latin, or Greek (not to speak of eastern and primitive dialects). And many words have been all these;—that is to say, have been Greek first, Latin next, French or German next, and English last: undergoing a certain change of sense and use on the lips of each nation; but retaining a deep vital meaning which all good scholars feel in employing them, even at this day. If you do not know the Greek alphabet, learn it; young or old—girl or boy—whoever you may be, if you think of reading seriously (which, of course, implies that you have some leisure at command), learn your Greek alphabet; then get good dictionaries of all these languages, and whenever you are in doubt about a word, hunt it down patiently. Read Max Müller's lectures thoroughly; to begin with; and, after that, never let a word escape you that looks suspicious. It is severe work; but you will find it, even at first, interesting, and at last, endlessly amusing. And the general gain to your character, in power and precision, will be quite incalculable.

Mind, this does not imply knowing, or trying to know, Greek, or Latin, or French. It takes a whole life to learn any language perfectly.

[9]From his *Account of the Life, Opinions, and Writings of John Milton*, 1885.

But you can easily ascertain the meanings through which the English word has passed; and those which in a good writer's work it must still bear.

And now, merely for example's sake, I will, with your permission, read a few lines of a true book with you, carefully; and see what will come out of them. I will take a book perfectly known to you all; no English words are more familiar to us, yet nothing perhaps has been less read with sincerity. I will take these few following lines of Lycidas:

[Ruskin here quotes 11. 108–29.]

Let us think over this passage, and examine its words.

First, is it not singular to find Milton assigning to St. Peter, not only his full episcopal function, but the very types of it which Protestants usually refuse most passionately? His "mitred" locks! Milton was no Bishop-lover; how comes St. Peter to be "mitred?" "Two massy keys he bore." Is this, then, the power of the keys claimed by the Bishops of Rome, and is it acknowledged here by Milton only in a poetical licence, for the sake of its picturesqueness, that he may get the gleam of the golden keys to help his effect? Do not think it. Great men do not play stage tricks with doctrines of life and death: only little men do that. Milton means what he says; and means it with his might too—is going to put the whole strength of his spirit presently into the saying of it. For though not a lover of false bishops, he *was* a lover of true ones; and the Lake-pilot is here, in his thoughts, the type and head of true episcopal power. For Milton reads that text, "I will give unto thee the keys of the kingdom of Heaven" quite honestly. Puritan though he be, he would not blot it out of the book because there have been bad bishops; nay, in order to understand him we must understand that verse first; it will not do to eye it askance, or whisper it under our breath, as if it were a weapon of an adverse sect. It is a solemn, universal assertion, deeply to be kept in mind by all sects. But perhaps we shall be better able to reason on it if we go on a little farther, and come back to it. For clearly, this marked insistance on the power of the true episcopate is to make us feel more weightily what is to be charged against the false claimants of episcopate; or generally, against false claimants of power and rank in the body of the clergy; they who, 'for their bellies' sake, creep, and intrude, and climb into the fold.'

Do not think Milton uses those three words to fill up his verse, as a loose writer would. He needs all the three; specially those three, and no more than those—"creep," and "intrude," and "climb;" no other words would or could serve the turn, and no more could be added. For they exhaustively comprehend the three classes, correspondent to the three characters, of men who dishonestly seek ecclesiastical power. First, those who "*creep*" into the fold; who do not care for office, nor name, but for secret influence, and do all things occultly and cunningly, consenting to any servility of office or conduct, so only that they may intimately discern, and unawares direct, the minds of men. Then those who "intrude" (thrust, that is) themselves into the fold, who by natural insolence of heart, and stout eloquence of tongue, and fearlessly perseverant self-assertion, obtain hearing and authority with the common crowd. Lastly, those who "climb," who by labor and learning, both stout and sound, but selfishly exerted in the cause of their own ambition, gain high dignities and authorities, and become "lords over the heritage," though not "ensamples to the flock."

Now go on:—

> Of other care they little reckoning make,
> Than how to scramble at the shearers' feast.
> *Blind mouths—*

I pause again, for this is a strange expression; a broken metaphor, one might think, careless and unscholarly.

Not so: its very audacity and pithiness are intended to make us look close at the phrase and remember it. Those two monosyllables express the precisely accurate contraries of right character, in the two great offices of the Church—those of bishop and pastor.

A Bishop means a person who sees.

A Pastor means one who feeds.

The most unbishoply character a man can have is therefore to be Blind.

The most unpastoral is, instead of feeding, to want to be fed,—to be a Mouth.

Take the two reverses together, and you have "blind mouths." We may advisably follow out this idea a little. Nearly all the evils in the Church have arisen from bishops desiring *power* more than *light*. They want authority, not outlook. Whereas their real office is not to rule; though it may be vigorously to exhort and rebuke; it is the king's office to rule; the bishop's office is to *oversee* the flock; to number it, sheep by sheep; to be ready always to give full account of it. Now it is clear he cannot give account of the souls, if he has not so much as numbered the bodies of his flock. The first thing, therefore, that a bishop has to do is at least to put himself in a position in which, at any moment, he can obtain the history from childhood of every living soul in his diocese, and of its present state. Down in that back street, Bill, and Nancy, knocking each other's teeth out!—Does the bishop know all about it? Has he his eye upon them? Has he *had* his eye upon them? Can he circumstantially explain to us how Bill got into the habit of beating Nancy about the head? If he cannot, he is no bishop though he had a mitre as high as Salisbury steeple; he is no bishop,—he has sought to be at the helm instead of the masthead; he has no sight of things. "Nay," you say, it is not his duty to look after Bill in the back street. What! the fat sheep that have full fleeces—you think it is only those he should look after, while (go back to your Milton) "the hungry sheep look up, and are not fed, besides what the grim wolf, with privy paw" (bishops knowing nothing about it) "daily devours apace, and nothing said?"

"But that's not our idea of a bishop." Perhaps not; but it was St. Paul's; and it was Milton's. They may be right, or we may be; but we must not think we are reading either one or the other by putting our meaning into their words.

I go on.

But, swollen with wind, and the rank mist they draw.

This is to meet the vulgar answer that "if the poor are not looked after in their bodies, they are in their souls; they have spiritual food."

And Milton says, "They have no such thing as spiritual food; they are only swollen with wind." At first you may think that is a coarse type, and an obscure one. But again, it is a quite literally accurate one. Take up your Latin and Greek dictionaries, and find out the meaning of "Spirit." It is only a contraction of the Latin word "breath," and an indistinct translation of the Greek word for "wind." The same word is used in writing, "The wind bloweth where it listeth;" and in writing,

"So is every one that is born of the Spirit;" born of the *breath*, that is; for it means the breath of God, in soul and body. We have the true sense of it in our words "inspiration" and "expire." Now, there are two kinds of breath with which the flock may be filled; God's breath, and man's. The breath of God is health, and life, and peace to them, as the air of heaven is to the flocks on the hills; but man's breath—the word which *he* calls spiritual,—is disease and contagion to them, as the fog of the fen. They rot inwardly with it; they are puffed up by it, as a dead body by the vapours of its own decomposition. This is literally true of all false religious teaching; the first and last, and fatalest sign of it is that "puffing up." Your converted children, who teach their parents; your converted convicts, who teach honest men; your converted dunces, who, having lived in cretinous stupefaction half their lives, suddenly awakening to the fact of there being a God, fancy themselves therefore His peculiar people and messengers; your sectarians of every species, small and great, Catholic or Protestant, of high church or low, in so far as they think themselves exclusively in the right and others wrong; and pre-eminently, in every sect, those who hold that men can be saved by thinking rightly instead of doing rightly, by word instead of act, and wish instead of work:—these are the true fog children—clods, these, without water; bodies, these, of putrescent vapour and skin, without blood or flesh: blown bag-pipes for the fiends to pipe with—corrupt, and corrupting,—"Swollen with wind, and the rank mist they draw."

Lastly, let us return to the lines respecting the power of the keys, for now we can understand them. Note the difference between Milton and Dante in their interpretation of this power: for once, the latter is weaker in thought; he supposes *both* the keys to be of the gate of heaven; one is of gold, the other of silver: they are given by St. Peter to the sentinel angel; and it is not easy to determine the meaning either of the substances of the three steps of the gate, or of the two keys. But Milton makes one, of gold, the key of heaven; the other, of iron, the key of the prison, in which the wicked teachers are to be bound who "have taken away the key of knowledge, yet entered not in themselves."

We have seen that the duties of bishop and pastor are to see, and feed; and, of all who do so, it is said, "He that watereth, shall be watered also himself." But the reverse is truth also. He that watereth not, shall be *withered* himself, and he that seeth not, shall himself be shut out of sight,—shut into the perpetual prison-house. And that prison opens here, as well as hereafter: he who is to be bound in heaven must first be bound on earth. That command to the strong angels, of which the rock-apostle is the image, "Take him, and bind him hand and foot, and cast him out," issues, in its measure, against the teacher, for every help withheld, and for every truth refused, and for every falsehood enforced; so that he is more strictly fettered the more he fetters, and farther outcast, as he more and more misleads, till at last the bars of the iron cage close upon him, and as "the golden opes, the iron shuts amain."

We have got something out of the lines, I think, and much more is yet to be found in them; but we have done enough by way of example of the kind of word-by-word examination of your author which is rightly called "reading;" watching every accent and expression, and putting ourselves always in the author's place, annihilating our own personality, and seeking to enter into his, so as to be able assuredly to say, "Thus Milton thought," not "Thus I thought, in mis-reading Milton." And by this process you will gradually come to attach less weight to your own "Thus I thought" at other times. You will begin to perceive that what *you* thought was a matter of no serious importance;—that your thoughts on any subject are not perhaps the clearest and wisest that could be arrived at thereupon:—in fact, that unless you are a very singular person, you cannot be said to have any "thoughts" at all; that you have no materials for them, in any serious matters;—no right to "think", but only to try to learn more of the facts. Nay, most probably all your life (unless, as I said, you are a singular person) you will have no legitimate right to an "opinion" on any business, except that instantly under your hand. What must of necessity be done, you can always find out, beyond question, how to do. Have you a house to keep in order, a commodity to sell, a field to plough, a ditch to cleanse? There need be no two opinions about these proceedings; it is at your peril if you have not much more than an "opinion" on the way to manage such matters. And also, outside of your own business, there are one or two subjects on which you are bound to have but one opinion. That roguery and lying are objectionable, and are instantly to be flogged out of the way whenever discovered;—that covetousness and love of quarrelling are dangerous dispositions even in children, and deadly dispositions in men and nations;—that in the end, the God of heaven and earth loves active, modest, and kind people, and hates idle, proud, greedy, and cruel ones;—on these general facts you are bound to have but one and that a very strong, opinion. For the rest, respecting religions, governments, sciences, arts, you will find that, on the whole, you can know NOTHING,—judge nothing; that the best you can do, even though you may be a well-educated person, is to be silent, and strive to be wiser every day, and to understand a little more of the thoughts of others, which so soon as you try to do honestly, you will discover that the thoughts even of the wisest are very little more than pertinent questions. To put the difficulty into a clear shape, and exhibit to you the grounds for *in*decision, that is all they can generally do for you!— and well for them and for us, if indeed they are able "to mix the music with our thoughts, and sadden us with heavenly doubts." This writer, from whom I have been reading to you, is not among the first or wisest: he sees shrewdly as far as he sees, and therefore it is easy to find out his full meaning; but with the greater men, you cannot fathom their meaning; they do not even wholly measure it themselves,—it is so wide. Suppose I had asked you, for instance, to seek for Shakespeare's opinion, instead of Milton's on this matter of Church authority?—or for Dante's? Have any of you, at this instant, the least idea what either thought about it? Have you ever balanced the scene with the bishops in Richard III against the character of Cranmer? the description of St. Francis and St. Dominic against that of him who made Virgil wonder to gaze upon him,—"disteso, tanto vilmente, nell' eterno esilio;" or of him whom Dante stood beside, "come 'l frate che confessa lo perfido asassin?" Shakespeare and Alighieri knew men better than most of us, I presume! They were both in the midst of the main struggle between the temporal and spiritual powers. They had an opinion, we may guess? But where is it? Bring it into court! Put Shakespeare's or Dante's creed into articles, and send *that* up into the Ecclesiastical Courts!

You will not be able, I tell you again, for many and many a day, to come at the real purposes and teaching of these great men; but a very little honest study of them will enable you to perceive that what you took for your own "judgment" was mere chance prejudice, and drifted, helpless, entangled weed of castaway thought: nay, you will see that most men's minds are indeed little better than rough heath wilderness, neglected and stubborn, partly barren, partly overgrown with pestilent brakes and venomous windsown herbage of evil surmise; that the first thing you have to do for them, and yourself, is eagerly and scornfully to set fire to *this*; burn all the jungle into wholesome ash heaps, and then plough and sow. All the true literary work before you, for life, must begin with obedience to that order, "Break up your fallow ground, and *sow not among thorns.*"

JOHN RUSKIN[10]

In "Lycidas" we have reached the high-water mark of English Poesy and of Milton's own production. A period of a century and a half was to elapse before poetry in England seemed, in Wordsworth's "Ode on Immortality" (1807), to be rising again towards the level of inspiration which it had once attained in "Lycidas."

MARK PATTISON[11]

"Lycidas" is probably the most perfect piece of pure literature in existence because every word and phrase and line is sonorous, ringing and echoing with music.

ARTHUR MACHEN[12]

Epitaphs and elegies are a good test of poetic seriousness; because they may tempt the poet to hollow rhetoric. I have already quoted Skelton's *Epitaph on Edward IV*, and Clare's *The Dying Child* and, by contrast, Dryden's fancy-dress *Epitaph on Lord Hastings.* Here are two more poems of the same solemn category from opposite ends of the social scale. What makes Surrey's *Epitaph on Clere of Cleremont* a good poem is that he remains uncompromisingly himself, with all the faults and virtues of his nobility, and that he feels a sincere grief:

> Norfolk sprang thee, Lambeth holds thee dead;
> Clere, of the County of Cleremont, thou hight.
> Within the womb of Ormond's race thou bred,
> And saw'st thy cousin crowned in thy sight. . . .

[10]From *Sesame and Lilies*, 1865.
[11]From his *Milton*, 1887.
[12]From his *Hill of Dreams*, 1907.

Shelton for love, Surrey for Lord, thou chase;
(Aye me! while life did last that league was tender)
Tracing whose steps thou sawest Kelsall blaze,
Laundersey burnt, and battered Bullen render,
At Mottrel gates, hopeless of all recure,
Thine Earl, half dead, gave in thy hand his will;
Which cause did thee this pining death procure,
Ere summers four times seven thou couldst fulfill.
　　Ah! Clere! if love had booted, care, or cost,
　　Heaven had not won, nor earth so timely lost.

What makes *The Night Before Larry Was Stretched*, a late eighteenth-century Dublin street-ballad, a good poem is that the writer, whoever he may have been (and one Harefoot Bill is generally credited with it) also remains uncompromisingly himself, with all the faults and virtues of his villainy, and he too feels a sincere grief:

　　　　The night before Larry was stretched,
　　　　　　The boys they all paid him a visit;
　　　　A bit in their sacks too they fetched,
　　　　　　They sweated their duds till they riz it;
　　　　For Larry was always the lad,
　　　　　　When a friend was condemned to the squeezer,
　　　　Would fence all the togs that he had
　　　　　　Just to help the poor boy to a sneezer,
　　　　　　　　And moisten his gob 'fore he died. . . .

　　　　The boys they came crowding in fast;
　　　　　　They drew their stools close round about him,
　　　　Six glims round his trap-case they placed;
　　　　　　He couldn't be well waked without 'em.
　　　　When one of us asked, could he die
　　　　　　Without having truly repented?
　　　　Says Larry, 'That's all in my eye,
　　　　　　And first by the clergy invented
　　　　　　　　To get a fat bit for themselves.'

　　. . . Then the deck being called for, they played
　　　　Till Larry found one of them cheated.

A dart at his napper he made,
  The lad being easily heated.
'So ye chates me because I'm in grief;
  O, is that, by the Holy, the rason?
Soon I'll give ye to know, you black thief,
  That you're cracking your jokes out of sason,
    I'll scuttle your nob with my fist.'

. . . When he came to the nubbling chit,
  He was tucked up so neat and so pretty;
The rumbler jogged off from his feet,
  And he died with his face to the city.
He kicked, too, but that was all pride,
  For soon you might see 'twas all over;
And after the noose was untied,
  Then at darky we waked him in clover,
    And sent him to take a ground sweat.

What (by your leave) makes *Lycidas* a bad poem, when judged by the
same standards, is that Milton has put on Theocritan fancy-dress;
and, as Dr. Johnson first pointed out, it must "not be considered the
effusion of real passion."

*   *   *

A poem (must I say again?) is addressed to the Goddess. She smilingly
forgives clumsiness in the young or uneducated—early poems have a
nap, or bloom, not found in later poems. And she appreciates the loving
care put into a poem by the more experienced; she dislikes slovens.
But she insists on truth, and ridicules the idea of using argument or
rhetorical charm to overbear her intuition of truth. Milton fell from
grace because he allowed his rhetorical skill, learned at Christ's, to dull
his poetic sense. While reading his "minor poems" one becomes aware
of poetry still struggling against the serpent coils. It is the unhappy
flutterings of its wings in *Comus* and the Nativity Ode—I am thinking
particularly of *Sabrina Fair* and "the yellow-skirted fays"—that give
these poems their poignant and, on the whole, distasteful character.
Earlier, when writing the sixth poem of his Latin *Silvae*, at the age of

twenty-three, Milton could energetically argue the cause of the "Golden Muse" against his father, on whom he depended for his allowance. Milton's father, a scrivener and a well-known musician, held that poetry was a pleasant relaxation for grave scholars and noblemen in the afternoon of their life, but that his son should choose some other sort of profession. Milton flatters him by saying: "Apollo made you a musician, and me a poet." Here is Skeat's translation:

> . . . Hence it is that as sire and son we win
> Dividual lot in his divinity.
> To hate my gentle Muse though thou dost feign,
> Thou canst not hate her, Father, I maintain:
> Since thou hast ne'er bid me to go where lies
> The broad highway and easier field of gain,
> Where hopes gleam sure of coin in mounded heap;
> Not hal'st me to the Bar and laws we keep—
> Too often wrench'd; nor with distasteful cries
> Mine ears dost peal: but seeking only power
> My mind well-stor'd with richer wealth to dower
> In deep retirement from the city's roar,
> Lettest me thus in jocund leisure stride
> As if at Phœbus's side,
> With benediction from our Muses' shore.

The poem ends with Milton's promise to celebrate his father's kindness in immortal verse.

So we come to the Theme of Fame. Skelton raised it; but only in joke. *The Garland of Laurell*, an account of his induction into the Temple of Fame, is a comic fantasy written for the Countess of Surrey, the Ladies Isabel and Miniall Howard, Lady Ann Dakers of the South, and his other women-friends at Court. Fame was no joke for Milton, but an obsession, as appears throughout the *Silvæ*, especially in his letter to Manso, and in *Lycidas*. Thirst for fame explains much that is dishonest and ruthless in his life, besides his passionate cultivation of polemical oratory. Milton appears never to have loved anyone, after the death of his friend Charles Diodati, except himself; and certainly had no women-friends with whom he could be on joking terms. Men became the objects of his adulation or execration only as they advanced or impeded his career. While an undergraduate, he wrote two elegies on bishops, and a Fifth of November poem in which he sentenced to "pains condign" (though the dupes of Satan) the treasonable wretches who tried to encompass the death of our devout King James; he had his eye, it seems, on a Royal Fellowship. But when the coveted fellowship went elsewhere, and a Bishop, a former tutor with whom he had quarrelled, proved to have been responsible, Milton lost all respect for bishops. In *Eikonoclastes* he justifies the judges who sentenced King James's devouter son Charles to similar "pains condign" at the block. His adulation of Queen Christina of Sweden in *The Second Defence of the English People* contrasts so revoltingly with his obscene libels on Charles in *The First Defence*, that nothing which he wrote later when influenced by the Muse "of Horeb and Sinai" can persuade me of his poetic sincerity; grapes are not gathered from thistles.

Poets have aimed at two kinds of poetic fame: the first, contemporary fame, is suspect because it is commonly acquired by writing for the public, or for the representatives of the public, rather than for the Muse —that is to say for poetic necessity. The second, posthumous fame, is irrelevant; though, if the poet falls in love and becomes obsessed with terrors of death, he may be forgiven (as we forgive Shakespeare) for contemplating the immortality bestowed on his beloved by means of a poem. Milton was obsessed by thoughts of his own fame. His strongest reaction to the news of Lycidas's drowning was: "Heavens, it might have been myself! Cut down before my prime, cheated of immortal fame!"

ROBERT GRAVES[13]

One might say that every poem shows some sign of a rivalry between Ariel and Prospero; in every good poem their relation is more or less happy, but it is never without its tensions. The Grecian Urn states Ariel's position; Prospero's has been equally succinctly stated by Dr. Johnson: *The only end of writing is to enable the readers better to enjoy life or better to endure it. . . .* Though every poem invokes *some* degree of collaboration between Ariel and Prospero, the role of each varies in

[13]From his *Crowning Privilege*, Cassell & Co., Ltd. (London, 1955). Reprinted by permission.

importance from one poem to another: it is usually possible to say of a poem and, sometimes, of the whole output of a poet, that it is Ariel-dominated or Prospero-dominated. . . .

It is also possible for a poet himself to be mistaken as to the kind of poem he is writing. For example, at first reading, "Lycidas" seems to be by *Prospero*, for it purports to deal with the most serious matters possible —death, grief, sin, resurrection. But I believe this to be an illusion. On closer inspection it seems to me that only the robes are Prospero's and that Ariel has dressed up in them for fun, so that it is as irrelevant to ask, "Who is the Pilot of the Galilean Lake?" as it is to ask, "Who is the Pobble who has no toes?" And He who walks the waves is merely an Arcadian shepherd whose name happens to be Christ. If "Lycidas" is read in this way, as if it were a poem by Edward Lear, then it seems to me one of the most beautiful poems in the English language; if, however, it is read as the Prospero poem it apparently claims to be, then it must be condemned, as Dr. Johnson condemned it, for being unfeeling and frivolous, since one expects wisdom or revelation, and it provides neither.

W. H. AUDEN[14]

A LIST OF ABBREVIATIONS USED IN THE NOTES

WORKS OF LITERATURE

Alciphron	*Ep.*	*Epistolæ*
Appolonius	*Arg.*	*Argonautica*
Ariosto	*O.F.*	*Orlando Furioso*
Cæsar	*B.G.*	*Commentarii de bello Gallico*
Cic: Cicero	*Arch.*	*Pro Archia*
	De Sen.	*De senectute*
	Off.	*De officiis*
	Tusc.	*Disputationes Tusculanæ*
Dante, *Divine Comedy*	*Inf.*	*Inferno*
	Purg.	*Purgatorio*
	Par.	*Paradiso*
Gellius	*Noct. Att.*	*Noctes Atticæ*

[14]From his *Dyer's Hand*, 1962.

Hor: Horace	*Ep.*	*Epistolæ*
	Epod.	*Epodi*
	Od.	*Odæ*
	Sat.	*Satiræ*
Milton	*Od. Nat.*	"Ode on the Morning of Christ's Nativity"
	C. D.	*Christian Doctrine*
Ovid	*A. A.*	*Ars Amatoria*
	Fast.	*Fasti*
	Met.	*Metamorphoses*
Pindar	*Nem.*	*Nemean Ode*
Pliny	*Nat. Hist.*	*Naturalis Historia*
Seneca	*Ep.*	*Epistolæ*
Soph: Sophocles	*Oed. T.*	*Oedipus Tyrannus*
Spenser	*Ecl.*	*Eclogues*, i.e., *The Shepheardes Calender*
	S. C.	*The Shepheardes Calender*
	F. Q.	*The Færie Queene*
Statius	*Theb.*	*Thebais*
Stradæ	*Prelu.*	*Prolusiones academica* of Famiano Strada
Virg.: Virgil	*Aen.*	*Aeneis*
	E.	*Eclogæ*
	G.	*Georgica*

PERIODICALS

JAP	*Journal of American Philology*
ELH	*[Journal of English Literary History]*
HLQ	*Huntingdon Library Quarterly*
JEGP	*Journal of English and Germanic Philology*
MLN	*[Modern Language Notes]*
N&Q	*Notes and Queries*
PMLA	*[Publications of the Modern Language Association of America]*
PQ	*Philological Quarterly*
RES	*Review of English Studies*
SP	*Studies in Philology*
TLS	*Times Literary Supplement*

LINE NOTES

1–14 See K. Rinehart, "A Note on the First Fourteen Lines of 'Lycidas,'" *N&Q*, CXCVIII (1953), 103, who calls the form of these lines "a broken sonnet, broken from the Italian sonnet pattern."

1 *Yet once more*: These words are to remind us that this is not the first poem of this sort written by our author. They refer, as I take it, to his poem "On the Death of a Fair Infant Dying of a Cough" (written *anno ætatis* 17, 1625), to his "Epitaph on Shakespeare" (written *anno ætatis* 22, 1630), and to his "Epitaph on the Marchioness of Winchester" (written whilst he was yet at Cambridge). PECK

An elegy on the death of the celebrated Countess of Pembroke, Sir Philip Sidney's sister, begins thus: "Yet once againe, my Muse." See *Songes and Sonnettes of Uncertain Auctours*, added to Surrey's and Wyat's Poems, edit. Tottell, fol. 85. . . . [The phrase] has a reference to [Milton's] poetical compositions in general, or rather to his last poem which was *Comus*. He would say, "I am again, in the midst of other studies, unexpectedly and unwillingly called back to poetry, again compelled to write verses, in consequence of the recent disastrous loss of my ship-wrecked friend, etc." Neither are the plants here mentioned, as some have suspected, appropriated to elegy. They are symbolical of general poetry. Theocritus, in an epigram which shall be cited in the next note, dedicates myrtles to Apollo. Doctor Newton, however, has supposed that Milton, while he mentions Apollo's laurel to characterize King as a poet, adds the myrtle, the tree of Venus, to show that King was also of "a proper age for love." . . . I would not exclude another probable implication: by plucking the berries and the leaves . . . he might intend to point out the pastoral or rural turn of his poem. WARTON

Milton had been compelled to forego the resolution to wait till time should ripen his powers and enable him to enter on that great poetic

251

work which he thought himself destined to achieve, "though of highest hope and hardest attempting." BROWNE

Milton's conceptions of a poet's work and of the preparation needed for it were of the highest. He was ever striving after "inward ripeness" (see "How Soon Hath Time . . .") and conscious how far he was from attaining it. . . . A little attention will show how these opening words cannot well be taken to mean, as by some readers and editors they are taken, "I am about to write another *In Memoriam* poem." It is true Milton had written a piece "On the Death of a Fair Infant Dying of a Cough" and also "An Epitaph on the Marchioness of Winchester"; but there is no manner of allusion to either of those poems here: laurels, and myrtles, and ivy are not funeral emblems. He should say, "I come to pluck your leaves, cypresses," if he wished to mention some sad sepulchral property; or "I come to cull flowers 'that sad embroidery wear.'" What he does say must mean, "Once more I must wear the poet's garland" (Comp. *Reas. of Ch. Gov.*: "For although a poet, soaring in the high reason of his fancies, with his *garland* and singing robes about him," etc.). HALES

See David S. Berkeley, "A Possible Biblical Allusion in 'Lycidas,' 1," *N&Q*, n.s. VIII (1961), 178, who cites Hebrews 12:26–7: "Yet once more I shake not the earth only, but also heaven. And this word, yet once more, signifieth . . ."

1, 2 *laurels, myrtles, ivy*: The laurel was sacred to Apollo, the god of learning; the myrtle, to Venus, the goddess of beauty; the ivy, to Bacchus, the god of wine; but here, by a more beautiful turn, they are all devoted to Lycidas, as a person full of learning, youth, and joy; and as he died young, gathered unripe to strew his cenotaph, which we may here suppose erected for him in the temple of the Muses. PECK

As evergreens they are also emblems of immortality, which is perhaps the leading idea intended to be conveyed. Cf. Drayton's *Pastoral Eclogue VI*: "nor mournful cypress nor sad widowing yew/ About thy tomb to prosper shall be seen;/ But *bay* and *myrtle*, which is ever new,/ In spight of winter flourishing and green." JERRAM

Cf. Virg. *E.* ii.54: "Et vos, o lauri, carpam, et te, proxima myrte."
. . . I am about again to invoke the Muses and write poetry. The laurel,
the myrtle, and the ivy were sacred to and the rewards of poets; and
the imagery here means: I come again for the poet's garland, but this is
not an occasion of my own choosing, but a forced one, and before the
mellowing year has matured for me such a wreath as I wish yet to wear.
BRADSHAW

Cf. Milton's "Epitaph on the Marchioness of Winchester" 55–58:
"Here be tears of perfect moan/ Wept for thee in Helicon,/ And some
Flowers and some Bays [i.e., laurels]/ For thy Hearse to strew the
ways." VERITY

Contrast Milton's confidence of winning the poet's laurel in "Ad
Patrem" 102: "Victricis hederas inter laurosque sedebo" ("I shall sit
with the ivy and laurel of a victor"). HUGHES

2 *Ye Myrtles brown*: *Brown* and *black* are classical epithets for the
myrtle: Theocritus *Epig.* i. 3; Ovid *A.A.* iii.690; Hor. *Od.* I.xxv.17.
WARTON

2 *Ivy*: as a reward of his learning: "doctarum ederae praemia
frontium" (Hor. *Od.* I.i.29). NEWTON

See Virg. *E.* vii.27 and viii.13: "Hanc sine tempora circum/ Inter
victrices hederam tibi serpere lauros." HALES

3 This beautiful allusion to the unripe age of his friend, in which
death "shatter'd his leaves before the mellowing year," is not antique,
I think, but of those secret graces of Spenser. [See "January" in *S.C.*]
The poet there says of himself under the name of Colin Clout, "Also
my lustful leaf is dry and sere," which explains too the old word in
the second line. RICHARDSON–NEWTON

Milton had most probably in his mind a passage in Cicero *De senectute*,
where the death of young persons is compared to unripe fruit plucked
with violence from the tree, and that of old persons to fully ripe mellow

fruit that falls naturally: "Et quasi poma ex arboribus, *cruda* si sint, *vi avellunter;* si matura et cocta, decidunt; sic vitam adolescentibus vis aufert, senibus maturitas." DUNSTER–TODD

3 *berries*: i.e., branches, with clusters of berries on them. He terms them "harsh and crude" perhaps simply on account of their bitterness. KEIGHTLEY

Those who imagine an allusion to the untimely death of Mr. King in the premature gathering of the laurels, etc., seem to overlook the fact that these plants represent, not the lost friend, but the verses offered to his memory. The metaphor by which an early death is compared to the plucking of unripe fruit (as in Cic. *De Sen.*) has therefore no application here, the reference being obviously to the poet's efforts in verse, which were, in his own opinion, yet "harsh and crude," but whose time of maturity a pious duty compelled him to forestall. Six years previously, in the Sonnet written at the age of twenty-three, he had expressed his resolution not to hasten the time of his "inward ripeness;" and in the accompanying letter he says: "I take no thought of being late, so it give advantage to be more fit." JERRAM

5 *mellowing year*: Here is an inaccuracy of the poet. The "mellowing year" could not affect the leaves of the laurel, the myrtle, and the ivy, which last is characterized before as "never sere." WARTON

6 So in Spenser *F.Q.* I.i.53: "Love of yourself, she said, and dear constraint/ Let me not sleep, but waste the weary night/ In secret anguish, and unpitied plaint." RICHARDSON–NEWTON

And Sidney thus addresses Time, *Arcadia* III: "Thou art the father of *occasion deare*." TODD

I.e., an occasion sad in itself, but concerned about a dear object (Spenser *F.Q.* I.i.53). But *dear* may mean "important," from its primary sense of "costly" (O.E. *deore*, G. *thueur*), an interpretation which is slightly favored by the occurrence of the word with the same meaning and connection in Sidney's *Arcadia*. Hence arose the peculiar use of "dear" in a sense apparently contradictory to its usual one, as in Shakespeare's "dearest foe," "dear peril," etc., which is to be explained ... by a natural transition from the original notion of importance into that of strong interest or emotion, whether of love or hatred.

The position of the noun between the two epithets is very common in Milton. . . . This order of words is imitated from the Greek. JERRAM

7 *compels*: instead of "compel," the "bitter constraint" and "sad occasion" being so nearly identical as to form one idea. . . . The Elizabethan writers and their immediate successors commonly made the verb agree in number with the nearest preceding noun. Many instances occur in the Bible, e.g., Prov. 1:27, and 2:6; Luke 5:10. JERRAM

8 Lycidas is the name of the shepherd in Theocritus's Idyl VII, and of one of the speakers in Virgil's Eclogue IX. It was used by later pastoral poets. VERITY

See E. E. Duncan-Jones, " 'Lycidas' and Lucan," *N&Q*, n.s. III (1956), 249, who cites *Pharsalia* iii. 638–639, as a possible source for the name.

8–9 The repetition resembles that in Spenser's *F.Q.* III.vi.45, and in his "Astrophel" 7–8: "Young Astrophel, the pride of shepherd's praise,/ Young Astrophel, the rustic lasses' love." BROWNE

See also Spenser's Eleventh Eclogue: "For dead is Dido, dead, alas! and drent;/ Dido the great Shepheard his daughter sheene." MASSON

9 *and hath not left his peer*: is the *quando ullum inveniet parem* of Hor. *Od.* I.xxiv.8. TUCKWELL

10 *he knew*: See John Diekhoff, " 'Lycidas,' Line 10," *PQ*, XVI (1937), 408–410, who explains the "he well knew" of the Trinity MS.

11 *build the lofty rhyme*: A beautiful Latinism, Hor. *Ep.* I.iii.24: "seu *condis* amabile carmen"; *A.P.* 436: "si carmina *condes*." NEWTON

"The lofty verse." This is unquestionably the sense of the word *rhyme* in *P.L.* I.16: "Things unattempted yet in prose or *rhyme*," from Ariosto *O.F.* I.ii: "Cosa non detta in *prosa* mai, ne in *rima*," where Harrington for once is a faithful and intelligent translator: "A tale in *prose* ne *verse* yet sung or said." WARTON

See Spenser *Ruines of Rome* XXV: "To builde, with levell of my loftie style,/ That which no hands can evermore compyle." TODD

The common spelling of this word (i.e., *rhyme*) owes its origin to a pedantic formation from Greek *rhythmos*, made by those who claimed for it a Greek derivation, but it is really the O.E. *rim*, "number," and the true orthography is *rime*, as Milton spelled it in the MS. JERRAM

12 *wat'ry bier*: So Jonson in *Cynthia's Revells* I.ii.58: "Sing some mourning straine/ Over his watrie hearse." WARTON

So Phineas Fletcher, of the dying swan, *Purple Island* I.xxx, "And, chaunting her own dirge, tides on her watry herse." TODD

14 *melodious tear*: *Tear* in this passage means a funeral elegy. Thus Harvey's verses on the death of Sir Thomas Smith are entitled *Musarum Lachrymae*. TODD

Compare the Heliconian "tears of perfect moan" in "An Epitaph on the Marchioness of Winchester," 55. HUGHES

15, 16 He means Hippocrene, a fountain consecrated to the Muses on mount Helicon, on the side of which was an altar of Heliconian Jupiter, as Hesiod says in the invocation for his poem on the generation of the gods: "Begin we from the Muses still to sing,/ That haunt high Helicon, and the pure spring,/ And altar of great Jove, with printless feet/ Dancing surround." This altar Milton calls the *seat* of Jupiter in imitation of the ancients. So Virgil calls the temple of Venus Erycina on the summit of Mount Eryx in Sicily, her *seat*, *Aen.* v.759: "Tum vicina astris Erycino in vertice *sedes*/ Fundatur Veneri. . . ." As he says *well* for *fountain*, using the old Anglo-Saxon word, which is often used in Chaucer and Spencer. RICHARDSON–NEWTON

Browne, in his *Brittania's Pastorals* (I.v.905), as Mr. Dunster also notices, calls Helicon "the *sacred well*." But Milton seems to have likewise borne in mind the poetry of Spenser, both in regard to Helicon and the address to the Muses. . . . See the *Teares of the Muses*, where the "sacred Sisters nine" are addressed as having poured forth their plaints as they "did sit beside the silver springs of Helicone." And at the end of the address, the poet calls on Clio to commence the doleful lay: "*Begin*, thou eldest Sister of the crew." Still Milton had in remembrance here his favorite Euripides, *Hipp.* 757. TODD

But here the allusion is to Pieria, the spring near Mount Olympus. BROWNE

No doubt in availing himself of Hesiod's hint, the poet wished to closely connect the Muses and their well with their great father—to connect the ministers of inspiration with its supreme author . . . In *P.L.* I.10–12 and III.25–32, he institutes a sort of analogy between the Aonian Mount and its waters, on the one hand, and Zion and its waters, on the other. As "Siloa's brook" flows "fast by the Oracle of God," so here he makes the Gentile stream spring from beneath the seat of Jove. HALES

The "sacred well" is Aganippe on Mount Helicon . . . and not, as Keightley supposes, "a fount of the poet's own creation," and the "seat of Jove" is the altar upon the same hill . . . Cf. "Il Penseroso" 47, 48; Spenser *Ecl.* IV.41, where the name of the mountain is transferred to the spring. "Well" in the sense of a natural fount occurs only here and in *P.L.* XI.416 (from Psalms 36:9). JERRAM

I.e., the Pierian Spring at the foot of Mount Olympus in Thessaly, the great Homeric seat of the Gods. This was the original birthplace and abode of the Muses, daughters of Zeus and Mnemosyne; though afterwards their worship was transferred to Mount Helicon in Boeotia, with its fountains Aganippe and Hippocrene. MASSON

In the Second Prolusion, he found a symbol of the divine harmony of the universe in the story—which "has prevailed from the very beginning of things . . . about the Muses dancing day and night about the altar of Jove." HUGHES

17 *sweep*: "E qui Calliopea alquanto surga," Dante *Purg*. i.9. MITFORD

19–22 See James A. S. Barrett, "A Line in 'Lycidas,'" *TLS*, Jan. 11, 1934, p. 28; and G. M. Gathorne-Hardy, a letter in *TLS*, Jan. 18, 1934, p. 44.

20 *Lucky words*: is the Latin *bona verba*. . . . and the liturgical *Favete linguis*, "speak lucky words or none" (Hor. *Od*. III.i.2), was a charge pronounced by the priest in opening the mysteries. TUCKWELL

See George O. Marshall, Jr., "Milton's 'Lycidas,' 15–22," *Explicator*, XVII (1959), no. 9, Item 66, who says Milton used the word in the sense of "having an unstudied or unsought felicity," a meaning the *OED* cites for 1700.

21 *he*: *He* for the Muse seems extraordinary. NEWTON

Muse is here used for the poet inspired by her. BROWNE

22 *my sable shroud*: Mr. Dunster has little doubt that Milton here means the "dark grave," *shroud* being the Miltonic word for "recess," "harbor," "hiding place." Yet he has overlooked the passages in Sylvester which occasioned, in my opinion, the introduction of *sable shroud* into Milton's monody. Cf. *Bethulian's Rescue* IV.13: "Still therefore, cover'd with a *sable shrowd*/ Hath she kept home; as to all Sorrow vow'd." In Sylvester's translation of *Du Bartas* we find: "O happy pair! upon your *sable toomb*/ May Mel and Manna ever showring come," and what further confirms me . . . is a passage from a funeral elegy of Sylvester: "From my sad cradle to my *sable chest*,/ Poor pilgrim I did finde few months of rest." TODD

There seems to be no necessity for rejecting the usual interpretation of "shroud" in the sense of grave-clothes. . . . As Milton's use of the word (as a noun) is confined to this and three other passages (*Comus* 147; *Od. Nat.* 218; *P.L.* X.1068), in all of which the context shows that it is employed metaphorically, these references prove nothing as to its meaning here. It may, however, mean the black pall that covers the coffin.   JERRAM

23   *For*: A new paragraph (as in l. 152) is often thus introduced; e.g., frequently in Lucretius; cf. "Namque canebat uti" (Virg. *E.*vi.32). But, Mr. Jerram takes these two lines as the conclusion of the invocation and says that the new paragraph begins with l. 25. Few readers will, I think, agree with him. The connection between "self-same hill," "same flock," and "together both" is so close that any decided break at the end of l. 24 ruins the rhythm of the thought, to say nothing of the fact that this passage of fourteen lines has probably an intentional similarity to a sonnet (as do lines 1–14, 50–63, 64–77).   COTTERILL

26   *opening eye-lids of the morn*: This personalizing everything that is the subject of imagination is a great part of the merit of ancient poetry. The present place is from Job, the most poetical of all books. Job curses the day in which he was born: "Let the stars of the twilight thereof be dark, let it look for light but have none, neither let it see the dawning of the day." The Hebrew (that Milton always follows) hath "neither let it see the eye-lids of the morning" (3:9).   RICHARDSON–NEWTON

opening eye-lids of the morn: Perhaps from Thomas Middleton's *Game at Chesse*, an old forgotten play, published about the end of the reign of James I, 1625: "Like a Pearl,/ Dropt from the *opening eyelids of the morn*/ Upon the bashful rose."   WARTON

Henry More and Sylvester used the same phrase, which occurs also in Sophocles *Antigone* 103. Cf. *Comus* 978; Sonnet II 5; "Il Penseroso" 141.   BROWNE

28   *What time*: "at the time when," *quo tempore*. Once a common idiom; cf. Psalms 56:3: "What time I am afraid, I will trust in thee." VERITY

Gray-fly: a brownish kind of beetle powdered with a little white commonly known by the name of the cock-chaffer or dor-fly. These in the hot summer months lie quiet all day feeding upon the leaves of the oaks and willows, but about sunset fly about with just such a sort of noise as answers the poet's description. The author could not possibly have chosen a circumstance more proper and natural for a shepherd to describe a summer's evening by, nor here expressed it in a more poetical manner. THYER–NEWTON

"We continued together till *noon*, and from thence, etc." The Gray-fly is called by the naturalists, the *Gray-fly* or *Trumpet-fly*. Here we have Milton's "horn," and "sultry horn" is the sharp hum of this insect at noon, or the hottest part of the day. But by some this has been thought the chaffer, which begins its flight in the evening. WARTON

A writer in the *Edinburgh Review* (July, 1868), suggests that the "gray-fly" may be the grig or cricket, O.E. *græg-hama*, i.e., "gray-coat," from it color. JERRAM

28 *sultry horn*: according to the classical usage by which an epithet is employed for an adverbial phrase denoting time. JERRAM

29 *Batt'ning*: See Edgar F. Daniels, "Milton's *Lycidas*, 29," *Explicator*, XXI (1963), Item 43, who suggests the meaning "enclosing."

30 Keightley remarks that the evening star "*appears*, not *rises*, and it is never anywhere but *on* 'heaven's descent,' " and he endeavours to save Milton from the charge of astronomical inaccuracy by interpreting the allusion of *any* star that rose about sunset. But the passage (*F.Q.* III. iv.51) "the golden *Hesperus* was mounted high in top of heaven sheen," which Keightley himself quotes in his note on *Comus* 93, shows that another poet was in fact guilty of the same error. Probably both remembered the *aulios aster* of Apollonius. (*Arg.* iv.1630), which is the same as Hesperus; and it is no necessary imputation of ignorance against Milton to suppose that he meant this star both here and in the *Comus*, since he was far more likely to have erred in company with the ancients than to have corrected their mistakes by the light of modern discovery. JERRAM

Milton evidently knew but little of stars, flowers, or animals, as Virgil, Dante, and Wordsworth knew them. As Dryden says, he regarded nature through the "spectacles of books." By the evening-star (Vesper or Hesperus) the planet Venus is generally meant, though Mercury, which is smaller and still nearer the sun, is sometimes given that name. Now, as the orbit of Venus lies between us and the sun, we have always to look somewhat in the direction of the sun to see her. As seen by us, she is never more than 48° from the sun. Consequently, at sunset her westering wheel has always travelled *at least* 42° (nearly half-way) down "heaven's descent," and is often much lower; so she does not "rise at evening," but appears in the western sky as the sunlight fails. COTTERILL

31 *westering wheel*: Drawing towards the west. A word that occurs in Chaucer *Troilus and Creseide* II.905: "the sonne/ Gan westrin fast and dounward for to wrie." NEWTON

Under the accepted interpretation "*any* star that so rose" will do. But Milton's known exactness is not satisfied with so easy an explanation that neglects the "westering wheel" as a mark of identification. To conceive of any star, a mere point of light, as a wheel would strain imagination, especially when such a conception is unnecessary. The words, I think, point to Arcturus, the brightest star in the constellation Bootes, the Waggoner, driver of the Wain (Ursa Major) (Homer *Il.* xviii.487–489, and Milton *Elegy V* 35,36). In the latitude of London the Wain does not set, but on the margin of the sky the wheel farther from the pole, sweeping around westward, seems down a slope from the wheel nearer the pole. "Westering," therefore, does not mean "passing to the west," as lexicographers instruct us, but "circling the west." This way of marking time in the night is one of extreme Arcadian simplicity and coincides with that in "Il Penseroso" 87. John A. Himes, *MLN*, XXXV (1920), 440.

33 *Temper'd to th' Oaten Flute*: Boethius III.12: "Illic blanda sonantibus/ *Chordis* carmina *temperans*." RICHARDSON–NEWTON

Probably the use is traceable to the *tennuis avena* of Virg. *E.* i.2. VERITY

34   *Rough Satyrs danc'd, and Fauns*: The like effects ascribed to
Silenus his singing. Virg. *E.* vi.27: "Tum vero in numerum Faunosque
ferasque videres/ Ludere." [Then, indeed, you might see Fauns and
fierce beasts play in rhythm."—Fairclough]   NEWTON

36   *old Damœtas*: Probably Dr. William Chappell, who had been
tutor to them both at Cambridge, and was afterwards Bishop of Cork
and Ross in Ireland.   NEWTON

Old Damœtas is a character in Sidney's *Arcadia*, the master of the
young shepherd Dorus, and described as a "suspicious, uncouth, arrant,
doltish clown." If Milton had this Damœtas in mind, the allusion to
Chappell under that name may possibly show that he had not quite
forgotten the old disagreement with his tutor which led to his temporary
"rustication" in 1626 (see *Elegy I* 11–20).   JERRAM

"Old Damœtas" may be . . . Dr. Bainbridge, the master [of Christ's]
. . . Chappell . . . was now Provost of Trinity College, Dublin; but
Joseph Meade, the Apocalyptic Commentator, who must have been
well known to them both, was still a fellow of the college, and one of the
noted characters of Cambridge. The pastoral name *Damœtas*, taken
from the Sixth Idyll of Theocritus and the Third Eclogue of Virgil,
has a sound of "Meade" in it.   MASSON

See Marjorie Nicolson, "Milton's 'Old Damœtas,' " *MLN*, XLI
(1926), 293–300, who suggests that by Damœtas Milton meant Joseph
Meade.

See E. S. De Beer, "Milton's Old Damœtas," *N&Q*, CXCIV (1949),
336–337, who notes that "Dametos" in Sidney's *Arcadia* ("first
eclogues") was an old man who presided over and judged the sports.

See Donald Leman Clark, "John Milton and William Chappell,"
HLQ, XVIII (1954–1955), 329–351, who supplies extensive information
about Chappell and his works and speculates about Milton's relations
with him.

See Harris Fletcher, "Milton's 'Old Damœtas,' " *JEGP*, LX (1961),

250–257, who suggests three possibilities: 1) William Chappell, tutor to Milton and King, 2) Michael Honywood, another tutor at Christ's, and 3) Abraham Wheelock, a young Cambridge poet.

39 *thee Shepherd, thee*: Lucretius and Virgil [*G.* iv.466], in similar repetitions, are here obvious. But see also Spenser's translation of Lucretius's address, in the opening of his first book to Venus: "*Te, dea, te* fugiunt venti, *te*, etc." *F.Q.* IV.x.44: "*Thee*, goddess, *thee* the winds, the clouds doe feare." But the passage most similar . . . in the opinion of Mr. Dunster [is] the lamentation for Orpheus in Ovid *Met.* xi.43: "*Te* mœstea volucres, Orpheu; *te* turba ferarum,/ *te* rigidi silices, etc." TODD

Resembling the opening lines of Spenser's "Colin Clout's Come Home Again." BROWNE

40 The common imagery under which the vine is represented is her marriage to her husband, elm; so that the poet represents her luxuriance, and leaving him to ramble after other supports, as "gadding abroad." WARBURTON–NEWTON

Gadding here simply describes the straggling nature of the vine (Cic. *De Sen.*, "Multiplici lapsu et *erratico*"), without any allusion to her desertion of the marital elm, as Warburton suggests (Hor. *Od.* IV.v.30; *Epod.* ii.10; Catullus lxii.49). *Gad*, from sb. *gad*, "a goad" (cf. "*gad-fly*"), Icel. *gaddr*, meant "to drive about," and was once common. Warton quotes from a Norfolk Register of 1534 "the *Gadynge* with S. Marye Songe," i.e. the going about with a carol to the Virgin. *Gadlyng* = "vagrant" in Chaucer, Wyatt, etc. Cf. . . . Bacon, *Essays*, "Envy is a gadding poison." The word is however specially used of wives roving from home, as in *Ecclus.* xxxv.25; xxvi.8, etc. A poet of the sixteenth century (probably John Heywood) speaks thus in praise of his lady—

> At Bacchus' feast none her shall meet,
> Ne at no wanton play;
> Nor gazing in the open street,
> Nor *gadding* as astray.

JERRAM

See A. S. Cook, " 'Lycidas,' 40 ff," *MLN*, XV (1900), 255, who refers to Virg. *E*. iv.19: "errantis hederas."

44   Cf. Virg. *E*. vi.28: "Tum rigidas motare cacumina quercus" ([While Silenus sang you might see] rigid oaks wave their tops.")

49   *to shepherd's ear*: As in Shakespeare *M.N.D.* I.i: "More tunable than lark to shepherd's ear." TODD

Todd ought to have quoted the next line to complete the parallelism: "When wheat is green, when hawthorn buds appear." MASSON

52, 53   *the steep,/ Where your old Bards*: Mr. Richardson's conjecture upon this passage, I think, is the best I have seen, that this . . . is a place called *Kerig y Drudion* in the mountains of Denbighshire, or *Druids stones*, because of the stone-chests or coffins, and other monuments there in abundance, supposed to have been of the Druids. See Camden [*Britannia*]. NEWTON

The *steep* is perhaps Penmaenmawr, which overhangs the sea opposite Anglesea. KEIGHTLEY

53   *Bards, the famous Druids*: The Bards and the Druids are distinguished by most authors, but Milton speaks of them as the same, and probably as priests they were Druids, and as poets they were Bards. For Cæsar, who has given us the best and most authentic account of the ancient Druids, says that among other things they learn a great number of verses: "Magnum ibi numerum versuum ediscere dicuntur" (*B.G.* VI.xiii). NEWTON

Cf. Milton's Latin epistle to Manso 42–43: "The Druids, an ancient folk occupied with the rites of the gods, used to sing the praises of heroes and their deeds so worthy of emulation." HANFORD

54   *Mona*: The isle of Anglesea was for a long time the principal residence of the Druids. Selden saith, "They made choice of it for its thick woods and groves, whence it was then called Inis-Dowil, the

dark isle." See his account of the name, profession, sacrifice, places of assembling, and subversion of the Druids, in his notes on Drayton's *Polyolbion*, Song IX. PECK

That the island was formerly well-wooded (cf. "*shaggy* top"), though now bare, we know from Tacitus. VERITY

55 *Deva*: Spenser (in the catalogue of English rivers who were present at the marriage of the Thames and Medway) mentions, "The *Dee*, which *Britons* long agone/ Did call divine." (*F.Q.* IV.xi.39). But Drayton is very full to our purpose:

> A Brook, it was suppos'd much bus'nesse to have scene,
> Which had an antient bound twixt *Wales* and *England* been,
> And noted was by both to be an *om'nous* Flood,
> That changing of his foards, the future ill, or good,
> Of either country told; of eithers warre, or peace;
> The sicknesses, or the health; the dearth, or the increase.
>
> (*Polyolbion*, Song X, 203) PECK

In Spenser the river Dee is the haunt of magicians. Merlin used to visit old Timon, in a green valley under the foot of the mountain Rauranvaur in Merionethshire, from which this river springs (*F.Q.* I.ix.4). The Dee has been made the scene of a variety of ancient British traditions. The city of Chester was called by the Britons the "Fortress upon Dee," which was feigned to have been founded by the giant Leon, and to have been the place of king Arthur's magnificent coronation.

But there is another and perhaps a better reason why Deva's is a "wisard stream." In Drayton this river is styled the "hallowed," and the "holy," and the "ominous flood." *Polyolbion*, Songs IV, IX, and X. . . . Compare Spenser as above, IV.xi.39; and Browne, in his *Britannia's Pastorals*, II, v. In our author's "At a Vacation Exercise," Dee is characterized, "ancient *hallowed* Dee" (line 91). Much superstition was founded on the circumstance of its being the ancient boundary between England and Wales: and Drayton, in his "Tenth Song," having recited this part of its history, adds, that by changing its fords, it foretold good or evil, war or peace, dearth or plenty, to either country. He then introduces the Dee, over which king Edgar had been rowed by eight kings, relating the story of Brutus. See also Songs III and XII. But in the "Eleventh Song," Drayton calls the Weever, a river of Cheshire, "the *wisard* river," and immediately subjoins, that in "prophetic skill" it vies with the Dee, Song XI. Here we seem to have the origin and the precise meaning of Milton's appellation. In *Comus*, *wisard* also signifies a "diviner" where it is applied to Proteus, v. 872: "By the Carpathian *wisard*'s hook."

Milton appears to have taken a particular pleasure in mentioning this venerable river. In the beginning of his first Elegy, he almost goes out of his way to specify his friend's residence on the banks of the Dee; which he describes with the picturesque and real circumstance of its tumbling headlong over rocks and precipices into the Irish sea. . . .

In the midst of this wild imagery, the tombs of the Druids, dispersed over the solitary mountains of Denbighshire, the shaggy summits of Mona, and the wisard waters of Deva, Milton was in his favorite track of poetry. He delighted in the old British traditions and fabulous histories. But his imagination seems to have been in some measure warmed, and perhaps directed to these objects, by reading Drayton; who in the Ninth and Tenth Songs of his *Polyolbion* has very copiously enlarged, and almost at one view, on this scenery. It is, however, with great force and felicity of fancy, that Milton, in transferring the classical seats of the Muses to Britain, has substituted places of the most romantic kind, inhabited by Druids, and consecrated by the visions of British bards. And it has been justly remarked how coldly and unpoetically Pope, in his very correct pastorals, has on the same occasion selected only the "fair fields" of Isis, and the "winding vales" of Cam.

But at the same time there is an immediate propriety in the substitution of these places which should not be forgotten and is not, I believe, obvious to every reader. The mountains of Denbighshire, the Isle of Man, and the banks of the Dee are in the vicinity of the Irish seas where Lycidas was shipwrecked. It is thus Theocritus asks the nymphs how it came to pass that when Daphnis died they were not in the delicious vales of Peneus, or on the banks of the great torrent Anapus, the sacred water of Acis, or the summits of mount Etna: because all these were the haunts or the habitation of the shepherd Daphnis. These rivers and rocks have a real connection with the poet's subject. WARTON

56   *Ay me*: "Ah me" in first ed., but "Ay me" is more pastoral.
PECK

56, 57   So these lines stand [i.e., so punctuated] in editions 1638, 1645, and 1673, the two last of which were printed under Milton's eye. Doctor Newman thus exhibits the passage:

> Ah me! I fondly dream
> Had ye been there, for what could that have done?

And adds this note: "We have here followed the pointing of Milton's manuscript in preference to all the editions; and the meaning plainly is, I fondly *dream of your having been there*, for what would that have signified?" But surely the words *I fondly dream had ye been there* will not bear this construction. The reading which I have adopted, to say nothing of its authority, has an abruptness which heightens the present sentiment, and more strongly marks the distraction of the speaker's mind. "Ah me! I am fondly dreaming! I will suppose you had been there—*but why should I suppose it*, for what could that have availed?" The context is broken and confused, and contains a sudden ellipsis which I have supplied with the words in italics.   WARTON

Surely Milton here but imitates the Latin *sed enim* (Greek *alla gar*), and uses *for* where *but* is more usual.   COTTERILL

See C. Alphonso Smith, "A Note on the Punctuation of 'Lycidas,' " *MLN*, XI (1896), 55, who says "Had ye been there" is the object of "dream."

58   *Orpheus*: was the son of the muse Calliope. It is said the Mœnades, the priestesses of Bacchus, tore him to pieces in the time of their sacrificing because he sang the praises of all the gods but him. Others say that all the women in general joined with these priestesses because, out of sorrow for the loss of his wife, he abandoned the company of all other women and persuaded others to do the like. Ovid goes farther and suggests a *pœderastia* for the reason

> Ille etiam Thracum populis fuit auctor amorem
> In teneros transferre mares—[*Met.* x.83]

It is added they threw his head and harp into the river Hebrus, which were thence born down by the stream to Lesbos. The harp, having seven strings (which represented the planets), was given him by his father Apollo. It was taken up into heaven and graced with nine stars, by the nine Muses. And Orpheus himself was turned into a swan. PECK

See *P.L.* VII.37. Lycidas, as a poet, is here tacitly compared with Orpheus. They were both victims of the water. WARTON

For the story see Ovid *Met.* xi.1–55, 61. This passage is partly repeated in *P.L.* VII.34ff. JERRAM

See C. W. Mayerson, "The Orpheus Image in 'Lycidas,' " *PMLA*, LXIV (1949), 189–207.

See David S. Berkeley, "The Revision of the Orpheus Passage in 'Lycidas,' " *N&Q*, n.s. V (1958), 335–336.

60   *Universal nature*: So "universal Pan" in *P.L.* IV.266.   WARTON

62   *gory visage*: See Rudolf B. Gottfried, "Milton and Poliziano," *N&Q*, n.s. V (1958), 195–196, who suggests that Milton's choice of "gory visage" was influenced by his knowledge of the Orpheus story in Poliziano's *Nutricia*.

63   *the swift Hebrus*: In calling Hebrus "swift," Milton, who is avaricious of classical authority, appears to have followed a verse in the *Æneid* i.321: "*Volucremque* fuga prævertitur *Hebrum.*" But Milton was misled by a wrong although a very ancient reading. Even Servius, in his comment on the line, with an aggravation instead of apology, blames his author for attributing this epithet to Hebrus, "Nam *quietissimus* est, etiam cum per hiemem crescit." . . .
When Milton copies the ancients, it is not that he wants matter of his own, but because he is fond of showing his learning; or rather, because the imagery of the ancients was so familiar to his thoughts. WARTON

Milton, I conceive, might be influenced, in the introduction of this disputed expression, not by the Virgilian passage, but by the words of an almost contemporary poet. See a copy of hexameter verses in Davison's *Poetical Rapsodie* (ed. 1611, p. 164): "As when Calliope's dear sonne . . . / Swift flowing Hebrus . . . ." TODD

The rapidity of this particular river has little to do with the matter; swiftness was a general attribute of rivers, and therefore became a commonplace poetical epithet of them. Thus in Virg. *Aen.* iii.76 Myconus is called "celsa," but "humilis" in Ov. *Met.* vii.463.   JERRAM

64-84   See J. Milton French, "The Digressions in Milton's 'Lycidas,'" *SP*, L (1953), 485-490, who suggests that this passage and 113-131 are "probably the core of the poem."

65   *the homely slighted Shepherds trade*: Cf. Spenser's *Shepheardes Calendar*, "June" 67: "And holden scorne of homely shepherds quill." TODD

66   Virg. *E.* i. 2: "Musam meditaris." "The thankless Muse," that earns no thanks, is not thanked by the ungrateful world; as *ingratus* in Latin is used in a passive as well as active signification. Virg. *Aen.* vii.425: "I nunc, *ingratis* offer te, irrise, periclis." NEWTON

Cf. *Comus* 547: "To meditate my rural minstrelsy."   BROWNE

Virgil ["musam meditaris"] meant simply "compose a *song*," a meaning which "Muse" will not bear in English, although it cannot go with "meditate" in any other sense. It is therefore doubtful whether Milton intended "thankless" to be intransitive, i.e., "the poetry which gets no thanks," or transitive, i.e., "the Muse who though courted with pains yet proves ungrateful."   JERRAM

67-69   *Were it not better done*, etc.: In this passage, hitherto not exactly understood, [Buchanan], who unbecomingly prolonged his "amorous descant" to graver years, is obliquely censured by Milton.

The Amaryllis to whom Milton alludes is the Amaryllis of Buchanan, the subject of a poem called "Desiderium Lutitiæ," a fond address of considerable length from an importunate lover: "O formosa Amarylli, tuo jam septima bruma/ Me procul aspectu, etc." It is allowed that the common poetical name *Amaryllis* might have been naturally and accidentally adopted by both poets; nor does it at first sight appear that Milton used it with any restrictive or implicit meaning. But Buchanan had another mistress whom he calls *Neæra*, whose golden hair makes a very splendid figure in his verses, and which he has complemented more than once in the most hyperbolical style. In his last Elegy, he raises the following extravagant fiction on the luxuriant tangles of this lady's hair. Cupid is puzzled how to subdue the icy poet. His arrows can do nothing. At length he hits upon the stratagem of cutting a golden lock from Neæra's head while she is asleep, with which the poet is bound; and thus "entangled" he is delivered a prisoner to Neæra (*El.* IX). This fiction is again pursued in his Epigrams (I, xlv). And to this Neæra many copies are addressed both in Buchanan's Epigrams, and in his Hende-capyllaths. Milton's insinuation "as others use" cannot therefore be doubted. . . . It should be remembered that Buchanan was now a popular and familiar modern Latin classic and that Milton was his rival in the same mode of composition. And of our author's allusions to him, instances have before occurred, and will occur again. I am obliged to an unknown critic for the leading idea of this very just and ingenious elucidation of a passage in "Lycidas." WARTON

It is true that the Amaryllis of Buchanan represents the city of Paris, and not an actual lady; but Milton may easily have overlooked or ignored this fact. The probability of the reference is strengthened by the first MS reading, "*Hid in* the tangles," etc., since our poet would hardly have committed the absurdity of representing a lover sporting with one mistress and at the same time being entangled in the hair of another, unless some such literary association had confused the two names in his mind. JERRAM

67 *Were it not better done*: These lines are modeled on Virg. *E.* ii. 14,15: "Were it not better to have endured the scorn of haughty Amaryllis?" HANFORD

67   *As others use*: alluding to the fashionable erotic poetry of the day (as represented by Herrick, Wither, Lovelace, etc.), with which Milton's severer taste did not accord.   JERRAM

68, 69   *Amaryllis and Neæra*: are two of the common representative names in ancient pastoral song. Cf. Virg. *E.* i.31; ii.14; iii.3,81; ix.22. *Amaryllis* (Greek ἀμαρύσσω), the "sparkling beauty," is the subject of Theocritus's Third Idyll. Both names occur together in *Ariosto O.F.* xi.12.   JERRAM

The names are mentioned by Spenser in *Colin Clouts Come Home Againe.*   HANFORD

See J. W. Saunders, "Milton, Diomede, and Amaryllis," *ELH*, XXII (1955), 254–286.

69   *tangles*: Cf. Lovelace, "To Althea": "When I lie tangled in her hair."   HALES

See P. Maas, " 'Hid in' in 'Lycidas,' 69," *RES*, XIX, (1943), 397–398, who points out that "a courtesan called Neæra, whose hair is praised, appears in Hor. *Od.* III.xiv.21 [and *Epode* XV]."

See A. J. Schoeck, "Milton and Neæra's Hair," *N&Q*, n.s. III (1956), 190–191, who says that "many of the verses of the *Basia* of Joannes Secundus are addressed to a Spanish beauty whom Joannes called Neæra." In these well-known poems of the renaissance Neæra is a symbol of eroticism. See F. A. Wright, ed., *The Love Poems of Joannes Secundus* (New York, 1930). Only in Secundus is the hair tangled.

70, 71   *Fame is the spur*, etc.: The reader may see the same sentiment enlarged upon in *P.R.* III.25–30, and confirmed by numerous quotations from the heathen philosophers in a note by Mr. Jortin [Newton's and Jortin's notes on this passage in *P.R.* refer to Cicero *Arch.* X; *Off.* I.viii; and *Tusc.* V.xxxvi; Tacitus *Hist.* IV.vi ("Even in the case of wise men the desire for glory is last cut off"); Seneca *Ep.* V.xxi, cii, cxiii; Horace *Ep.* I.i; Marcus Aurelius *passim*; Epictetus *Enchir.* xlv; and Plato *Rep.* i.]   NEWTON

Mr. Gifford, the learned editor of Massinger's plays, notices a similar expression in the *Very Woman* (1634) (V, iv) of that author. TODD

See *Catiline* (1616): "Ambition, like a torrent, ne'er looks back,/ And is a swelling, and the last affection/ A high mind can put off." And Feltham, *Resolves* XV, "Of Fame" (1636): "Doubtless, even in this [Fame], man is ordered by a power above, which hath instructed in the minds of all men an ardent appetition of a lasting fame. Desire of glory is the last garment that even wise men lay aside. For this we may trust Tacitus." BRADSHAW

But Milton's line is an exact quotation from the play *Barnevelt* (1622). HANFORD

70 The expressions in this line may be compared with Spenser's *Teares of the Muses* 454: "Due *praise*, that is the *spur* of dooing well." And with Drummond's third sonnet for Galatia: "that dragon, which doth keep/ Hesperian fruit, the *spur* in you doth *raise*." *Clear spirit* occurs in *The Remonstrants' Defence*: "Certainly never any clear spirit nursed up from brighter influences, with a soul enlarged to the dimensions of spacious art and high knowledge, ever entered [the Cave of Mammon] but with scorn." Drayton, in one of his elegies, has the same expression (ed. 1631, p. 268): "Had not my *cleare spirit* in fortunes scorne/ Mee above earth and her affections borne." TODD

"Clear spirit" Keightley takes to mean "illustrious," It. *chiaro*. JERRAM

Fame is the spur, etc.: Mr. Bowle observes that Abate Grillo in his *Lettere* has called "Questa sete di fama et gloria, ordinaria *infirmita* de gli *animi generosi* (Lib. ii, p. 210, edit. Ven. 1604, 4to). WARTON

Such also is Sir Henry Wotton's observation in his *Panegyrick to King Charles*, speaking of King James I: "I will not deny his appetite of glory, *which generous minds do ever latest part from*." TODD

"Quasi hic subesset ingens *Cupido gloriae* quae *etiam* sapientibus *novissima* exuitur." *Stradae Prelu.* p. 161, ed. Ox. MITFORD

Cf. Peele *Battle of Alcazar* I.i: "Honour, the *spur* that pricks the princely mind/ To follow rule, and climb the stately chair." KEIGHTLEY

Cf. *P.R.* III.25: "glory, the reward/ That role excites to high attempts, the flame/ Of most erected spirits, most temper'd pure/ Ethereal, who all pleasures else despise,/ All treasures and all gain esteem as dross," and *P.L.* I.668: "Mammon, the least erected spirit that fell/ From heaven." A "clear spirit" is therefore one so "nursed up" and "erected" as to have breathed the pure ethereal atmosphere and to scorn the temptations of Mammon. . . . Cf. Virgil's "aurai simplicis ignem"—the pure ethereal flame. COTTERILL

See R. J. Schoeck, *N&Q*, n.s. II (1955), 235–237, who quotes John of Salisbury *Entheticus* (875): "Haec est praestantes quae deserit ultima mentes."

See H. MacL. Currie, "Silius Italicus' 'Fax Mentes Honestae' and Milton," *N&Q*, n.s. V (1958), 106–107.

See John S. Coolidge, "Boethius and 'That Last Infirmity of Noble Mind,' " *PQ*, XLII (1963), 176–182.

75 *blind Fury*: But what have the furies to do with the "abhorred shears"? The fates indeed (who may be elegantly called *fairies*) are often and not improperly said to be blind (because no man can foresee what his fate or fortune will be), and the "abhorred shears" are expressly said to belong to Atropos, one of the three. And for these reasons I read, "Blind fairie." PECK

Milton here has made the Fates the same with the Furies; which is not quite destitute of authority, for so Orpheus in his hymns, two of which are addressed to these goddesses, styles them. SYMPSON–NEWTON

Milton does not here confound the Fates and the Furies. He only calls Destiny a Fury. In Spenser we have "blind Fury." "Ruins of Rome" xxiv: "If the *blinde Furie* which warres breedeth oft." WARTON

Atropos, the Fate whose duty it was to cut the threads of men's lives after her sisters had spun them out. See "Arcades," 63–69. Milton called her *blind* because she works indiscriminately, like the goddess Fortune. He called her a Fury, perhaps thinking of Prometheus' saying that those who guide the helm of Necessity are the "Fates triple-formed, the Furies unforgetting" (Aeschylus *Prometheus* 516). HUGHES

76 *thin-spun life*: see Tibullus *Eleg.* I.vii.1,2: "Parcæ fatalia nentes/ Stamina, non ulli dissoluenda deo." HALES

But not the praise: Cf. *Shepheardes Calender*, "October" 13:

Cuddie   The dapper ditties that I wont devise
          To feede youthes fancie, and the flocking fry,
          Delighten much: what I the bett for thy?
          They han the pleasure, I a sclender prise:
          I beate the bush, the byrds to them doe flye:
          What good thereof to Cuddie can arise?
Pires   Cuddie, the prayse is better than the prise
          The glory eke much greater than the gayne.
                                                  HANFORD

77 Cf. Virg. *E.* vi. 3: "Cynthius aurem/ vellit et admonuit" [Apollo touched my ear and warned me" (i.e., against ambition)]. PECK

Conington [the commentator on Virgil] remarks that touching the ear was a symbolical act, the ear being the seat of memory. JERRAM

But Milton's "touched my trembling ears" is utterly different from Virgil's "aurem vellit," and involves a subtle meaning, the very opposite in effect to that in Virgil's lines. To this day it is a popular humour that the tingling of a person's ears is a sign that somewhere people are talking of him and saying good or ill of him in his absence. The superstition was an old one in Milton's time. "When our cheek burneth or ear tingleth," says Sir Thomas Browne, in his *Vulgar Errors* (V.23), "we usually say that somebody is talking of us; which is an ancient conceit, and ranked among superstitious opinions by Pliny: "Absentes tinnitu aurium præsentire sermones de se receptum est." I have no doubt that the significance of the phrase "my trembling ears" rests on this allusion. What Milton had been saying about poetic fame was evidently applicable to himself personally, and would, he saw, be so understood by his readers. He had therefore the sensation described; he felt, at that moment, as if absent people were weighing his words, and appraising, cooly, or perhaps ill-naturedly, the chances *he* had of ever obtaining the "fair guerdon." MASSON

Scholars will remember the "oppono auriculam" of Hor. *Sat.* i.9. The action denoted impressing something on the memory.
COTTERILL

The allusion is probably to the story of Midas, who, declaring that Pan was a better musician than Phœbus, had his ears changed by the offended god to those of an ass, to indicate his stupidity. Milton likens his own doubtful utterance to the foolishness of Midas, and his ears tremble in anticipation of Phœbus's reproof. Cf. the phrase "Midas ears" in the "Sonnet to Henry Lawes." HANFORD

78–84 I think I remember the sublime morality of part of this allegory in Pindar. But I cannot readily turn to the passage. WARTON

Cf. Pindar *Nem.* vii.45: "true honor is theirs whose glorious fame the god exalteth, an aid to their memory after death." JERRAM

79 As much as to say it is not leaf-gold, it is true sterling. Cf. Spenser *F.Q.* I.iv.4, and IV.v.15. NEWTON

Milton's words admit of a twofold construction. The first is—"Nor is it (Fame) set off to the world in (i.e., *by*) the glistering foil, nor does it lie (consist) in a wide reputation." In this case "foil" must be understood in a sense which it often bears elsewhere, of a dark substance (originally a thin *leaf* of metal), in which jewels were placed to set off their luster. . . . But this mode of taking the words fails to give a suitable meaning to the passage. It is not Fame itself which is "set off to the world," but the life and actions of the man, the display of which before the eyes of the public constitutes fame—at least according to the vulgar notion which Milton is here combatting. The true sense seems to be this: "Nor does it (true Fame) consist in the specious appearance *which is* displayed to the world, nor in a widespread renown." *Fame* will then be the subject of the verb *lies*, and *set off* a participle agreeing with *foil*; the preposition *in* before "glistering foil" will have the same construction and sense as the *in* before "broad rumour," both phrases being constructed after *lies*. And the meaning of "foil" will be, not exactly "leaf-gold," as Newton takes it, but *tinsel*, i.e., some baser metal which glitters like gold, and makes a fair show to the eye. [John] Scott [in *Critical Essays* (1785)] doubts "whether the metaphor of 'plant' is continued to this line or not," and imagines "a plant with leaves artificially gilded." Perhaps the idea of "foil" (*folium*) was suggested by the word "plant," but the metaphor itself is not resumed till l. 81 in the words "lives and spreads," which describe the growth of a tree. JERRAM

I believe Milton had in mind Virgil's description (*Aen.* vi) of the golden branch with its crackling leaves of *bractea* (thin metal, or foil), and that the sense is, "fame grows not on mortal soil nor in that glistering foil (with that glittering, tinsel-like foliage) which attracts the gaze of the world, not lies it spreading broad-expanded, like some great banian-tree, occupying the realm of human praise, but spreads *aloft*." COTTERILL

80–84 The lines bear comparison with St. Thomas Aquinas's faith in the beatific vision as the reward of those who are not blinded by earthly prizes (*Summa contra gentiles* III.lxiii.5) and with Dante's glimpse of the souls in the heaven of Mercury (*Par.* VI.112–117) who have striven after earthly glory and "thereby dimmed the beams of love." HUGHES

81 *by*: probably = "near," i.e., "in presence of." Shakespeare *Twelfth Night* III.i, "Thou mayest say the king lives *by* a beggar, if a beggar dwell *near* him." So we still say "hard *by*." This seems better than Keightley's explanation, "by means of." JERRAM

those pure eyes: Perhaps from Scripture [Habak. 1:13]: "God is of purer eyes than to behold iniquity." And hence an epithet sufficiently

hackneyed in modern poetry. *Comus* 213: "Welcome *pure-eyed* Faith."
WARTON

85 *Arethuse*: one of the Nereids, a companion of Diana, and beloved
of the river Alpheus. Diana turned her into a fountain, called after her
Arethusa, at Elis in Peloponnesus, whose waters, to avoid mixing with
the Alpheus, run underground by secret channels, and broke out again
about Syracuse in Sicily, whither also Alpheus pursues her. PECK

For the story of Arethusa see Ovid *Met.* v.579ff. JERRAM

In giving Arethusa the distinctive appellation of *fountain*, Milton
closely and learnedly attends to the ancient Greek writers. See more
particularly the scholiast on Theocritus *Idyll.* i.117. WARTON

85, 86 *Arethuse* and *Mincius*: Now Phœbus, whose strain was of a
higher mood, has done speaking, he invokes the fountain Arethuse of
Sicily, the country of Theocritus, and Mincius, the river of Mantua,
Virgil's country, which river he calls *honored flood* to show his respect
to that poet, and describes much in the same manner as Virgil himself
has done, *G.* iii.14: "Tardis ingens ubi flexibus errat/ Mincius, et tenera
prætexit arundine ripas" ["Where great Mincius wanders in slow
windings and fringes his banks with tender reeds."—Fairclough]. It
was the more necessary for him to call to mind these two famous pastoral
poets as now his own "oaten pipe proceeds." NEWTON

86 *Mincius*: a river of Venice, now called *Mencio* and *Menzo*;
which makes the city of Mantua, famous for the birth of Virgil, thence
called the *Mantuan swan*, the smoothness and music of whose verse is
here insinuated by the gentleness of the stream and the great plenty of
reeds growing on its banks. PECK

See A. S. Cook, "Four Notes," in *SP*, XVI (1919), 177–186, who
gives parallels for "smooth-sliding," "crown'd," and "vocall reeds."

87 *a higher mood*: "I'll tune my reed unto a higher key." Browne's
Brit. Past. IV.41. MITFORD

mood: = "character," from *modus*, signifying a particular arrangement of intervals in the musical scale, the study of which formed so important an element in the Greek system of education (Plato *Rep.* iii; Aristotle *Politics* viii). The word has nothing to do with a "mood" or "state of mind," Cf. *P.L.* I.550; *S.A.* 661. JERRAM

89 *Herald of the Sea*: i.e., Triton, son of Neptune by the nymph Salacia. He was a man to the middle and a dolphin below, with forefeet like a horse, and two circled tails. He swims (like a herald) before his father's chariot, sounding his conch. PECK

90 Keightley understands "Neptune's plea" to mean the judicial enquiry which Neptune deputed Triton to hold; and he instances the "Court of Common *Pleas*," etc., as examples of the word in this signification. But it seems better to take it in its usual sense of a statement made by the defendent to satisfy (*placere*) the court—here the excuse offered by Neptune and conveyed by Triton. Milton probably intended to represent Neptune himself as involved in the blame and desirous to clear himself by a strict enquiry applied to his subordinates. JERRAM

93 *question'd*: "And *question'd* each wind that came that way". Beaumont's *Psyche* XVIII.lvi. MITFORD

94 *each beaked promontory*: Cf. Drayton's *Polyolbion*, Song I: "The utmost end of Cornwall's furrowing *beak*." WARTON

Pliny *Nat. Hist.* x.49 uses "rostrum" for the promontory of an island in the Nile. JERRAM

96 *Hippotades*: is no very common or familiar name for Aeolus the son of Hippotas. It is not in Virgil, the great storm-painter, and who appears to be so perfectly acquainted with the poetical family of the winds. Perhaps I may be mistaken, but it occurs only in four classic poets: Homer (*Od.* x.2; v.36); Apollonius Rhodius, a Greek poet whom I have frequently traced in Milton (*Argon.* iv.819); in Ovid . . .; and in Valerius Flaccus (*Argon.* i.610). The name is seldom mentioned

even by the mythologists. I must not forget that it is found in the geographical poem of Dionysius, with an allusion to the *Odyssey* v.462. WARTON

Cf. Ovid *Met.* xiv.224: "Aeolon Hippoteden, cohibentem carcere ventos." HUGHES

sage: Hippotades is called *Sage* from foreknowing the weather. RICHARDSON–NEWTON

The epithet *sage* may refer to the prudence with which he is described governing the winds committed to his care; Virg. *Aen.*i.62: "qui fœdere certo/ Et premere et laxas *sciret* dare jussus habenas." DUNSTER –TODD

Richardson's is a later and rationalized form of the story, and one which Milton as a poet is not likely to have chosen, since even when writing history he professes himself unwilling to give up the myths entirely, rejecting only those which are "impossible and absurd" (*Hist. of Britain* I, and see Grote *Hist. of Greece* I.xvii). JERRAM

Called *sage* perhaps because Diodorus Siculus says that he invented sails and taught the art of predicting storms. (*Historical Library*, 5, 7). HUGHES

99 *Sleek Panope*: a sea-nymph: the word itself signifies that pure calm and tranquility that gives an unbounded prospect over the smooth and level brine; therefore *sleek* Panope. RICHARDSON–NEWTON

Alciphron *Ep.* I.xix.74, ed. Bergler. MITFORD

Panope is mentioned in the *Aeneid* v.240 as if she were the greatest of the Nereids and one of the gods who have "the empire of the sea." ... Milton's ultimate source was Hesiod's *Theogony* 240–64, but he was indebted to a later tradition for the idea that the Nereids befriended sailors. HUGHES

See C. W. Brodribb, "Milton and Valerius Flaccus," *N&Q*, CLXXV (1937), 299, who notes that Panope is a nymph in Valerius Flaccus.

100, 101   *that fatal and perfidius bark*, etc.: Although Doctor Newton mentions the "Ille et nefasto" [*Od*. II.xii.1] and "Mala soluta navis exit alite" [*Epod*. x.1] of Horace as two passages similar to this, yet he has not observed how much more poetical and striking is the imagery of Milton, that the ship was "built in the eclipse" and "rigged with curses." DR. J. WARTON–WARTON

100   See the inscription prefixed to the *Cambridge Verses* of 1638 [i.e., to the section of English poems in the *Justa Edovardo King*, the original collection of verses to King; this section is separately entitled]: "navi in scopulum allisa, *et rimis et ictu fatiscente*." JERRAM

Here (and perhaps elsewhere in "Lycidas") there may be a reminiscence of Propertius *Elegies* iii.7. F. R. B. Godolphin [*MLN*, XLIX (1934), 162–166] compares Propertius's doomed voyagers in the line (100) "portabat sanctos alreus ille viros" (*Elegies*, IV,vi,16). HUGHES

101   See G. G. L., "Milton! Built in th'eclipse ['Lycidas,' 100]," *N&Q*, CLXXIX (1940), 9 (and T. O. Mabbott, *ibid*., 141–142) on the possibility that *eclipse* means "the waning of the moon," a period of eight days.

103   *Next Camus, reverend sire*: The river Cam is fitly introduced upon this occasion, and is called *reverend sire*, as both Mr. King and Milton were educated at Cambridge. NEWTON

So in Spenser's *Pastorall Æglogue* the Thames, Humber, Severn, and other rivers mourn for their favorite bard Phillisides. Cowley, "Complaint" 6, speaks of "reverend Cam." "Sire" is the usual mythological designation of a river, as a presiding and protecting power. Cf. Livy ii.10: "Tiberine pater"; Virg. *Aen*. viii.31. JERRAM

Cf. Giles Fletcher, *Christ's Victorie on Earth*, 15: "At length an aged syre farre off He sawe/ Come slowely footing." VERITY

Milton makes Camus as mysterious and venerable as Virgil did the river god of the Tiber, the "Father Tiber" to whom Aeneas prays (*Aen.* viii.72). HUGHES

See J. Mitchell More, "A Pun in 'Lycidas,'" *N&Q*, n.s. V (1958), 211, who thinks "footing" includes a pun on "pedant."

went footing slow: The Cam is described according to the nature of that river. "Went footing slow," as it is a gentle winding stream, according to Camden, who says the British word *Cam* signifies crooked. NEWTON

Slow footing: is an expression of Spenser, *F.Q.* I.iii.10: "A damzel spyde *slow-footing* her before." But see Giles Fletcher's *Christ's Triumph on Earth* (stanza 15), to which Mr. Dunster refers: "At length an *aged sire* far off he saw/ Come *slowly footing*." *Footing slow*, Mr. Dunster observes, as meant to mark the sluggish course of the river Cam, is exactly Claudian's description of the Mincius, "*tardusque meatu Mincius.*" TODD

104 The Cam abounds with reeds and sedge, for which reason "His mantle [is] hairy, and his bonnet sedge." NEWTON

104, 105 Alluding to the fabulous traditions of the high antiquity of Cambridge. But how Cam was distinguished by a "hairy mantle" from other rivers which have "herds" and "flocks" on their banks, I know not—unless "the *Budge* doctors of the Stoic *fur*," as Milton calls them in *Comus*, had lent him their academic robes. WARBURTON–WARTON

See Milton's Elegy I: "Stat quoque iuncosas Cami remare paludes" (line 89) ["It is also fixed that I return to the sedgy marshes of the Cam"—Mackellar] and line 11: "Iam nec arundiferum mihi cura revisere Camum" ["Meanwhile I care not to revisit the reedy Cam"—Mackellar]. It would be difficult to ascertain the meaning of "figures dim." Perhaps the poet himself had no very clear or determinate idea, but in obscure and mysterious expressions leaves something to be supplied or explained by the reader's imagination. WARTON

Mr. Dunster remarks that on sedge leaves, or flags, when dried or even beginning to wither, there are not only certain *dim*, or indistinct, and dusky streaks, but also a variety of dotted marks "scrawl'd over" (as Milton had first written) on the edge, which withers before the rest of the flag. TODD

Editors speak of the "dusky streaks" on dried sedge. They are not very perceptible, and I do not believe Milton had eyes for such things. He was probably thinking of the "figures dim" on the oracular leaves of the Sibyl (*Aen*. v.74). COTTERILL

106 *sanguin flower inscribed with woe*: the hyacinth, which sprung according to the poets from the blood of the boy Hyacinthus or of Ajax; the leaves were imagined to be marked with the mournful letters *AI AI*. For these particulars you may consult the poets, especially Ovid *Met*. x.210 ff. NEWTON

Cf. Drummond, "Epitaph on Prince Henry": "That sweet flower that bears/ In sanguine spots the tenour of our woe." JERRAM

The flower is the ancient *hyakinthos*—probably are of the various "hyacinthi" mentioned by Virgil, or the "vaccinium"—but *not* the modern hyacinth. . . . [On the golden larkspur (*Delphinium Ajacis*, "larkspur of Ajax") the AIAI can be clearly seen.] At present I am inclined to think (1) that the original *hyakinthos* was a *dark* flower, that it is our dark-blue garden larkspur (a native of Greece and Asia Minor); (2) that this was what Virgil calls *vaccinium*; (3) that there may be other flowers with similar marks, which may have been regarded by later writers as the true *hyakinthos*. . . . Milton called it "sanguine" because the marks were said to be derived from the blood of Ajax or Hyacinthus. In the first draft of "Lycidas" he speaks of the "vermeil grain" of the same flower, and in his lines "On the Death of a Fair Infant," where he calls the flower "purple"—evidently Ovid's "purpureus," which may be anything between violet and scarlet. COTTERILL

Camus is personified as wearing an academic robe with colors like the dark reeds on its bank, but relieved by the crimson of a "sanguine flower," the hyacinth of Theocritus *Idy*. x.28. HUGHES

107   *my dearest pledge*: as children were simply called by the Latins *pignora*, pledges.   RICHARDSON–NEWTON

Mr. Bowle compares this line with one in the *Rime spirituali* of Angelo Grillo. It is a part of the Virgin's lamentation on the Passion of Christ: "Deh, disse, ove ne vai mio caro *pegno?*" "Alas, quoth he, where goest thou, my dear pledge?" And he adds that *reft* was here perhaps immediately taken from a passage in Spenser's "Daphnaida," (ll. 159–160) where the subject is the same: "And reft from me my sweet companion,/ And reft from me my love, my life, my hart." WARTON

Pignus in this sense is very common. . . . Milton has "pignora cara," Elegy IV 42. Cf. *P.L.* II.818; "At a Solemn Musick," 1; Spenser, *F.Q.* I.x.4; Bacon, *Essay on Marriage.*   JERRAM

108–131   From this . . . one would think our poet had read *Il divortio Celeste*, fathered (but some think not very justly) on Ferrante Pallavicini. The author, whoever he was, a Roman Catholic, supposes "That Jesus Christ, observing that the church of Rome his spouse, being become a prostitute to the lusts of many pontiffs, and particularly to Urban VIII, resolved to divorce himself from her and to cohabit no longer with an adultress. . . . Immediately upon the publication of this divorce, Luther, Calvin, and others go and offer their respective churches to Christ as a spouse for him, but Christ, calling to mind the injuries he had received from his Romish spouse, resolves for the future to lead a life of celibacy (Bayle, *Crit. Dict.* Vol. VIII. 127a).   PECK

109   *The pilot of the Galilean lake*: Milton finely raises the character of St. Peter by making him the *pilot* of the lake of Genesareth in Galilee. See how artfully he takes this hint from Luke 5:3.   RICHARDSON–NEWTON

It seems somewhat extraordinary to introduce St. Peter after Apollo, Triton, etc., a Christian bishop among heathen deities; but here Milton's imagination was dazzled, his taste corrupted, and his judgement perverted by reading the Italian poets.   NEWTON

In calling the apostle the "Pilot of the Galilean *Lake*" (i.e., inland sea, cf. Luke 8:22, 23) Milton may have used some medieval belief. VERITY

See E. S. de Beer, "St. Peter in 'Lycidas,' " *RES*, XXIII (1947), 60–63, who gives several reasons for St. Peter's presence in the poem.

See John M. Steadman, "St. Peter and Ecclesiastical Satire: Milton, Dante, and 'La Rapprisentazione del Di del Guidizio,' " *N&Q*, n.s. V (1958), 141–142.

See Ralph E. Hone, " 'The Pilot of the Galilean Lake,' " *SP*, LVI (1959), 55–61, who suggests that Milton here meant Christ, not St. Peter.

110, 111 *Two massy keys*, etc.: The *two keys* (which he hath likewise painted poetically) Christ himself gave him. See Matt. 16:19. RICHARDSON—NEWTON

Mr. Bowles thinks this an allusion to the Italian proverb "Con le chiavi d' oro s'apre ogna porta," to which one in Spanish corresponds. St. Peter's two keys in the Gospel seem to have supplied modern poetry with the allegoric machinery of two keys, which are variously used. In Dante's *Inferno* xiii, the ghost of a courtier of the Emperor Frederick tells Virgil that he had possessed two keys with which he locked and unlocked his master's heart. WARTON

Mr. Warton afterwards added, from Jonson's *Masque of Hymen*, the figure of Truth holding in her left hand "a curious bunch of *golden keys*,/ With which *Heaven's gate* she locketh and *displays*." . . . But Milton here perhaps, as in *Comus* also, had in view Phineas Fletcher's description of the Pope *Locusts* [iii.16]: "Three *mitred* crownes the proud Imposter weares,/ For he in earth, in hell, in heav'n, will raigne:/ And in his hand two *golden keys* he beares/ To *open* heav'n and hell, and *shut* againe." The same author, in his *Purple Island* [vii.61], gives Sedition "*two keys*, with which to open and shut the gates of heaven and hell." TODD

"In either hand she held a massie key. . . . The one of beaten burnish'd *gold*. . . . That in her left of swarthy *iron* is." Beaumont's *Psyche* XVI.cxl, cxli. MITFORD

The distinction between the two metals—one denoting the value of the benefits secured by admission, the other stern severity in exclusion—is our poet's own; in the parallel passage of Dante, *Purg.* ix.120ff., both a golden and a silver key are used by the angel to *open* the gate. The Italian proverb quoted by Mr. Bowles [see above] alludes to the influence of money, and has therefore nothing to do with the "power of the keys." JERRAM

112 *Miter'd locks*: It is much that this inveterate enemy of prelacy would allow Peter to be a bishop. But the whole circumstance is taken from the Italian satirists. Besides I suppose he thought it sharpened his satire to have the prelacy condemned by one of their own order. WARBURTON–NEWTON

It would be unfair to construe this admission of the *mitre* into a precise statement of Milton's religious views at this period or to [agree] with Warburton. . . . As St. Peter here speaks with episcopal authority, he is made to wear the distinctive dress of his order. JERRAM

114, 115 He here animadverts on the endowments of the church, at the same time insinuating that they were shared by those only who sought the emoluments of the sacred office, to the exclusion of a learned and conscientious clergy. See *P.L.* IV.193, 194, and the sonnet to Cromwell. During the usurpation he published a pamphlet entitled *The Likeliest Means to Remove Hirelings out of the Church*, against the revenues transferred from the old ecclesiastic establishment to the presbyterian ministers. WARTON

115 See John 10:8 ff.; and in l. 117 there seems to be an allusion to Jude 12, in the Greek. KEIGHTLEY

By intrusion into the fold Milton does not imply absence or invalidity of orders; his matured views concerning credentials were afterwards clearly set forth in the treatise on *Christian Doctrine*, chapters 29 and 31. These are a minister's "spiritual knowledge and sanctity of life," to be tested by previous trial, and the choice is to belong to the people collectively. JERRAM

Cf. John 10:1: "He that entereth not by the door into the sheepfold, but climbeth up some other way, the same is a thief and a robber." HANFORD

Cf. John Skelton's *Colin Clout* 75–81: "Laye men say indede/ How they take no hede/ Theyr sely shepe to fede,/ But plucke away and pull/ The fleeces of theyr wull,/ Vnethes they leue a locke/ Of wull amonges theyr flocke." HUGHES

See A. S. Cook, " 'Lycidas,' 113 ff.," *MLN*, XVI (1901), 92, who refers to Bale's characterization of John Capgrave (*Script. Illus.*, p. 582): 'Not shepherds but hirelings, who leave the sheep to the wolves, caring only for the milk and fleece."

118 Cf. Matt. 22:8: "they which were bidden were not worthy." HANFORD

119 *Blind mouthes! that scarce themselves know how to hold*, etc.: See instances of the like construction in *P.L.* V.711–718; Psalms 54:7; Matt. 20:15; Prov. 30:17, Spenser *Epithalamion* 154–164; Hor. *Sat.* II.ii.39–40. PEARCE–NEWTON

The phrase "blind mouthes" may be illustrated from the classical usage of transferring to one bodily sense the functions of another: e.g., Soph. *Oed. T.* 371: τυφλὸς τὰ ὦτα; Val. Flacc. ii.461: "cæcus clamor"; Plin. *Nat. Hist.* xxxvii. 18: "surdus color," etc. The shepherds are emphatically termed "mouths," first for their gluttony, secondly in reference to their preaching. . . . As to the relative importance of *preaching*, Milton places it foremost among ministerial duties, even above the administration of sacraments. (*C. D.*, Ch. 29). To a Puritan "a non-preaching ministry" was a crying evil. JERRAM

Cf. Ezekiel 34:2–3.

Ruskin's comment (*Sesame and Lilies* 22) is illuminating: "A 'Bishop' means 'a person who sees.' A 'Pastor' means 'a person who feeds.' The most unbishoply character a man can have is therefore to be Blind. The most unpastoral is, instead of feeding, to want to be fed—to be a mouth." HANFORD

Ruskin's interpretation of *Blind mouths* as meaning the greed of the bishops is challenged by John A. Himes, *MLN*, XXXV (1920), 441, on the ground that the term *blind-mouthed* was applied by Strabo to rivers with shallow outlets to the sea. Thus shallowness rather than greed is Milton's charge against the clergy. HUGHES

See William Elton, "Two Milton Notes," *N&Q*, CXCII (1947), 428–429, who refers to "cieca cupidigia" in Dante *Inf*. xii.49 and *Par*. xxx.139. Robert Kane, *MLN*, LXVIII (1953), 239–240, adds nothing.

123, 124 Allusion to Virgil *E*. iii.26: "non tu in triviis, indocte, solebas/ Stridenti miserum stipula disperdere carmen" ["To ruin a miserable song on a scrannel straw"—Fairclough] PECK

This probably alludes to the Arminian doctrines which they taught, and which Calvinists have at all times spoken of with aversion and contempt. KEIGHTLEY

See W. J. Harvey, "Milton and the 'Late Fantasticks,' " *N&Q* n.s. IV (1957), 523–524, who says *lean* means *spare, naked, unornamented*— the "trimming slight" in "At a Vacation Exercise."

124 *scrannel*: I remember not to have seen this word in any other author, nor can I find it in any dictionary or glossary that I have consulted; but I presume it answers to the *stridenti* of Virgil. NEWTON

scrannel is "thin," "lean," "meagre." "A scrannel pipe of straw" is contemptuously for Virgil's "tenuis avena." WARTON

The word does not seem to have been used by any *previous* writer. . . .

In the Lancashire dialect it means "thin" or "meagre," and it is a question whether Milton was aware of its existence there, or whether he coined it to express the sound, after the analogy of *crane, screech* (G. *schreien*), etc. The former hypothesis is more probable, considering the extent of his information, and the improbability of his indulging in a license which would be questionable in point of view of taste, and of which there would be no other instance in his poems. It has also been suggested that the word may be connected with *cranny*, and that if so, it would well express the squeaking noise produced from a pipe not perfectly air-tight. But this is doubtful. JERRAM

124 For the stanza of Ottava Rima commencing here, see [my] *Life of Milton*, p. 293, where it should have been observed that this close junction of stanzas occurs occasionally in the *Amadigi* of B. Tasso, but we have no proof of Milton's ever having read that poem. KEIGHTLEY

126 *swoln with wind*: Dante (*Par.* ix and xxix. 106–107) complains that "the pope himself of a shepherd is become a wolf;" and again, that "vain questions and fables echo from the pulpit all the year long, and the poor sheep come back 'fed with wind' " (*Crit. Dict.* Vol. IV. p. 516 b.). PECK

Cf. Virg. *G.* iii.504 (of the cattle-plague): "Imaque longo Ilia singultu tendunt" and the λὺγξ κενὴ in Thucydides' description of the pestilence at Athens (ii.49). Here of course there is a direct allusion to the "windy" words of the preacher, which may be illustrated by the Homeric phrase ἀνεμώλια βάζειν (*Il.* iv.355), and the German *windreden* "to talk vainly." JERRAM

126 *the rank mist*: Cf. Song of the Priest of Pan in Fletcher's *Faithful Shepherdess*: "Mists unsound,/ Damps and vapors fly apace,/ Hovering o'er the wanton face/ Of these pastures, where they come/ Striking dead both bud and bloom." JERRAM

127 Milton may here have remembered Lucretius vi.1129 (of a vitiated atmosphere): "Et cum spirantes mixtos hinc *ducimus auras*,/

Illa quoque in corpus pariter *sorbere* necesset"; also *ibid.* 1235: "Nullo cessabant tempore apisci/ ex aliis alios avidi *contagia morbi.*" T. Becon in his *Supplication* uses similar language of popish pastors: "Instead of thy blessed communion they feed thy sheep with vile stinking devilish masses; and into these unwholesome and pestilent pastures they drive the sheep." JERRAM

See William B. Hunter, Jr., "A Note on 'Lycidas,'" *MLN*, LXV (1950), 544, who says "rot inwardly" comes either from a description of diseases of sheep in Aristotle's *Parts of Animals* 672 a–b, or from "some renaissance adaptation" of it.

See Edward S. Le Comte, "'Lycidas,' Petrarch, and the Plague," *MLN*, LXIX (1954), 402–404, who cites a parallel passage in Petrarch's Ninth Eclogue.

128, 129 Milton meant to accuse Archbishop Laud of privily introducing popery and therefore in his zeal threatened him with the loss of his head, which notion was suggested to me by Dr. Pearce, the Lord Bishop of Bangor. . . . [Or perhaps Milton meant] besides what the popish priests privately pervert to their religion; and Spenser in his Ninth Eclogue describes them under the same image of wolves, and complains much in the same manner. NEWTON

It has been conjectured that Milton in this passage has copied the sentiments of Piers, a protestant controversial shepherd, in Spenser's Eclogue "May." Of this there can be no doubt, for our author, in another of his puritanical tracts, written 1641, illustrates his arguments for purging the church of its rapacious hirelings and insidious wolves by a quotation of almost the whole of Pier's speech, observing that Spenser puts these words into the mouth of his righteous shepherd "not without some presage of these reforming times" (*Animadversions*). WARTON

The language which Milton here employs respecting the "wolf" presents at least a twofold objection to [the notion that Milton meant to refer to Archbishop Laud]. First, the evil is an *external* one, being distinguished from the abuses previously mentioned as existing *within* the fold—the word "besides" indicates this—and secondly, the expression "privy paw," denoting secrecy, would be a most unfit one if it were intended to describe the doings of Laud and the High Commission Court, whose attacks on Nonconformity were open and undisguised; nor was there perhaps any character more prominent at this time than that of the Archbishop. Both the required conditions are satisfied if we adopt Newton's alternative explanation, "besides what the Papish priests privately pervert to their religion," in support of which view Masson in his *Life of Milton* brings forward the instances of Sir Toby Matthews, Sir Kenelm Digby, and others, who had been most active in this matter for some years before the publication of *Lycidas*. He goes on to show that Laud himself strongly disapproved of these perversions, as appears from his letter of remonstrance to Sir K. Digby (March 27, 1636) upon his change of religion, and from his strict injunctions to Dr. Bayly, Vice-chancellor of Oxford (Aug. 29, 1637), to take strong measures against the Jesuits, who were seducing the students in that University. It may have been the case that "as he valued his theory of a possible union of the churches, the floating off of atoms vexed and annoyed him" (Masson), but even the fact that he did desire such a union is mainly supported by the assertion of Montague, Bp. of Chichester, to Panzani, a Papal agent sent to decide certain disputes among the English Catholics, but with special instructions not to have any dealings whatever with Laud (Lingard, *Hist. of England*, VII, v). Taken in connection with this injunction, the circumstances attending the offer of a cardinal's hat, made to Laud a short time before, and rejected by him on the ground of dissatisfaction with Rome "as it then was" (*Diary*, Aug. 4, 1633) serve to show that the distrust between the two parties was at least mutual; for it is certain that this offer was made without cognizance of the Pope, who even refused to ratify it when the request to do so was laid before him. We know also that the news of Laud's death in 1646 was hailed at Rome with great rejoicing, on the ground that "the greatest enemy of the Church of Rome in England was cut off, and the greatest champion of the Church of England silenced." (Testimony of Sir Lionel Tolmache, as reported to the Rev. J. Whiston, his chaplain, about 1666). All this agrees very well with Laud's own assertions in answer to the charges brought against him by the Puritans in

1640, "that he hath traytorously endeavoured to reconcile the Church of England with the Church of Rome, and permitted a Popish hierarchy in this kingdom, etc." To this he replies, "I did never desire that England and Rome should meet, but with the forsaking of error and superstition, if some tenets of Rome on one side and some deep disaffections on the other have not made this impossible, *as I much doubt they have*. But that I should practice with Rome *as it now stands* is utterly untrue. Secondly, I have hindered as many from going to the Roman party as any divine in England hath done. (Twenty-two names are here quoted, many of whom are of high rank and quality.) Thirdly, many Recusants think that *I have done them and their cause more harm than they which have seemed more fierce against them.*" The obvious fact is that the vital differences between the religious theory of Laud and that of the Roman Church, patent to either party and too great to allow the possibility of a union, were ignored by the Puritans in their zeal against the Laudian movement, which they either did not care to distinguish from actual Popery, or considered as even something worse. (See speech of Lord Falkland, Feb. 9, 1641.) Nor is it very likely that Milton, young as he was at this time, surrounded by Puritan influences, and having a strong natural bias in the same direction, would be enabled to form a juster estimate of the facts than the rest of his party did; it is therefore quite likely that he may have wished to include Laud among even the foremost of the Romanisers in the Church of England, though we deny that the allusion in the present passage is directly or exclusively intended for him. JERRAM

129 *And nothing sed*: This agrees very well with the popular clamors of that age against the supposed connivance of the court at the propagation of popery. NEWTON

Some suppose that our author in this expression insinuates the connivance of the court at the secret growth of popery. But perhaps Milton might have intended a general reflection on what the puritans called "unpreaching prelates," and a liturgical clergy, who did not place the whole of religion in lectures and sermons three hours long. Or, with a particular reference to present circumstances, he might mean the clergy of the church of England were silent, and made no remonstrances

against these encroachments. It is, in the meantime, certain that the verb *to say* was a technical term for the performance of divine service, as in [William Warner's] *Albion's England* IX.liii. He is speaking of ignorant enthusiasts intruding into the churches, and in contempt of order praying after their own way: "Each sot impugning order *saith*, and doth his fantasie;/ Our booke of Common Prayer, though most sound divinitie,/ They will not reade; nor can they preach, yet up the pulpit towre,/ There making tedious preachments of no edifying powre."
WARTON

It is a matter of surprise that this violent invective against the Church of England and the hierarchy, couched indeed in terms a little mysterious yet sufficiently intelligible, and covered only by a transparent veil of allegory, should have been published under the sanction and from the press of one of our universities, or that it should have escaped the severest animadversions at a period when the proscriptions of the Star-chamber, and the power of Laud, were at their height. Milton, under pretence of exposing the faults or abuses of the episcopal clergy, attacks their establishment, and strikes at their existence. WARTON

I must further observe how surprising it is that the passage should have escaped the notice of Laud, who, in the preceding year, had entered the following memorandum in the *Diary of His Own Life*: "A note was brought to me of a short libel pasted on the cross in Cheapside that the *arch-wolf of Canterbury* had his hand in persecuting the saints" (July 7, 1637). See [Henry] Wharton's life of Laud. TODD

The expression . . . is plainly an imputation upon the Court and hierarchy for their remissness in dealing with the evil we have just been considering. As regards the letter, if we take Laud as its representative, it is probable (to quote again from Professor Masson) that "the Puritans, not knowing his measures [against the Catholic agents], or not thinking them enough, found in the increasing number of perversions a fresh condemnation of him and his adherents." But the policy of Charles I towards the Papists was by no means uniform. His treaty of marriage with the Princess Henrietta in 1624 had contained a promise of immunity to the Catholics for the peaceable exercise of their worship, though he had sworn in conjunction with his father a few months before that in case of his marriage with a Catholic the said immunity should extend only to herself and her own family. In 1629 he adopted a middle course, exempting them from the extreme penalites of recusancy in respect of fines for non-attendance at the services of the established Church, yet not allowing them absolute freedom in their own religious worship; and even this concession was loudly reprobated by the Puritans. At the present time (1637) the queen's private influence was considerable. By the strenuous efforts of Con, the successor of Panzani, she had been induced to take a warm interest in the work of individual proselytism, which had superseded the former scheme of reunion of the Churches, and the autumn of this year was marked by a large accession of perverts to Rome. On the whole therefore we may conclude that Milton's words *little* (or *nothing*) *said* are a rather moderate statement of the real grievance, and one with which the Puritans generally would by no means have contented themselves.

Warton is surprised that the University should have allowed these lines, and that they should have escaped "the severest animadversions" from the High Court of Commission and the Star Chamber. But there had long been a decided Puritan element at Cambridge, the leading man at the time of Charles' accession being Dr. Preston, Master of Emmanuel, "the greatest pupil-monger in England," according to Fuller, formerly a favorite with the Duke of Buckingham, and one of the king's chaplains (Masson, I, 94). As to the civil and spiritual tribunals, perhaps Milton was then too obscure to demand their notice. JERRAM

See E. S. de Beer, "St. Peter in 'Lycidas,'" *RES*, XXIII (1947), 60–63, who explains "nothing sed."

130, 131 *that two-handed engine*, etc.: That is, the ax of reformation is upon the point of smiting once for all. It is an allusion to Matt. 3:10; Luke 3:9: "And now also the ax is laid unto the root of the trees." An ax is properly "a two-handed engin." "At the door," that is, this reformtion is now ripe, and at hand; "near, even at the doors," Matt. 24:33. "Behold the judge standeth before the door," James 5:9. And it was to be a thorough and effectual reformation. "Stand ready to smite once and smite no more," in allusion to the language of the Scripture,

1 Sam. 26:8: "Let me smite him, I pray thee, with the spear, even to the earth at once, and I will not smite him the second time." This explication is the more probable as it agrees so well with Milton's sentiments and expressions in other parts of his works. His head was full of these thoughts, and he was in expectation of some mighty alteration in religion, as appears from the earliest of his prose-works, which were published not four years after this poem. In the second book of his treatise *Of Reformation in England*, he employs the same metaphor of "the ax of God's reformation, hewing at the old and hollow trunk of papacy," and presages the time of the bishops to be but short, and compares them to a wen that is going to be cut off. And in his *Animadversions*, addressing himself to the Son of God he says: "But thy kingdom is now at hand, and thou standing at the door. 'Come forth out of thy royal chambers, O Prince of all the kings of the earth'—for now the voice of thy bride calls thee, and all creatures sigh to be renewed." The reading of these treatises of Milton will sufficiently make appear what his meaning must be, and how much about this time he thought of lopping off prelatical episcopacy. NEWTON

These are the last words of Peter predicting God's vengeance on his church by his ministry. The making him the minister is in imitation of the Italian poets, who in their satiric pieces against the church always make Peter the minister of vengeance. The "two-handed engine" is the two-handed Gothic sword, with which the painters draw him. "Stands ready at the door" was then a common phrase to signify a thing imminent. "To smite once and smite no more" signifies a final destruction, but alludes to Peter's single use of his sword in the case of the high priest's servant. WARBURTON–NEWTON

In these lines our author anticipates the execution of Archbishop Laud by a "two-handed engine," that is, the ax; insinuating that his death would remove all grievances in religion, and complete the reformation of the church. . . . The expression is a periphrasis for an ax, which the poet did not choose to name in plain terms. . . .

In the meantime, it coincides just as well with the tenor of Milton's doctrine to suppose that he alludes in a more general acceptation to our Savior's metaphorical ax in the Gospel. WARTON

On the whole, we must first seek Milton's *general* meaning. That is plain enough. He has been describing the Church of England in its Laudian era, and he winds up by prophesying a speedy Reformation of that Church. This Reformation presents itself in the image of a "two-handed engine at the dorr," standing ready to smite. One immediately fancies that this means to smite on the door, and the picture accordingly that rises to the mind is that of a strong man wielding a huge axe, like the Black Knight at the postern gate of Front-de-Boeuf's castle in *Ivanhoe*, and ready to batter down the opposing timbers, so as to let the besiegers in. Possibly Milton meant no more than this; and it is worth while to notice that, in one case out of the two in which the word "engine" occurs in the Authorized Version of the Bible, it is in this sense of a battering engine, Ezek. 26:9: "And he [Nebuchadnezzar] shall set engines of war against thy [Tyre's] walls, and with his axes shall he break down thy towers." It is not unlike Milton, however, to have had some subtler meaning in the name given to his battering engine here, and either to have construed it out of some Apocalyptic metaphor in Scripture, or else to have invented it to describe the particular agency by which he himself foresaw that the English Church Reformation would be effected. If the former, we are directed, I think, to the first three chapters of the Book of Revelation, where St. John sees the awful vision of "one like unto the Son of Man," and receives from him the messages that are to be sent to the Seven Churches of Asia. Part of the description of the divine figure is that "he had in his right hand seven stars" and that "out of his mouth went *a sharp two-edged sword*" (Rev. 1:16. The Greek phrase for the implement [implies] a very large sword which might require two hands). Now this "two-edged sword" figures in the subsequent messages to at least one of the Churches. Thus, Rev. 2:12–16: "To the angel of the Church in Pergamos write: These things saith he *which hath the sharp sword with two edges*; I know thy works, and where thou dwellest. . . . Thou holdest fast my name, and hast not denied my faith. . . . But I have a few things against thee, because thou hast there them that hold the doctrine of Balaam . . . . Repent; or else I will come unto thee quickly, and will fight against them with *the sword of my mouth*." Connect this with the words spoken, at the end, as part of the message to the church of Laodicea: "Behold I *stand at the door* and knock"; where, though the subsequent words are "If any man hear my voice, and open the door, I will come in to him and sup with him," yet we are to remember that he who stood at the door was the figure from whose mouth came the two-edged sword, the use of which had been threatened against the Church of Pergamos. Notwithstanding the difference of the conceptions suggested by the two images—(1) "a sharp two-edged sword," described as proceeding from the mouth of a figure standing at a door, and (2) a "two-handed engine" described as at a door, and standing ready to smite—it is not improbable that Milton's use of the second image is a poetic variation of the first. The Apocalyptic agency for the reform of a corrupt Church is certainly the "two-edged sword" of St. John's Vision, and Milton is not likely to have overlooked this. Moreover, the words in the text of *Lycidas* are supposed to be spoken by St. Peter; and it is at least a coincidence that in the Second Epistle of St. Peter, where he is describing the future corruption of the Church of Christ by "false teachers" and the "damnable heresies" which they will bring in, he particularises as one of these heresies that very "following the way of Balaam" for which, among other errors, punishment by the "two-edged sword" is denounced against the Church of Pergamos in the Apocalypse (2 Peter 2:15, 16). There remains, however, the hypothesis that Milton did not take his image from the Bible, but invented one to describe the agency by which, in his own historical speculations he foresaw that the English Church would be reformed. In that case we have not far to seek. We know the agency by which, three or four years after *Lycidas* was written, the reformation in question . . . *was* effected. It was that of *the English Parliament with its two Houses.* . . . For eight years prior to 1637 Charles had not called a Parliament. It was the "Reign of Thorough," when it was all but treason to use the word *Parliament*; and yet this word was in the hearts of all, and it was to a coming Parliament with its two Houses that all looked forward for the rectification of the accumulated abuses in Church and State. MASSON

The two hands may represent the two Houses of Parliament. The engine seems like a symbol of its power to establish true liberty, like the "wholesome and preventive Shears" which Milton foresaw the Long Parliament using against "the New Forcers of Conscience" (*On the New Forcers* etc., 1. 15). HUGHES

Among the many articles on these lines several include summaries of earlier interpretations; see Donald C. Dorian, *PMLA*, XLV (1930), 204–215; E. M. W. Tillyard, *Milton* (London, 1930), Appendix F; Edward S. Le Comte, *SP*, XLVII (1950), 589–606; W. Arthur Turner, *JEGP*, XLIX (1950), 562–565; Leon Howard, *HLQ*, XV (1951–1952), 173–184; William J. Grace, *SP*, LII (1955), 578–591; George W. Whiting, *Milton and This Pendant World* (Austin, 1958), pp. 29–58. There is a good summary and bibliography of articles in C. A. Patrides, *Milton's "Lycidas," the Tradition and the Poem* (New York, 1961), pp. 240–241. The history of the curiosity and ingenuity, as well as the occasional good sense, exercised on these lines may be traced in the following notes and articles: *Athenaeum*, June 30, 1900, p. 815; April 14, 1906, pp. 451–452; April 28, 1906, p. 515; May 5, 1906, p. 547. *TLS*, June 16, 1927, p. 424; July 28, 1927, p. 520; Nov. 22, 1928, p. 909; Dec. 6, 1928, p. 965; April 11, 1929, p. 295; April 25, 1929, p. 338; June 12, 1930, p. 496; April 25, 1936, p. 356; July 25, 1936, p. 616; August 29, 1936, p. 697; June 5, 1943, p. 271; June 12, 1943, p. 283; June 19, 1943, p. 295; July 3, 1943, p. 319. *N&Q*: Ser. VI, No. xi (1885) pp. 428, 516; Ser. VI, No. xii, p. 351; CLXXXI (1941), 273, 320; CXCIII (1948), 338, 503; n.s. II (1955), 58–59, 235–237; n.s. III (1956), 67–68, 249, 335; n.s. VI (1959), 364–366, 366–367; n.s. VII (1960), 237. *English Journal*, XXVI (1937), 148–151. *Italica*, XX (1943), 121–126. *MLN*, XXXIII (1918), 211–215; LXVIII (1953), 229–231. *MLR*, XXXI (1936), 57–60. *PMLA*, LXVII (1952), 1181–1184. *PQ*, XXIX (1950), 444–445. *RES*, I (1925), 339–341; XXIII (1947), 60–63; n.s. V (1954), 25–36. *SP*, XLIX (1952), 548–550; L (1953), 488; LIX (1962), 184–200.

132 *Alpheus*: a river of Arcadia, near Elis, runs down by Pisae into Greece, and is there swallowed up and runs underground and passes thence through the sea without mingling with it, till he arrives at Sicily, where he blends his current with the fountain Arethusa near Syracuse— insomuch that anything thrown into the river on the side of Greece shows itself in Arethuse. The mythologists by this fable suggest that as Alpheus (i.e., ἀλφός, a spot or imperfection) follows Arethusa (i.e., ἀρετὴ virtue) so matter desires form as its proper good; and the soul, virtue, as its proper form. But our author here makes Alpheus to sink

into the earth at the stern voice and speech of St. Peter. Which thought is very beautiful, and a much better reason for his disappearing than his supposed pursuit of *Arethusa*. PECK

As he had before distinguished the voice of Apollo, so here he far more exalts that "dread" one of St. Peter, that quite "shrinks" up the "stream" of Alpheus. Now this "is past, return Sicilian Muse," Sicelides Musæ Virg. *E.* iv.1. Now comes pastoral poetry again, and calls the vales to cast their flowers on Lycidas his hearse, according to the custom of the ancients. RICHARDSON–NEWTON

See D. C. Allen, "Milton's *Alpheus*," *MLN*, LXXI (1956), 172–173, who suggests an anagogical implication.

134–153   On this passage see: Henry Hitch Adams, "The Development of the Flower Passage in 'Lycidas,'" *MLN*, LXV (1950), 468–472; Wayne Schumaker, "Flowerets and Sounding Seas: A Study in the Affective Structure of 'Lycidas,'" *PMLA*, LXVI (1951), 485–494 as reprinted in C. A. Patrides' ed. of *Lycidas* (New York, 1961), pp. 125–135; W. Lawrence Thompson, "The Source of the Flower Passage in 'Lycidas,'" *N&Q*, CXCVII (1952), 97–99.

138   *the swart Star sparely looks*: The swart star is the dog-star, Sirius ardens, burning and drying up things, and making them look black and swarthy. But he "sparely looks" on these valleys, as he approaches not Horace's fountain of Blandusia, *Od.* III.xii.9: "Te flagrantis atrox hora caniculæ/ Nescit tangere." NEWTON

Milton is more likely to have here had an eye to Beaumont and Fletcher's *Philaster* (V.i): "Whose still shades/ The worthier beasts have made their layers, and slept/ Free from the Sirian Star." WARTON

Looks on is the astrological term for starry influence; "*seu Libra seu me scorpios aspicit*," Hor. *Od.* II.xvii.17. TUCKWELL

139   *eyes*: The term *eyes* is technical in the botany of flowers. WARTON

142–150   Mr. Bowles observes that here is an undoubted imitation of Spenser in "Aprill"

> Bring hither the pinke, and purple cullumbine,
>   With gilliflowres;
> Bring coronations, and sops in wine,
>   Worne of paramours:
> Strowe me the ground with daffadowndillies,
> And cowslips, and kingcups, and loved lillies;
>   The prettie pawnce,
>   And the chevisawnce,
> Shall match with the faire flowre delice.
>   WARTON

See original reading, and cf. Quarles' *Emblems* V.ii:

> The *purple vi'let* and the pale-fac'd lily,
> The *pansy* and the organ *columbine*,
> The flow'ring thyme, the gilt-breast *dafodilly*,
> The lowly *pink*, the lofty eglantine;
> The blushing *rose*, the queen of flowers and best
> Of Flora's beauty; but above the rest
> Let *Jesse's* sov'reign flower perfume my qualming breast.

The last is a play on "jessamine."   JERRAM

There is no need to suppose that Milton directly imitated the *Shepheardes Calender*, "April." Of the many similar passages which might be quoted, here is one from Ben Jonson's pastoral masque, *Pan's Anniversary*; it has the merit of having escaped the editors. Several nymphs are dressing the altar of Pan while a shepherd looks on with approval:

> Well done, my pretty ones, raine roses still,
> Untill the last be dropt: Then hence: and fill
> Your fragrant prickles for a second shower,
> Bring Corn-flag, Tulips, and *Adonis* flower,
> Faire Oxe-eye, Goldy-locks, and Columbine,
> Pinkes, Garlands, King-cups, and sweet Saps-in-wine,
> Bleu Harebells, Paglis, Pansies, Calaminth,
> Flower-gentle, and the fair hair'd Hyacinth,

> Bring rich Carnations, Floure-de-luces, Lilies,
> The chequ'd and purple-ringed Daffodillies.

And so on through six more verses, mentioning eleven other flowers.
VERITY

142–151 This passage has been the subject for that kind of insect-criticism, as one may call it, from which nothing is too classic in literature to be safe, and which seems to have fastened of late on Milton more particularly, as if from a disposition to avenge openly on his poetry, wherever possible, some secret dislike or awe felt for him as a man. Is the passage botanically correct? it is asked. Is "glowing" a correct epithet for the violet, or "wan" for the cowslip; or, should these be conceded, is the particular assemblage of diverse flowers which the passage demands—eleven or twelve of them in all—such as could possibly have been gathered together from field or garden, at one and the same time? Are they not, or some of them, flowers of different seasons? . . . The critics will [say] . . . "We do not say that [Milton] had to tie himself to any one month; but what we mean is that, whatever month he imagined, or whether he imagined any one month or not, he was bound to respect botanical possibility!" Was he? Most certainly not *here*, wherever else that might have been the right rule. He is engaged in a wish or invocation,—a prayer to the Pastoral Muse to bid all the meads and all the valleys, all the shadiest banks of brooks and streamlets, in whatsoever landscape of the earth, real or ideal, near or far, contribute their choicest flowers of melancholy tinge or hue to the required memorial. What cared he whence they came, or from what season or sequence of seasons, or whether they could come at all; and what do his sympathetic readers care either? MASSON

142 The primrose, being an early flower, is at first very acceptable, and being a lasting flower, it continues till it is put out of countenance by those which are more beautiful, and so "dies forsaken" and neglected. JORTIN–NEWTON

The flowers here selected are either peculiar to mourning or early flowers, suited to the age of Lycidas.

"That forsaken dies" is imitated from Shakespeare, as Mr. Warburton observed with me: *The Winters Tale*, IV, iv: "Pale primroses,/ That die unmarried." NEWTON

The particular combination of "rathe primrose" is perhaps from a pastoral called a "Palinode" by E. B., probably Edmond Bolton, in *England's Helicon* (ed. 1614, sig. B.4): "And made the rathe and timely primrose grow." . . . But why does the primrose die "unmarried"? . . . Because it grows in the shade uncherished or unseen by the sun, which was supposed to be in love with some sorts of flowers. . . . Compare our author's *Prolusion I*: "Quinetiam et moesta Clytie, totam fere noctem converso in orientem vultu, Phoebum præstolata suum, jam arridet, et adblanditur appropinquanti amatori," ["Moreover the heliotrope, after mourning almost all night with her face turned eastward in expectation of her lover, Phoebus, now welcomes his approach with a caressing smile"—Hughes]. WARTON

Rathe, one of the really antiquated words in "Lycidas." JERRAM

143 *The tufted crow-toe*: The hyacinth. RICHARDSON–NEWTON

Identified by most editors with the crow-flower (see *Hamlet*, IV, vii, 170) formerly used of the Ragged Robin but now of the buttercup. VERITY

Tufted by no means suits the blue-bell with its one-sided raceme, whereas it is fairly descriptive of a luxuriant specimen of Meadow Ranunculus. . . . Perhaps by *crow-toe* Milton meant *crowfoot* a name given to several species of Rannuculus that have each segment of the leaf divided into three lobes, having often a striking resemblance in form to the footprint of a large bird. . . . Some botanists (including Gerarde) give the name "crow-toe" to the hyacinth. Milton, therefore, *perhaps* means the "blue-bell hyacinth"—which is really a "scilla." COTTERILL

143 *Jessamine*: The only jessamine that Milton knew is not pale, but dazzling white; and it is not an English flower, but introduced from the East (Persian *jasmin* = fragrant). COTTERILL

144   *The white Pink*: Gerarde mentions white wild pinks, [but] the only English white pink grows in gardens. . . . The flower is not named from the color, but the color from the flower (pink = pincé, "stiff"). COTTERILL

144   *freakt with jet*: Mr. Meadowcourt proposes to read "streakt with jet," which is a more usual word; but *freakt* is the word in Milton's manuscript as well as in all editions, and I suppose he means the same as *freckled* or spotted. NEWTON

See C. E. H., " 'The Pansy Freaked with Jet' [*Lycidas*, 144]," *N&Q*, CLXXVII (1939), 98, and E. H. V. & Wm. Jaggard, *ibid.*, 139 and 175.

147   *cowslips wan*: borrowed from Shakespeare's "pale primrose," and spoilt in the borrowing, for primroses differ from cowslips just in regard to pallor. When writing his "Song on May Morning," Milton saw more accurately (though through spectacles) "the yellow cowslip and the pale primrose." COTTERILL

149   *Amaranthus*: actually the flower is also called "love-lies-bleeding," but in Milton's mind it is rather the mythical flower which was supposed never to fade (the literal meaning of the word "amaranthus"), and which was therefore a symbol of immortality. TILLYARD

See D. C. Allen, "Milton's Amarant," *MLN*, LXXII (1957), 256–258, who notes a possible source for this, the only alien flower for Lycidas's hearse.

150   *daffadillies*: a rustic form (the imaginary speaker is a shepherd) of *daffodil*. VERITY

151   *laureat herse*: "The *herse* was a platform, decorated with black hangings and containing an effigy of the deceased. Laudatory verses were attached to it with pins, wax, or paste" (Stanley, *Memorials of Westminster Abbey*, p. 341). Cf. King's "Elegy on Donne": "Each quill can drop his tributary verse,/ And pin it like the hatchments to the herse." JERRAM

Derived from Latin *hirpex*, "a harrow," *hearse* originally meant a triangular frame shaped like a harrow, for holding lights at a church service, especially the services in Holy Week. . . . Later it was applied to the illumination at a funeral, and then to almost everything connected with a funeral. Thus it could signify the dead body, the coffin, the pall covering it, the framework of wood on which a coffin was placed in the church before the altar, the bier, the funeral car (as always now), the service (cf. the Glosse to the *Shepheardes Calender*, "November"), and the grave. See Way's *Promptorium*, p. 236.   Verity

154   *Ay me!*: Milton repeats this exclamation, as Spenser often does in his elegies. See l. 56, above. It seems to have been once so hackneyed a phrase that it is ridiculed in *The Scourge of Villanie* (1598), VIII, iii: "Puling *aye mee*, ô valour's obloquie." Again, in *The Woman Hater* (1607), III, i: "Draw sonnets from the melting lover's braine,/ *Aymees* and *elegies*." Todd

Whilst thee, etc.: See Statius *Theb.* ix.358: "Jacet ipse procul, qua mixta supremum/ Ismenon primi mutant confinia ponti" ["He himself lies far off, where on the bounds of mingling sea and river Ismenos suffers his last change"—J. H. Mozley]. Richardson–Newton

Mr. Jortin says *shores* is improper, and fancies it should be *sholes*, the shallow waters, *brevia*. In the Mask 115, "The sounds and seas"—the sounds, *freta*. If Milton wrote *shores*, he perhaps had in his mind this passage of Virgil, *Aen.* vi.362, where Palinurus, who, like Lycidas, had perished in the sea, says: "Nunc me fluctus habet, versantque in litore venti." On which line Pierius observes, "*Litus* non tam de sicco, quam de asperginibus et extrema maris ora, intelligitur." But, yet, though a dead body may be said to be washed on the shore by the returning tides, the shore can hardly be said to wash the body, and the expression is harsh and uncouth. "Far away," that is, in some remote place, whatsoever it be. He seems rather to mean *in* some place, than *to* some place. Newton

154   *shores*: shallow waters, as contrasted with "sounding seas."
Tillyard

157   *under the whelming tide*: In the manuscript, and the edition of 1638, it is "humming tide," in reference to the distant sound of the waters over his head . . . . By every person accustomed to diving, the propriety of this epithet is fully understood. Clarence, in his dream, talks of "the noise of waters in his ears," while he supposes himself sinking to the bottom of the sea. Where also "the bottom of the monstrous world" is finely described. Milton altered *humming* to *whelming* as Lycidas is now dead. WARTON

For the reading in the 1638 ed., cf. *Pericles* III.i.64: "humming water must *o'erwhelm* thy corpse." Perhaps *o'erwhelm* afterwards suggested *whelming*. VERITY

See T. H. Banks, "A Source for 'Lycidas' 154–158," *MLN*, LXII (1947), 39–40, who adds a bit to Verity.

158   Virg. *Aen.* vi.729: "Et quæ marmoreo fert monstra sub æquore pontus." So classical is Milton in every part of this poem. NEWTON

The sea, the world of monsters, Hor. *Od.* I.iii.18: "Qui siccis oculis monstra natantia." WARTON

Thus Drummond in one of his sonnets: "And Proteus' *monstrous* people in the deep." TODD

159   *moist vows*: Our *vows* accompanied with tears. As if he had said *vota lachrymosa*. But there may be a quaint allusion to the water. WARTON

160–162   Milton, doubting which way the waves might carry the body of Lycidas, drowned in the Irish sea, imagines it was either driven northward beyond the Hebrides, or else so far southward as to lie sleeping near the fable, or fabulous mansions of old Bellerus, where the great vision of the guarded mount looks towards the coast of Spain. But where can we find the place which is thus obscurely described in the language of poetry and fiction? The place here meant is probably a promontory in Cornwall, known at present by the name of the Land's End, and called by Diodorus Siculus *Belerium promontorium*, perhaps from Bellerus, one of the Cornish giants, with which that country and the poems of old British bards were once filled. A watch-tower and lighthouse formerly stood on this promontory and looked, as Orosius says, towards another high tower at Brigantia in Gallicia, and consequently towards "Bayona's hold". See Orosius and Camden, who concludes his account of this part of Cornwall with saying that no other place in this island looks directly to Spain. MEADOWCOURT–NEWTON

It may be farther observed that Milton in his manuscript had written *Corineus*, and afterwards changed it for *Bellerus*. Corineus came into this island with Brute and had that part of the country assigned for his share, which after him was named *Cornwal*. "To Corineus," says Milton in the first book of his History of England, "Cornwal, as we now call it, fell by lot; the rather by him liked for that the hugest giants in rocks and caves were said to lurk still there; which kind of monsters to deal with was his old exercise." Of this race of giants, we may suppose, was Bellerus; but whoever he was, the alteration in Milton's manuscript was certainly for the better, to take a person from whom that particular promontory was denominated, rather than one who gave name to the country at large. The "fable of Bellerus" and "the vision of the guarded mount" is plainly taken from some of our old romances, but we may perceive what place is intended. NEWTON

Not far from the Land's End in Cornwall is a most romantic projection of rock, called *Saint Michael's Mount*, into a harbor called Mounts Bay. It gradually rises from a broad basis into a very steep and narrow, but craggy, elevation. Towards the sea the declivity is almost perpendicular. At low water it is accessible by land; and not many years ago it was entirely joined with the present shore, between which and the mount is a rock called Chapel Rock. Tradition, or rather superstition, reports that it was anciently connected by a large tract of land, full of churches, with the Isles of Scilly. On the summit of Saint Michael's Mount a monastery was founded before the time of Edward the Confessor, now a seat of Sir John Saint Aubyn. The church, refectory, and many of the apartments still remain. With this monastery was incorporated a strong fortress regularly garrisoned, and in a patent of Henry the Fourth, dated 1403, the monastery itself, which was ordered to be repaired, is styled *Fortalitium* (Rym. *Foed.* viii. 102, 340, 341). A stone lantern in one of the angles of the tower of the church is called *Saint Michael's Chair*. But this is not the original Saint Michael's Chair. We are told by Carew, in his *Survey of Cornwall*: "A little without the Castle (this fortress), there is a bad (dangerous) seat in a craggy place called *Saint Michael's Chair*, somewhat dangerous for access, and therefore holy for the adventure" (ed. 1602, p. 154). We learn from Caxton's *Golden Legend*, under the history of the Angel Michael that "Th'apparacyon of this angell is manyfold. The fyrst is when he appeared in mount of Gargan, etc." (ed. 1493, fol. cclxxxii.a). William of Worcestre, who wrote his travels over England about 1490, says in describing Saint Michael's Mount, there was an "Apparicio Sancti Michaelis in monte Tumba antea vocato *Le Hore Rok in the wodd*" (*Itenerar.* ed. Cantab., 1778, p. 102). The "Hoar Rock in the Wood" is this Mount or *Rock* of Saint Michael, anciently covered with thick wood, as we learn from Drayton and Carew. There is still a tradition that a vision of Saint Michael seated on this crag, or Saint Michael's *Chair*, appeared to some hermits, and that this circumstance occasioned the foundation of the monastery dedicated to Saint Michael. And hence this place was long renowned for its sanctity, and the object of frequent pilgrimages. Carew quotes some old rhymes much to our purpose (p. 154. ut supr.): "Who knows not Mighel's Mount and Chaire,/ The pilgrim's holy vaunt?" Nor should it be forgot that this monastery was a cell to another on a Saint Michael's Mount in Normandy, where was also a vision of Saint Michael.

But to apply what has been said to Milton. This "great vision" is the famous apparition of Saint Michael, whom he with much sublimity of imagination supposes to be still throned on this lofty crag of Saint Michael's Mount in Cornwall, looking towards the Spanish coast. The "guarded mount" on which this "great vision" appeared is simply the "fortified" Mount, implying the fortress above-mentioned. And let us observe that *Mount* is now the peculiar appropriated appellation of this promontory. So in Daniel's "Panegyricke on the King," stanza 19: "From Dover to the Mount."

With the sense and meaning of the line in question is immediately connected that of the third line next following, which here I now for the first time exhibit properly pointed: "Look homeward, Angel, now, and melt with ruth." Here is an apostrophe to the Angel Michael, whom we have just seen seated on the Guarded Mount: "O Angel, look no longer *seward* to Namancos and Bayona's hold; rather turn your eyes to another object. Look *homeward*, or *landward*, look towards your *own coast now*, and view with pity the corpse of the shipwrecked Lycidas floating thither." . . . Lycidas was lost on the seas near the coast, "Where the great vision, etc." The great vision and the Angel are the same thing, and the verb *look* in both the two last verses has the same reference. The poet could not mean to shift the application of *look*, within two lines. Moreover, if in the words "Look homeward angel now" the address is to Lycidas, a violent, and too sudden, an apostrophe takes place, for in the very next line Lycidas is distantly called "the hapless youth." To say nothing that this new "angel" is a "hapless youth," and to be "wafted by dolphins."

Thyer seems to suppose that the meaning of the last line is, "You, O Lycidas, now an angel, *look down* from heaven, etc." But how can this be said to look homeward? And why is the shipwrecked person to melt with ruth? That meaning is certainly much helped by placing a full point after *surmise*, line 153. But a semicolon there . . . is the point of the first edition; and to show how greatly such a punctuation ascertains or illustrates our present interpretation, I will take the paragraph a few lines higher, with a short analysis. "Let every flower be strewed on the hearse where Lycidas lies, so to flatter ourselves for a moment with the notion that his corpse is present; and this (ah me!) while the seas are wafting it here and there, whether beyond the Hebrides, or near the shores of Cornwall, etc." WARTON

Besides the poetical citation from Carew relating to St. Michael's Mount . . . the notice of this romantic place by Spenser must not be omitted (*S.C.*, "July" 41): "St. Michael's Mount who does not know,/ That wardes the Westerne coast?" TODD

162 *Namancos*: I once thought that this name was designed for the celebrated Numantia, and that Milton had adopted the spelling from

some romance. In the *Monthly Magazine* for June, 1800, it is observed that "Namancos must have been intended for the ancient Numantia, near Tarragona, on the coast of Catalonia, and that Milton has given a Spanish termination to the word." The observer adds, "I am aware that this place was on the opposite side to Bayona; but let it be remembered that they are no common eyes which look upon the scene; that they are no less than those of an archangel." Mr. Dunster, noticing the preceding criticism, observes that "Milton scarcely meant to make his arch-angel look two ways at once. Acceding," he says, "to Namancos being the ancient Numantia, I shall not hesitate to consider 'Bayona's hold' as the French Bayonne with its citadel, a very strong fortress. To this, Mounts Bay, or the Guarded Mount, looks, I believe, more directly than to the Spanish Bayona; and the line of vision directed to it would pass at no great distance from that part of the Spanish coast which lies nearest to the site of the ancient Numantia.

It will however appear that the ancient Numantia and the French Bayonne were not the present objects of Milton's consideration. I have been directed by a literary friend to Mercator's Atlas (ed. fol., Amsterdam, 1623, and again in 1636); and in the map of Galicia, near the point Cape Finisterre, the desired place occurs thus written "Namancos T.' In this map the castle of Bayona makes a very conspicuous figure. Milton most probably recollected this geographical description of the Spanish province. TODD

Probably the source consulted by Milton was the first English edition of that great work [*Mercator's Atlas*], published recently (1636). In that *Atlas* the part of Galicia just west of Namancos is shaded to represent mountains, which gives it prominence as a feature of the coast-line to which the angel gazes. But Namancos was not a headland (as M. may have thought), nor a town, but a district or county, and the correct form of the name (so attractive for the scansion) was "Nemancos." "Namancos" had appeared in an older map and the misprint was copied into later maps. [See A. S. Cook, "Two Notes on Milton," *MLR*, II (1907), 121–128.] VERITY

163   The obvious and striking contrast between the "look homeward" of this line and the looking "towards Namancos, etc." of the one

preceding clearly justifies Warton's supposition that St. Michael, and not Lycidas, is the person here addressed. Still, the arguments in favor of the contrary interpretation ought to be fairly stated. It has been objected that if a full stop be placed at "surmise," the present line is required to complete the sentence beginning at "whilst thee, etc.," which would otherwise be unfinished, and of which Lycidas is the subject throughout; and that, even with the semicolon there (l. 152), St. Michael's apparition is merely introduced parenthetically, as part of a local description, and never directly apostrophised. This is perhaps strictly true; but a poet is not always bound by the strict laws of grammatical construction, and the sudden turn of address from Lycidas to the archangel (who is now a prominent figure in the description) strikes powerfully upon the reader's imagination. Another argument (which at first sight appears plausible) is founded upon the coincidence of the present passage and of ll. 183ff. in structure, language, and sentiment, with certain lines in the First Eclogue of Sannazaro (ca. 1520), in which a drowned man is thus addressed by his mourning friends: "At tu, *sive* altum felix colis æthera, *seu* jam/ Elysios inter Manes, etc. . . ./ *Aspice nos* mitisque veni, *tu numen aquarum/ Semper eris semper lætum* piscantibus *omen*." But even admitting, as we surely may (cf. especially l. 184), that Milton had the above passage generally in view, we need not assume that he copied his original with such exactness as to make the subject of his "look homeward" correspond with that of "aspice" in Sannazaro. JERRAM

The "Angel" is Michael, who is imagined as standing on St. Michael's Mount, looking southward. In Jewish and often in Christian tradition he is the patron of mariners and is so recognized in the church of Mont St. Michel on the Norman coast. HUGHES

See L. H. Kendall "'Melt with ruth,'" *N&Q* CXCVIII (1953), 145, on earlier uses of *ruth*.

164 Alluding to what Pausanius says of Palæmon toward the end of his *Attics*, that "a dolphin took him up and laid his body on the shore at Corinth where he was deified." RICHARDSON–NEWTON

Stories of the amiability of dolphins were common in ancient times.
Besides the familiar legend of Arion (Herod. I.i.24; Ovid *Fast.*
ii.105ff.), we have the one quoted from Apion by Gellius *Noct. Att.*
vii.8, of a dolphin who carried a boy on his back daily from Baiæ to
Puteoli, and on the death of the boy pined away with grief. Pliny *Nat.
Hist.* ix.8, describes the animal as "maxime homini amicum" (cf. Arist.
De Animalibus ix.35), and especially notices its care of its own species,
when dead or wounded. Some of these tales about dolphins may (as
Liddell and Scott suppose, see their *Greek Lexicon* under *delphis*) be
due to the fact of their playing in stormy weather and so warning
mariners of danger. JERRAM

On one occasion the sailors of a ship in which [Arion] was returning
with many treasures from Sicily to his home at Corinth plotted his
murder; whereupon he threw himself into the sea and was carried
safely to land by a dolphin which had been touched by the strains of his
lute. The notion of dolphins being fond of music is often alluded to in
poetry. VERITY

See B. A. Wright, "Milton's Use of the Word *Waft*," *N&Q*, n.s. V
(1958), 341.

165 Keightley (*Poems of John Milton* I.140) has a long note to
prove that the line should be read: "Weep nó more, woeful shepherds,
weep no móre," a line suggested, he says, by "sigh nó more, ladies,
sigh no móre." But in the corresponding line of the song, the accent
surely falls thus: "Oñe foot in séa and oñe on shóre." COTTERILL

165–181 Cf. [Thomas] Watson, *Eclogue on the Death of the Right
Honourable Sir Francis Walsingham* (1590): "Injustlie judge we
Melibœus' death,/ As though his worth was buried in his fate;/ Now
Melibœus in comparelesse place/ Drinks nectar, eates divine ambrosia."
JERRAM

165 *Weep no more*: See William G. Madsen, "The Voice of Michael
in 'Lycidas,'" *SEL*, III (1963), 1–7, who suggests that this is the beginning of a speech by Michael that ends at l. 181.

166 *is not dead*: So in Spenser's "Astrophel," stanza 48: "Ah no!
it is not dead, ne can it die,/ But lives for aye in blissful Paradise."
WARTON

167 *watry floor*: Dante *Purg.* ii.15: "Sovra 'l suol marino."
Davison's *Poet. Rhapsodie*, p. 78. MITFORD

168 *So sinks the day-star*: The thought of a star's being washed
in the ocean and thence shining brighter is frequent among the ancient
poets; and at the first reading I conceived that Milton meant the morning
star alluding to Virgil *Aen.* viii.589 "Qualis ubi oceani perfusus
Lucifer unda" etc.; but upon farther consideration I rather think that
he means the sun, whom in the same manner he calls the "diurnal
star" in *P.L.* X.1069; and Homer, if the hymn to Apollo be his,
compares Apollo to a star in mid-day. See v. 441. NEWTON

Cf. also Ov. *Fast.* vi.718, where "stella serena" is said of Phœbus;
also *Met.* i.429; Tibull. II.i.47, where "sidus" is similarly used. The
chief advantage of this interpretation would be to save Milton from the
astronomical blunder involved in making the same planet a morning and
an evening star in one day; but here, as in l. 30 (see note), he is most
likely to have followed the usage of the ancients, who commonly speak
of Lucifer and Hesperus in this way. Catullus (lxii.34) describes the
evening star as returning next morning, "mutato nomine"; Horace
(*Od.* II.ix.10) measures a night's duration by the rising and setting of
Hesperus; and Virgil (*E.* viii.17, 30) makes Lucifer and Hesperus
appear during the same day. Moreover, the present passage is evidently
copied from Virg. *Aen.* viii.589: "Qualis ubi Oceani perfusus Lucifer
unda" etc., compared with the original in Hom. *Il.* v.6, thus translated
by Lord Derby: "Like autumn's star, that brightest shines/ When
newly risen from his ocean bath." Compare also the closely similar
language in Giles Fletcher's *Christ's Triumph after Death*, ll. 89ff.:
"So fairest Phosphor, the bright morning-star,/ But newly washed in
the green element,/ Before the drowsy night is half aware,/ Shooting
his flaming locks with dew besprent,/ Springs lively up into the orient."
JERRAM

Probably the sun . . . . Cf. Sylvester: "While the bright day-star rides his glorious round." VERITY

Those who think Milton uses the word here to mean Lucifer (as identical with Hesperus) are at great pains to prove that he had classical authority for [doing so] . . . but that he should have believed . . . that the evening-star sinks in the ocean behind the sun and (on the next morning, as Mr. Jerram interprets) rises before the sun, is scarcely credible—although his ideas on the subject of the even-star certainly do seem to have been a little vague (see on l. 30). Surely if he had meant it thus he would have said that the even-star, not the day-star, sinks in the ocean, for it is as Hesper that the star sets. To speak of tomorrow's morning-star setting would be a conceit to which surely Milton would not have stooped. COTTERILL

171   Cf. *Coriolanus* II.i.57, 58: "One that converses . . . with the forehead of the morning." VERITY

173   Of him over whom the waves of the sea had no power. It is a designation of our Saviour, by a miracle which bears an immediate reference to the subject of the poem. WARTON

174   See Virg. *Aen.* vi.641: "solemque suum, sua sidera norunt." And as Mr. Richardson adds, Ariosto when he brings Astolfo to the moon to look for Orlando's wit that was lost (XXXIV.lxxii): "These other rivers stream, smile other fields/ Than here with us, and other plains are stretch'd,/ Sink other valleys, other mountains rise." NEWTON

175   Like Apollo in Hor. *Od.* III.iv.61: "Qui rore puro Castaliæ lavit/ crines solutos." NEWTON

Cf. "On the Death of a Fair Infant," 49, "thy nectared head." Nectar with ambrosia is said to have been used by way of ablution to preserve immortality, as well as for the food and drink of the gods. Hom. *Il.* xiv.170; xix.39. In *Comus*, 836 ff., the deification of Sabrina is effected by "nectared lavers" and "ambrosial oils." JERRAM

oozy locks: Since "ooze" properly means moisture of any kind (O.E. *wos*, "juice"), it would be possible to understand "oozy" of the effect of the nectar, according to the common classical figure called *prolepsis* . . . . But as the word is generally, if not invariably, used of slime or mud, it probably here refers to the sea water which is washed away by the nectar, and may be compared with Hom. *Il.* xiv.170. JERRAM

176 *the unexpressive nuptial song*: This is the song in Rev. 14:3, 4: "which no man could learn but they who were not defiled with women, and were virgins." NEWTON

So in [Milton's] Latin poem "Ad Patrem," line 37: "Immortale melos, et inenarrabile carmen." WARTON

The reference should rather be Rev. 19:6 and 7, the song at "the marriage supper of the Lamb." JERRAM

177 That is, "in the blest kingdoms of meek joy and love," a transposition of the adjective which we meet with also in *P.L.* IX.318: "So spake domestic Adam in his care," in which verse *domestic* is without doubt to be joined to *care*, and not to *Adam* as the common opinion is. So also in the same book, line 225: "and the hour of *supper* comes *unearned*." THYER–NEWTON

Even here, after Lycidas is received into heaven, Milton does not make him an angel. He makes him, indeed, a being of a higher order, "the Genius of the shore." If the poet in finally disclosing this great change of circumstances, and in this prolix and solemn description of his friend's new situation in the realms of bliss after so disastrous a death had exalted him into an angel, he would not have forestalled that idea, according to Thyer's interpretation. WARTON

179 Compare *P.L.* XI.80; VII.198; X.86, 460; I.128, 315, 360; II. ll, 310; V.591, 601, 772, 840. Milton's angelic system, containing many whimsical notions of the associations and subordinations of these

sons of light, is to be seen at large in Thomas Aquinas and Peter Lombard. But it was not yet worn out in the common theology of his own times. This doctrine, which makes such a figure in *P.L.*, he very gravely delivers in his *Church Government*, I, i: "The Angels themselves are distinguished and quaternioned into their celestial princedoms and satrapies." The same system, which afforded so commodious a machinery for modern Christian poetry, is frequent in the Italian poets. WARTON

There is no necessary allusion in this line to the "angelic system" . . . as "saints" and not angels are here specified. The Christian doctrine of the *Communion of Saints* needs no illustration. JERRAM

181 From Scripture: Isaiah 25:8; Rev. 7:17 and 21:4: "And God shall wipe away all tears from their eyes." TODD

183 This is said in allusion to the story of Melicerta or Palæmon, who with his mother Ino was drowned and became a sea deity propitious to mariners. Ovid *Met.* iv.522; *Fast.* vi.485; Virg. *G.* i.436. And as Mr. Jortin observes, it is pleasant to see how the most anti-papistical poets are inclined to canonize and then to invoke their friends as saints. See "On the Death of a Fair Infant," st. 10. NEWTON

Many will agree with Todd in wishing that "after the sublime intimation of angels wiping the tears from the eyes of Lycidas [he] had not been converted into the classical Genius of the shore." For although the individual Genius is a conception in many points similar to that of the guardian angel, the *Genius loci* can have no counterpart in modern religious belief, being a product of that localizing tendency of Pagan theology which it was one special aim of Christianity to abolish (John 4:21ff.). The mention of him here serves, somewhat inartistically, to mark a return to the pastoral form in which the poem is chiefly set. . . . The language in the text is perhaps hardly definite enough to make the reference [to Melicerta] certain. JERRAM

185 *perilous*: pronounced as a dissyllable everywhere in Milton except in *P.L.* II.420. JERRAM

186   See Thomas K. Sidney, "The 'Uncouth Swain' in Milton's 'Lycidas,' " *MLN*, XXIII (1908), 92.

188   *various quills*: in allusion to the varied strains of the elegy (at ll. 76, 88, 113, 132, 165). This almost amounts to a recognition on the part of the poet of the irregularity of style, the mixture of different and even opposing themes, which some have censured as a defect.   JERRAM

189   He calls it *Doric lay* because it imitates Theocritus and other pastoral poets who wrote in the Doric dialect. Though Milton calls himself as yet "uncouth," he "warbles with eager thought his Doric lay," earnest of the poet he was to be, at least—as he promises in the motto to these juvenile poems of edit. 1645: "baccare frontim/ Cingite, ne vati noceat mala lingua futuro" (Virg. *E.* vii.28). This looks very modest, but see what he insinuates. The first part of Virgil's verse is "Aut si ultra placitum laudarit."   RICHARDSON–NEWTON

190   See Virg. *E.* i.83: "*Et jam* summa procul villarum culmina fumant,/ *majoresque cadunt altis de montibus umbræ.*"   NEWTON

192   *twitcht*: i.e., snatched up from where it lay beside him. Or according to Keightley, "drew tightly about him on account of the chillness of the evening." In any case the word expresses haste, as if the setting sun had surprised him while "eager" in his singing.   JERRAM

192   Cf. *Hudibras*: " 'Twas Presbyterian true blue."   BROWNE

blew: Blue was also a common color for servant-men. Ben Jonson speaks of servants as "the blue order"; also of a "blue waiter." In Beaumont and Fletcher a footman is called a "blue-bottle," a familiar phrase still.   HALES

blew: the color of a shepherd's dress, and the poet impersonates a shepherd (Hales, *Longer English Poems*). It is not probable that Milton meant anything more than this, though other explanations, more or less fanciful, have been offered.   JERRAM

Grey, however, seems to be the color more often mentioned. Thus Greene more than once describes the shepherd Paris as "all clad in grey" when he wooed Oenone. See Greene's *Friar Bacon and Friar Bungay* III.69, where Dr. Ward's note gives numerous instances. Browne (*Eclogue II*) speaks of an extravagant shepherd who had two suits, one of either color. VERITY

See Robert C. Fox, "Milton's 'Lycidas,' 192–193," *Explicator*, IX (1951), No. 54, who notes that blue is the symbolic color for hope (Spenser *F.C.* I.x.14).

193 Mr. Richardson conceives that by this last verse the poet says (pastorally) that he is hastening to, and eager on new works; but I rather believe that it was said in allusion to his travels into Italy, which he was now meditating, and on which he set out the spring following. NEWTON

Compare Phineas Fletcher *Purple Island* VI. 77: "To morrow shall ye feast in pastures new,/ And with the rising sunne banquet on pearled dew." WARTON

An accomplished scholar writes to me: "The reason for the shepherd's going to new haunts is that the old ones are associated with Lycidas, and so he cannot bear to feed his sheep there alone—a very just idea— and an admirable exit." I have not the least doubt that this explanation . . . gives correctly the primary purport of the line.

Nor does it seem to me inconsistent with the commonly accepted view that there is an underlying allusion to Milton's tour in Italy. He tells us in the *Second Defence* that on the death of his mother he became anxious to travel. She died in April, 1637. . . . The Italian scheme, therefore, may have occurred to him before he began this poem.

Another theory with reference to the line is that it is a covert way of saying that Milton has finally separated himself from the Anglican and Court party, and means to identify himself with the Puritans. This seems to me very farfetched. The danger of reading "allusions" into a writer's words is that there can be no definite limit to the process: each may start his own theory. VERITY

PRINCIPAL EDITIONS FROM WHICH NOTES HAVE BEEN TAKEN

PECK *New Memoirs of the Life and Poetical Works of Mr. John Milton,* etc., by Francis Peck, M.A. (London, 1740).

NEWTON *"Paradise Regained," a Poem in Four Books. To which is added "Samson Agonistes"; and Poems upon Several Occasions,* ed. Thomas Newton (London, 1752). [The names of commentators quoted by Newton are joined to Newton's name with a dash, as –Newton.]

WARTON *Poems upon Several Occasions: English, Italian, and Latin, with Translations,* ed. Thomas Warton (London, 1785; rev. ed., 1791).

TODD *The Poetical Works of John Milton,* ed. H. J. Todd, 6 vols. (London, 1801; rev. ed., 1809; 3rd ed., 1826).

MITFORD *The Poetical Works of John Milton,* ed. John Mitford, 3 vols. (London, 1832).

BRYDGES *The Poetical Works of John Milton,* ed. Sir Egerton Brydges, 6 vols. (London, 1835).

KEIGHTLEY *The Poems of John Milton,* ed. Thomas Keightley, 2 vols. (London, 1859).

BROWNE *English Poems by John Milton,* ed. R. C. Browne (Oxford, 1866; rev. ed., 1894).

HALES *Longer English Poems,* ed. John W. Hales (London, 1872).

JERRAM *The "Lycidas" and "Epitaphium Damonis" of Milton,* ed. C. S. Jerram (London 1874; rev. ed., 1881). [In many ways this is the finest, richest, most useful of all editions of the poem.]

MASSON *The Poetical Works of John Milton,* ed. David Masson, 3 vols. (London, 1874; rev. ed., 1890).

BRADSHAW *The Poetical Works of John Milton,* ed. John Bradshaw, 3 vols. (London, 1878).

VERITY *Milton's "Ode on the Morning of Christ's Nativity" "L'Allegro," "Il Penseroso," and "Lycidas,"* ed. A. W. Verity (Cambridge 1891).

COTTERILL *Milton's "Lycidas,"* ed. H. B. Cotterill (London, 1902).

TUCKWELL *"Lycidas:" A Monograph,* ed. W. Tuckwell (London, 1911).

HANFORD   *The Poems of John Milton*, ed. James Holly Hanford (New York, 1936; rev. ed., 1953).

HUGHES   *Milton: Paradise Regained, the Minor Poems, and Samson Agonistes*, ed. Merritt Y. Hughes (New York, 1937).

HUGHES   *John Milton: Complete Poems and Major Prose*, ed. Merrit Y. Hughes (New York, 1957).

TILLYARD   Comus *and Some Shorter Poems of Milton*, ed. E. M. W. Tillyard (London, 1952).

When the forthcoming Variorum edition of Milton's minor poems appears, it will furnish students of "Lycidas" with an extensive selection of critical comment on the poem.

Bibliographies

BOOKS AND ARTICLES ON
PASTORAL POETRY

Carrara, Enrico *La Poesia Pastorale* (Milan, 1909).

Chambers, Sir Edmund "The English Pastoral," in *Sir Thomas Wyatt and Some Collected Studies* (London, 1933), pp. 146–180.

Congleton, J. E. *Theories of Pastoral Poetry in England, 1684–1798* (Gainesville, 1952).

Cory, Herbert E. "The Golden Age of the Spenserian Pastoral," *PMLA*, XXV (1910), 241–267.

Gerhardt, Mia I. *La Pastorale, essai d'analyse littéraire* (Assen, 1950).

Greg, Walter W. *Pastoral Poetry and Pastoral Drama* (London, 1906).

Hall, H. M. *Idylls of Fishermen* (New York, 1914).

Harrison, Thomas P., Jr. "The Latin Pastorals of Milton and Castiglione," *PMLA*, L (1935), 480–493.

Harrison, Thomas P., Jr., ed. *The Pastoral Elegy* (Austin, 1939).

Hughes, Merritt Y. *Virgil and Spenser* (Berkeley, 1929).

Hughes, Merritt Y. "Spenser and the Greek Pastoral Triad," *SP*, XX (1923), 184–215.

Lang, Andrew *Theocritus, Bion and Moschus* (London, 1880), pp. xi–xliii.

. Mustard, Wilfred P. "Later Echoes of the Greek Bucolic Poets," *AJP*, XXX (1909), 245–283.

Norlin, George "The Conventions of the Pastoral Elegy," *AJP*, XXXII (1911), 294–312.

Rand, E. K. *The Magical Art of Virgil* (Cambridge, Mass., 1931), pp. 68–175.

Shackford, Martha H. "A Definition of the Pastoral Idyll," *PMLA*, XIX (1904), 583–592.

Wirtzmann, Francis W. "Notes on the Elizabethan Elegie," *PMLA*, L (1935), 435–443.

BOOKS AND ARTICLES ABOUT "LYCIDAS"

Abrams, M. H. "Five Types of 'Lycidas,'" in *Milton's "Lycidas,"* ed. C. A. Patrides (New York, 1961), pp. 212–231. Reprinted as "Five Ways of Reading 'Lycidas,'" in *Varieties of Literary Experience*, ed. Stanley B. Burnshaw, (New York 1962), pp. 1–29.

Adams, R. P. "The Archetypal Pattern of Death and Rebirth in Milton's 'Lycidas,'" *PMLA*, LXIV (1949), pp. 183–188.

Allen, Don Cameron *The Harmonious Vision* (Baltimore, 1954), pp. 41–70.

Arnold, Robert F. "Milton's 'Lycidas' deutsch," *Z. f. franz. und engl. Unterricht*, XXI (1922), 241–253.

Auden, W. H. "Robert Frost," in *The Dyer's Hand* (New York, 1962), pp. 337–341.

Austin, W. B. "Milton's 'Lycidas' and Two Latin Elegies by Giles Fletcher the Elder," *SP*, XLIV (1947), 41–55.

Baskerville, Charles Read "Two Parallels to 'Lycidas,'" *Nation*, XCI (1910), 546–547.

Battestin, Martin C. "John Crowe Ransom and 'Lycidas': A Reappraisal," *College English*, XVII (1956), 223–228.

Beum, Robert "The Pastoral Realism of 'Lycidas,'" *Western Humanities Review*, XV (1961), 325–329.

Brett, R. L. "Milton's 'Lycidas,'" in his *Reason and Imagination* (London, 1960), pp. 21–50.

Brooks, Cleanth and John Edward Hardy *Poems of Mr. John Milton* (New York, 1951), pp. 169–186.

Candy, Hugh C. H. "Milton's Autograph Established," *Library*, 4th ser. XIII (1932–1933), 192–200.

Clark, Evert Mordecai "Milton's English Poetical Vocabulary," *SP*, LIII (1956), 220–238.

Coffman, George R. "The Parable of the Good Shepherd, *De Contemptu Mundi*, and 'Lycidas': Excerpts from a Chapter on Literary History and Culture," *ELH*, III (1936), 101–113.

Daiches, David *Milton* (London, 1957), pp. 73–92.

Diekhoff, John S. "Milton's Prosody in the Poems of the Trinity Manuscript," *PMLA*, LIV (1939), 177–183.

Diekhoff, John S. "Critical Activity of the Poetic Mind: John

Milton," *PMLA*, LV (1940), 748–772.

Finney, Gretchen "A Musical Background for 'Lycidas,'" in her *Musical Backgrounds for English Literature*: 1580–1650 (New Brunswick, 1962), pp. 195–219.

Fleischauer, Warren "Johnson, *Lycidas*, and the Norms of Criticism," in *Johnsonian Studies*, ed. James L. Clifford and Donald J. Greene (Cairo, 1962), pp. 235–256.

Fraser, G. S. "Approaches to 'Lycidas,'" in *The Living Milton*, ed. Frank Kermode (London, 1960), pp. 32–54.

French, J. Milton "The Digressions in Milton's 'Lycidas,'" *SP*, L (1953), 485–490.

Friedland, Louis S. "Milton's 'Lycidas' and Spenser's 'Ruines of Time,'" *MLN*, XXVII (1912), 246–250.

Frye, Northrop "Literature as Context: Milton's 'Lycidas,'" in *The Proceedings of the Second Congress of the International Comparative Literature Association*, ed. W. P. Friederick (University of North Carolina Studies in Comparative Literature, XXIII [1959]), I, 44–55. Reprinted in his *Fables of Identity* (New York, 1963) pp. 119–129.

Godolphin, F. R. B. "Milton, 'Lycidas' and Propertius," *MLN*, XLIX (1934), 162–166.

Graves, Robert *The Common Asphodel* (London, 1949), pp. 321–325.

Hanford, James Holly "The Pastoral Elegy and Milton's 'Lycidas,'" *PMLA*, XXV (1910), 403–447.

Hanford, James Holly "The Youth of Milton: An Interpretation of his Early Literary Development," in *Studies in Shakespeare, Milton, and Donne* (University of Michigan Publications: Language and Literature, I [1925]), 89–163.

Hazlitt, William "On Milton's 'Lycidas,'" in *The Round Table; Works*, ed. P. P. Howe (London, 1930), IV, 31–36.

Hughes, Merritt Y. "Milton and the Sense of Glory," *PQ*, XXVIII (1949), 107–124.

Jones, Katherine "A Note on Milton's 'Lycidas,'" *American Imago*, XIX (1962), 141–155.

Jones, William M. "Immortality in Two of Milton's Elegies," in *Myth and Symbol*, ed. Bernice Slote (Lincoln, Nebraska, 1962), pp. 133–140.

Kellett, E. E. "Edward King and Milton," *Cambridge Review* XXXVII (1915), 326–327.

Lawry, Jon S. " 'Eager Thought': Dialectic in 'Lycidas,' " *PMLA*, LXXVII (1962), 27–32.

Le Comte, Edward S. *Yet Once More: Verbal and Psychological Patterns in Milton* (New York, 1953), pp. 24–26.

Lloyd, Michael "*Justa Edovardo King*," *N&Q*, n.s. V (1958), 432–434.

Lloyd, Michael "The Two Worlds of 'Lycidas,' " *Essays in Criticism*, XI (1961), 390–402.

Mac Caffrey, Isabel G. "*Lycidas*: The Poet in a Landscape," in *The Lyric and Dramatic Milton*, ed. Joseph H. Summers (New York, 1965), pp. 65–92.

McKenzie, Kenneth "Echoes of Dante in Milton's 'Lycidas,' " *Italica*, XX (1943), 121–126.

Madsen, William G. "The Voice of Michael in 'Lycidas,' " *SEL*, III (1963), 1–7.

Miles, Josephine *The Primary Language of Poetry in the 1640s* (Berkeley, 1948), pp. 86–90.

More, Paul Elmer "How to Read 'Lycidas,' " *The American Review*, VII (1936), 140–158. Also in *On Being Human* (Princeton, 1936), pp. 184–202.

Nicolson, Majorie Hope *John Milton: A Reader's Guide to His Poetry* (New York, 1963), pp. 87–111.

Ogden, H. V. S. "The Principles of Variety and Contrast in Seventeenth-Century Aesthetics, and Milton's Poetry," *JHI*, X (1949), 159–182.

Oras, Ants "Milton's Early Rhyme Schemes and the Structure of 'Lycidas,' " *MP*, III (1954), 12–22.

Patrides, C. A., ed. *Milton's 'Lycidas': The Tradition and the Poem* (New York, 1961).

Prince, F. T. *The Italian Element in Milton's Verse* (Oxford, 1954), pp. 71–88.

Ransom, John Crowe "A Poem Nearly Anonymous," in his *The World's Body* (New York, 1938), pp. 1–28.

Roberts, Donald Ramsay "The Music of Milton," *PQ*, XXVI (1947), 329–344.

Ross, Malcolm M. "Milton and the Protestant Aesthetic," in his *Poetry and Dogma* (New Brunswick, 1954), pp. 201–204.

Saintsbury, George "Milton and the Grand Style," in *Collected Essays and Papers* (London, 1923), III, 175–196.

Sandys, Sir John "The Literary Sources of Milton's 'Lycidas,'" *Transactions of the Royal Society of Literature*, 2nd series, XXXII (1914), 233–264.

Saunders, J. W. "Milton, Diomede and Amaryllis," *ELH*, XXII (1955), 254–286.

Shawcross, John T. "Division of Labor in *Justa Edovardo King Naufrago* (1638), "*The Library Chronicle of the University of Pennsylvania*, XXVII (1961), 176–179.

Shawcross, John T. "Establishment of a Text of Milton's Poems Through a Study of 'Lycidas,'" *PBSA*, LVI (1962), 317–331.

Shuster, George N. "Milton and the Metaphysical Poets," in *The English Ode from Milton to Keats* (New York, 1940), pp. 64–92.

Strathman, Ernest A. "'Lycidas' and the Translation of 'May,'" *MLN*, LII (1937), 398–400.

Stroup, Thomas B. "'Lycidas' and the Marinell Story," in *SAMLA Studies in Milton*, ed. J. Max Patrick (Gainesville, 1953), 100–113.

Taylor, George Coffin "Milton's English," *N&Q*, CLXXVIII (1940), 56–57.

Tillyard, E. M. W. *Milton* (London, 1930), pp. 80–85, 385–389.

Tillyard, E. M. W. *The Miltonic Setting* (London, 1938), pp. 35–42.

Tillyard, E. M. W. *Poetry Direct and Oblique* (London, 1945), pp. 81–84.

Toynbee, Paget *Dante in English Literature* (New York, 1909), I, 123–124.

Tuve, Rosemond *Images and Themes in Five Poems by Milton* (Cambridge, Mass., 1957), pp. 73–111.

Wagenknecht, Edward "Milton in 'Lycidas,'" *CE*, VII (1946), 393–397.

Wallerstein, Ruth "The Laureate Hearse: The Funeral Elegy and Seventeenth-Century Aesthetic," in her *Studies in Seventeenth-Century Poetics* (Madison, 1950), pp. 3–150.

Whiting, George W. *Milton's Literary Milieu* (Chapel Hill, 1939), pp. 101–107.

Whiting, George W. *Milton and This Pendant World* (Austin, Texas, 1958), pp. 29–58.

Woodhouse, A. S. P. "Milton's Pastoral Monodies," in *Studies in Honour of Gilbert Norwood*, ed. M. E. White (Toronto, 1952), pp. 261–278.

Index

Auden, W. H., 248–249

Basore, John W., 41 n.
Bastwicke, Dr., 196, 207–219
Bion, 21–25
Boccaccio, Giovanni, 54–57
Bradshaw, John, 253
Bridgewater, Earl of, 165
Brief Relation of certain . . . passages, and speeches in the Starre-Chamber . . . at the censure of Dr. Bastwicke, Mr. Burton and Mr. Prynne, A, 207–219
Browne, R. C., 251–252, 255, 257, 258, 259, 263, 269, 315
Bryskett, Lodowick, 95–101
Buckingham, Duke of, 180, 193, 194
Bunyan, John, 190
Burghley, Lord, 186
Burton, Robert, 196, 207–219

Castiglione, Baldassare, 67–72
Charles I, king of England, 180–182, 188, 194, 195, 196, 198
Clement VI, Pope, 45 n.
Cleveland, John, 154–157
Coke, Sir Edward, 192
Cotterill, H. B., 259, 261, 267, 273, 274–275, 276, 282, 301, 302, 310, 312
Cowley, Abraham, 139–144
Cromwell, Oliver, 183

Derby, Countess Dowager of, 165
Diodati, Charles, 164, 173–174
Donne, John, 126–129
Dryden, John, 30 n.
Durling, Robert M., 67 n.

Elizabeth I, queen of England, 186, 188, 189

Fletcher, Giles, 117–120
Fox, George, 190

Gollancz, Sir Israel, 54 n.
Graves, Robert, 244–248
Guerlac, Rita Carey, 107 n.

Hales, John W., 252, 253, 257, 271, 315
Hall, W., 158–159
Hallam, Henry, 235–236
Hanford, James Holly, 270, 274, 286, 287
Harrison, Thomas P., Jr., 74 n., 79 n.
Harsnet, Bishop of Norwich, 204
Hayden, John, 204
Hazlitt, William, 232–235
Henrietta Marie, queen of England, 194, 195
Henry II, king of France, 79 n.
Henry VIII, king of England, 190
Hughes, Merritt Y., 253, 256, 258, 274, 276, 279, 280, 281, 282, 286, 287, 296
Huntly, George, 203
Hurd, Richard, 227–228

Jackson, Sir John, 182
James I, king of England, 187, 188
Jerram, C. S., 252, 254–255, 256, 257, 259, 260, 262, 263, 268, 269, 271, 274, 275–276, 277, 278, 279, 280, 282, 283, 285–286, 287–291, 292–293, 299, 301, 302, 308–309, 310, 311, 312, 313, 314, 315
Johnson, Samuel, 228–230
Jonson, Ben, 165–166
Justa Edovardo King, 150–160
Juxon, Bishop of London, 192

Keightly, Thomas, 236–237, 264, 273, 285, 287, 288
King, Edward, 147–149
King, Henry, 148, 150, 151–154

329

Lang, Andrew, 15 n., 21 n., 25 n.
Laud, William, 183–195
Lawes, Henry, 165
Leon, Harry Joshua, 74 n., 79 n.
Letter to Charles Diodati (Milton), 173–174
Lilburne, John, 197

Machen, Arthur, 244
MacKendrick, Paul, 45 n.
Marot, Clement, 72–75
Masson, David, 257, 262, 295–296, 300
Milton, John, 3–9, 130–139, 167–175, 220–224; early training and aspirations, own account of, 167–170; life from 1608 to 1637, 163–166; *An Apology for Smectymnuus*, 167–170; *Epitaphium Damonis*, 130–139; *A Letter to a Friend*, 170–173; "Lycidas," 3–9; *Of Reformation Touching Church Discipline in England*, 220–224; *The Reason of Church Government Urged Against Prelaty*, 174–175.
Mitford, John, 258, 272, 277, 278, 279, 285, 311
More, W., 157–158
Moschus, 25–30
Mozley, J. H., 42 n.

Newton, Thomas, 227, 253, 254, 255, 256–257, 258, 259, 260, 261, 262, 263, 264, 269, 271, 273, 275, 277, 279, 280, 281, 283, 284, 285, 286, 289, 291, 293–294, 298, 300–301, 302, 303, 304–305, 309, 311, 312, 313, 314, 315, 316

Obsequies to the Memorie of Mr. Edward King, 151–160
Olivier, Isaac, 159–160

Pattison, Mark, 244
Peck, Francis, 251, 252, 264–267, 273, 274, 276–277, 278, 283, 287, 288, 297–298
Petrarch, 45–67
Phillips, Edward, 147 n.
Prynne, William, 196, 197–206, 207–219
Puttenham, George, 112–114
Pym, John, 192

Ronsard, Pierre de, 76–81
Rupert, Prince, 194
Ruskin, John, 237–244

Saville, Lord, 182
Scaliger, Julius Caesar, 107–111
Seneca, 41–42
Smart, Peter, 203
Spenser, Edmund, 82–94
Stalbridge, Henry, 206
Statius, Publius Papinius, 42–44

Theocritus, 15–21
Tillyard, E. M. W., 302, 303
Todd, H. J., 254, 256, 257, 258, 263, 264, 269, 272, 279, 281, 282, 284, 292, 303, 304, 307–308, 314
Tourneur, Cyril, 121–125
Trevelyan, G. M., 179–197
Tuckwell, W., 255, 258, 298
Tyndall, William, 201

Verity, A. W., 253, 255, 259, 265, 280, 284, 299–300, 301, 302, 303, 304, 308, 310, 312, 316
Virgil, 30–40

Waddell, Helen, 130 n.
Warton, Joseph, 227
Warton, Thomas, 230–231, 251–254, 256, 259, 260, 267–268, 269–270, 272, 273, 275, 277, 278–279, 280, 281, 283, 284, 287, 289, 291–292, 294, 298–299, 301, 304, 305–307, 311, 312, 313–314, 316
Wraughton, William, 206

LYCIDAS

In this Monodie the author bewails a lerned freind unfortunatly
drownd in his passage from Chester on the Irish seas 1637.

Yet once more O yee Laurells, and once more
yee myrtle's browne wth Ivie never sere
I come to pluck yor berries harsh and crude
and wth forc't fingers rude
shatter yor leaves before the mellowing yeare.
bitter constraint, and sad occasion deare
compells me to disturbe yor season due
for Lycidas is dead, dead ere his prime
young Lycidas, and hath not left his peere
who would not sing for Lycidas? he well knew
himselfe to sing, and build the loftie rime
he must not flote upon his watrie beare
unwept, and welter to the parching wind
without the meed of some melodious teare
Begin then Sisters of the sacred well
that from beneath the seate of Jove doth spring
begin, and somewhat loudly sweepe the string
hence wth denial vaine, and coy excuse
so may some gentle muse
wth luckie words favour my destin'd urne
and as he passes turne
and ~~to~~ bid faire peace be to my sable shroud
for wee were nurs't upon the selfe same hill
fed ye same flock by fountaine, shade, and rill
Together both ere the high launs appear'd
under the ~~glimmering~~ eyelids of the morne   opening
wee drove afeild, and both together heard
what tyme the gray fly winds her sultrie horne
batning our flocks wth the freshe dews of night
oft till the ~~ev'n~~ starre ~~bright~~ that rose in Evning bright
towards heavens descent had sloapt his ~~burnisht~~ weele   westring
meane while the rurall ditties were not mute
tempd to th' oaten flute
rough Satyrs danc't; and Fauns wth clov'en heele
from the glad sound would not be absent long
and old Damoetas lov'd to heare our song
But O the heavie change now thou art ~~gone~~   gone
now thou art gon, and never must returne
thee shepeard, thee the woods and desert caves
wth wild Thyme, and the gadding vine oregrowne
and all thire ~~Eccho~~ Echo's mourne
the willows, and the haze'l copses greene
shall now no more be seene
fanning thire joyous leavs to thy soft lays
as killing as the canker to the rose
or taint-worme to the weanling heards that graze
or frost to flowrs that thire gay ~~buttons weare beare~~   wardrope weare
when first the white thorne blows
such Lycidas thy losse to shepeards eare
where were yee nymphs when ye remorselesse deepe
clos'd ore the head of y^r ~~youn~~ lov'd Lycidas
for neither were yee playing on the steepe
where yor old bards the famous Druids lie
nor on the shaggie top of Mona high
nor yet where Deva spreds her wisard streame   whome universal nature
ay mee I fondly dreame   might lament
~~had yee~~ bin there for what could that have don?   ~~and heaven and hel deplo[re]~~
~~what could the golden hayrd Calliope~~   when his divine head downe
for her inchaunting son   the streame was sent
~~when shee beheld (the gods farre sighted bee)~~   downe the swift Hebrus to [the]
~~his goarie scalpe rowle downe the Thracian lee~~   Lesbian shore.